English Romanticism and the French Tradition

English Romanticism and the French Tradition

Margery Sabin

Harvard University Press
Cambridge, Massachusetts
London, England

Copyright © 1976 by the President and Fellows of Harvard College
All rights reserved
Printed in the United States of America
Second printing 1977
Publication of this book has been aided by a grant from the
Andrew W. Mellon Foundation
Library of Congress Cataloging in Publication Data
Sabin, Margery, 1940-
    English romanticism and the French tradition.
    Includes bibliographical references and index.
    1. English literature—19th century—History
and criticism. 2. French literature—19th century—
History and criticism. 3. Literature, Comparative
—English and French. 4. Literature, Comparative—
French and English. I. Title.
PR129.F8S2   809'.91'4   75-43959
ISBN 0-674-25686-7

To Jim

Preface

Every time we arrange or rearrange books on a shelf, we enjoy in crude form one of the basic pleasures of literary criticism. To place one particular book next to another or in a certain grouping expresses a literary judgment and even the interpretation of a text. There always seem alternate possibilities, different arrangements which would express different perceptions. Does James go with English or American fiction? Where do we put T. S. Eliot? We might have a shelf of French fiction or of the "realistic" novel in several languages.

Many possible arrangements have been designed for the period of Western literature from the mid-eighteenth to the mid-nineteenth centuries, the period loosely called Romanticism. Babbitt, Lovejoy, and Trilling come to mind among many other "comparatistes" and historians of particular national literatures. The custom for scholars of comparative literature has been to favor arrangements according to period or genre across national boundaries. Their groupings have thus tried to show the shared characteristics of certain literary forms or the common developments of thought and sensibility in different nations at the same time. Comparative studies have, characteristically, tried to trace the international voyage of ideas like "creative imagination" and "the sublime." Or they have followed the international influence of a writer: Rousseau in England, Byron or Poe in France; or they have measured the consequences of a writer's exposure to foreign air: Coleridge in Germany, Chateaubriand in London.

In this book I pursue a somewhat different approach to the comparative study of literature. Instead of reducing the importance of

national characteristics, as comparative studies generally do, I try to
show that national traditions of thought and language have a deter-
mining influence through the Romantic period in England and in
France.

A similar, equally interesting argument can be made, I believe, for
the distinct identity of German literature in the Romantic period, even
considering the pervasive influence of German thought on European
Romanticism generally. I concentrate here exclusively on the English
and the French traditions in the Romantic period, partly because this
subject offers complications enough, and partly because the separateness of the best French from the best English writing in this period is a
conspicuous yet widely ignored phenomenon. Moreover, the effort to
characterize the English and the French traditions helps to focus larger
questions about the common vocabulary of criticism for this period in
literary history. The familiar generalizations about European Romanticism seem especially confusing and artificial when French and
English texts are read together; the common critical terms are inadequate to describe the sharp sense of contrast experienced in the reading
of particular French and English writers. Nor do the common critical
categories explain the persistent coolness of literary relations between
the English and the French. Why did Coleridge think that serious
poetry could not be written in the French language? Why, in turn,
have Wordsworth and Coleridge never seriously been read in France?
Although recognizing common concerns in the writings of this period,
I wish to suggest the fundamental ways in which English and French
writers were using different, perhaps untranslatable languages.

The subtlety of written criticism over the arranging of bookshelves
becomes apparent. It is difficult, literally, to put Baudelaire's criticism
next to Coleridge and, at the same time, far away, or to place *Middlemarch* near *Madame Bovary*, but even closer to *The Prelude*. My
study is arranged as a sequence of pairings which start from obvious
analogies between writers or texts but then reveal even more
fundamental contrasts.

A comparison of Rousseau and Wordsworth constitutes the first
half of the book, for both the analogies and the differences between
French and English Romanticism stand out most strikingly in the *Confessions* and *The Prelude*. Moreover, the great influence of these two
writers at least in part accounts for the course of what follows for several generations. In their separate ways Rousseau and Wordsworth

each discovered the autobiographical theme and made it into the major subject of modern literature. In talking about themselves, they also renewed the old themes of all literature with an emphasis that seems in each distinctively new, whether we call it Romantic or modern.

Historians of literature have applauded (or lamented) the achievement of Rousseau and Wordsworth, but by praising or blaming them *together* they have, it may be argued, diminished their individual stature and confused the significance of the legacy each left behind. The *Confessions* and *The Prelude* are equally original, masterful, and profoundly influential works of art partly because each is so distinctive, so remarkably unlike the other.

The second half of this book pursues the comparison of English and French writings further into the nineteenth century in three genres: poetry, criticism, and fiction. The examples are, obviously, intended to be suggestive rather than exhaustive. I do not intend a rigid definition of either the French or English mind, nor a tight classification to which there are no exceptions. Since I began the study partly out of discomfort with the widespread application of identical critical terms to writings felt to be fundamentally different, I am reluctant to impose other, perhaps equally inadequate or overrestrictive labels. My general categories are deliberately tentative, as responsible as possible to the recurrent effects of particular books and writers.

My first and last impression has been that French and English writers in this period have not done the same things well. For the most part, and at their best, they were not even trying to express the same sense of life at all. The idea of the "transcendental imagination" never takes hold in French Romanticism as it does in English. Wordsworth's heroic ideal of the marriage between mind and nature in a universe enlivened by eternal spirit does not inform the writings of Rousseau, Hugo, Baudelaire, or Flaubert. It even seems alien to their common preoccupation with the isolated human spirit, thrown back on its own human resources of feeling, conscience, or faith.

In the writings of Wordsworth, Coleridge, and George Eliot, the pulse of life within the self is, in some way, taken to be a version of a larger, universal vitality, even though the pulse of the individual life may slacken, or fail to achieve full union with the spirit beyond it. The French writings I examine have a more plaintive or ironic tone. Human vitality resides in the urgency of desires which reality generally fails to satisfy. The private certainty of personal human emotion is the ultimate irreducible reality, and it survives independent of any response to desire from the universe.

It is not necessary, or perhaps even possible, to choose between these deeply different perceptions of life. Each of us at times may lean toward one view or the other, though for the most part everyday life proceeds without scrutiny of the assumptions about reality and self implicit in our very categories of thought and language. The promise of this sort of study, like one promise of literature itself, is the articulation of convictions ordinarily taken for granted without reflection. The writers I discuss all have the power of great writers to bring to consciousness what usually goes without saying—or, stated another way, to intensify awareness of what is implicit in different ways of saying things. My aim is to be as fully responsive as possible to the individual visions of these different writers, while at the same time defining the features we vaguely recognize under the loose designations of culture or tradition.

Many teachers, friends, and colleagues have generously helped me by their encouragement and perceptive criticism. My oldest debt is to Paul de Man, whose superb teaching first drew me to the study of Comparative Literature. I received invaluable help in the early stages of this work (now the sections on Rousseau and Wordsworth) from Herbert Dieckmann and the late Reuben Brower. Other colleagues and friends have since read all or part of the manuscript: Leo Bersani, Anne Ferry, David Ferry, Robert Garis, David Kalstone, Patrick F. Quinn, Patricia Meyer Spacks, and William Youngren. Their provocative objections have been as helpful as their enthusiasm. My husband, James Evan Sabin, has watched patiently over the growth of this book for a long time, sustaining my work by his confidence in it and, especially, by his astute judgments and suggestions.

Preliminary work for this book was aided by a Fellowship from the American Association of University Women. The generosity of Wellesley College, in subsidizing a leave from teaching in 1973-74, enabled me to complete the book. A shorter version of Chapter 4 appeared as an article, "Imagination in Rousseau and Wordsworth," and is reprinted by permission of Comparative Literature, 22 (1970), 328-345.

The English translations of citations from Rousseau's Confessions are from Jean-Jacques Rousseau, The Confessions, translated by J. M. Cohen (Penguin Classics, 1954), pp. 1 and passim, copyright © J. M.

Cohen, 1954, and are here reprinted by permission of Penguin Books, Ltd. The English translations of Baudelaire's art criticism are from the translation by Jonathan Mayne, published as *The Mirror of Art: Critical Studies by Baudelaire* (Doubleday Anchor Books, 1956), copyright © 1955, and are reprinted by permission of Phaidon Press, Ltd. The English translations of Montaigne are from *The Complete Works of Montaigne*, translated by Donald M. Frame (Stanford University Press, 1948).

I wish also to thank Marie-Hélène Gold for so expertly helping me to translate the other French texts. Not surprisingly, the difficulties encountered in translating these texts often seemed to confirm the main theses of the book. Because my argument is so often about the details of language, I have included the original French as well as a translation of all quotations except those from modern French criticism.

The excerpt from "The Circus Animals' Desertion" is reprinted by permission of Macmillan Publishing Co., Inc., New York, from *The Collected Poems of W. B. Yeats,* © 1940 by Georgie Yeats, renewed 1968 by Bertha Georgie Yeats, Michael Butler Yeats, and Anne Yeats, and also by permission of M. B. Yeats, Anne Yeats, and Macmillan of London and Basingstoke. "The Darkling Thrush" is reprinted from *Collected Poems of Thomas Hardy*, copyright 1925, by permission of Macmillan Publishing Co., Inc., Macmillan Press, Ltd. of London and Basingstoke, and Macmillan of Canada, Ltd. Citations from Wordsworth's *The Prelude* are reprinted by permission of Oxford University Press, from *The Prelude*, ed. Ernest de Selincourt and Helen Darbishire, © 1959.

Contents

Part Four Ideas of the Symbol in Coleridge and
   Baudelaire

Part Five Nature and Imagination in *Middlemarch*
   and *Madame Bovary*

English Romanticism and
the French Tradition

Part One

Rousseau and Wordsworth
Autobiography and the Language of Feeling

1
The Story of a Life

I sought a theme and sought for it in vain,
I sought it daily for six weeks or so.
Maybe at last, being but a broken man,
I must be satisfied with my heart, although
Winter and summer till old age began
My circus animals were all on show,
Those stilted boys, that burnished chariot,
Lion and woman and the Lord knows what.

In "The Circus Animals' Desertion," Yeats re-creates a familiar Romantic experience. The writing of autobiography, in the Romantic period and since, often reflects a mood of enervation or uncertainty but at the same time the act of self-examination releases new creative energy. In "The Circus Animals' Desertion," autobiography at first seems to the poet only the enumerating of old themes, since his heart, more or less disguised, had always been in his poetry. But to be satisfied with his heart also means that what he calls "heart-mysteries" look different to him now. His own past provides therefore a new poetic theme with new images arising to express his fresh attitude.

"The Circus Animals' Desertion" dramatizes the renewal of poetic power through the activity of memory, itself an old theme which Yeats re-creates in new terms. Wordsworth, in Book I of *The Prelude*, also "sought a theme in vain" and then settled for the history of his own heart as memory and introspection began to revive his "genial mood." Rousseau's autobiographical project in the *Confessions*, written about forty years earlier, seems bolder and more deliberate from the start. Yet Rousseau also sought in autobiography a release from the old forms of past literature and from the disguising images of his own earlier writings.

The simplest terms of analogy between Rousseau and Wordsworth as autobiographical writers are familiar and easy to state. We can still use Hazlitt's remarks in his essay about Rousseau written in 1816: "The writer who most nearly resembles him [Rousseau] in our own times is the author of the *Lyrical Ballads*. We see no other difference between them, than that the one wrote in prose and the other in poetry. . . . Both create an interest out of nothing, or rather out of their own feelings; both weave numberless recollections into one sentiment; both wind their own being round whatever object occurs to them."[1] Hazlitt inaugurates the tendency to trace the subjective or egotistical character of modern literature to Rousseau and Wordsworth.[2] With mixed admiration and reproach, Hazlitt calls Rousseau and Wordsworth "two of the greatest egotists we know of." Their egotism makes them the leading spokesmen for the character of the new age, in politics as well as literature. The modern writer, like the political revolutionary, is essentially an egotist, Hazlitt explains, for he "tolerates only what he himself creates; he sympathizes only with what can enter into no competition with him. . . . He sees nothing but himself and the universe."[3]

Hazlitt, like many other and more recent critics of literature and life, proceeds as if "egotism" named a single trait of character or a uniform stance in relation to experience. The only distinction to Hazlitt between Rousseau and Wordsworth is that the one wrote in prose and the other in poetry. To him, it is a minor distinction, to be mentioned only in passing. To us, it may signify the proper starting point of an essential contrast. To re-create the self in poetry or in prose—that alternative suggests the range rather than the sameness of human egotism. We shall see that "heart-mysteries," whatever their substance, look altogether different when rendered in prose and in poetry, particularly when we are comparing eighteenth-century French prose and nineteenth-century English blank verse. The simple difference in form has immense implications for both Rousseau and Wordsworth, partly because their choice of form reflects their affiliations with two distinct earlier traditions.

Rousseau announces the character of his autobiography at the very beginning of the *Confessions*:[4] "Voici le seul portrait d'homme, peint exactement d'après nature et dans toute sa vérité, qui existe et qui probablement existera jamais" (3). (Here is the only portrait of man, painted exactly and in every way according to the truth of nature, which exists and will probably ever exist.) Rousseau calls us to witness a unique personal performance, unprecedented and inimitable. But it is important to see also that he is announcing this claim in relation to a particular literary tradition. The proposed form of his work, "un portrait," and the promise of fidelity to nature recall distinguished precedents in the French prose tradition. One thinks, first, of Montaigne's effort to draw a portrait (or what he calls a "peinture") of himself according to the truth of nature:

Les autres forment l'homme; je le recite et en represente un particulier. . . . Or les traits de ma peinture ne fourvoyent point, quoy qu'ils se changent et diversifient. . . . Est-il aussi raison que je produise au monde, où la façon et l'art ont tant de credit et de commandement, des effects de nature crus et simples, et d'une nature encore bien foiblette?[5]

(Others form man; I tell of him, and portray a particular one. . . . Now the lines of my painting do not go astray, though they change and vary. . . . Is it reasonable too that I should set forth to the world, where fashioning and art have so much credit and authority, some crude and simple products of nature, and of a very feeble nature at that?)

The precedents evoked by Rousseau's project are not limited to earlier self-portraiture. La Bruyère uses similar language to introduce his portraits of society, Les Caractères ou les moeurs de ce siècle. The public may contemplate, La Bruyère writes in the Preface, "ce portrait que j'ai fait de lui d'après nature"[6] (this portrait of it that I have made, following nature). Further, one hears echoes of Pascal's introduction to his portrait of man, "L'Homme sans Dieu": "Mais j'ai cru trouver au moins biens des compagnons en l'étude de l'homme, et que c'est la vraie étude qui lui est propre. J'ai été trompé: il y en a encore moins qui l'étudient que la géometrie."[7] (But I thought I would at least find many companions in the study of man, in that it is his true and proper study. I was mistaken; there are even fewer who study that than geometry.)

Pascal, it is true, seems wryly disappointed to be so alone in his study of man, while Rousseau glories in his uniqueness. Rousseau's arrogance, his presumption to solitary possession of truth, marks his distance from the seventeenth century. Yet the worth of his project and even the claim of new fidelity to truth derive from the values asserted by the seventeenth-century moralists and Montaigne.[8] Rousseau assumes an audience trained to value "l'étude de l'homme," and

accustomed to seek the truth of human nature in forms of biography
and portraiture. The pretensions of this great French prose tradition
provide the standard by which Rousseau asserts his own superiority:

> Des histoires, des vies, des portraits, des caractéres! Qu'est-ce que
> tout cela? Des romans ingenieux bâtis sur quelques actes extérieurs,
> sur quelques discours qui s'y rapportent, sur de subtiles conjectures
> où l'Auteur cherche bien plus à briller lui-même qu'à trouver la
> vérité. ("Ebauches des Confessions," 1149)

> (Stories, lives, portraits, characters! What does it all come to? In-
> genious novels built out of some external actions, some speeches
> that fit together, some subtle conjecture through which the author
> tries much harder to make himself shine than to find the truth.)

Rousseau claims to be unique among writers, perhaps among men,
in his singleminded pursuit of truth. When he dismisses other works of
biography or portraiture as "des romans ingenieux," he implies a
necessary distinction between truthfulness and the show of literary
skill: "On saisit les traits saillans d'un caractére, on les lie par des traits
d'invention, et pourvu que le tout fasse une physionomie, qu'importe
qu'elle ressemble? Nul ne peut juger de cela" ("Ebauches des Confessions," 1149). (One seizes on the striking traits of a character, links
them together by invented traits and, provided that it adds up to a
physiognomy, what is the difference whether it is a resemblance? No
one can judge that.) Rousseau chastises "false" portrait painters as if
they were in some way cheating, trying to deceive an audience, or to
distract from truth by the dazzle of a literary performance. This kind
of egotism Rousseau loudly abjures. His portrait of himself will be different because he has diligently pursued total and exact truth, the
truth of "ressemblance" rather than "vraisemblance."

Rousseau makes his repudiation of literary values seem a kind of
humility. He sacrifices the glamour of literature to serve the stark but
noble principle of truth. The enterprise demands a similar austerity
from the reader. In the Preface to Rousseau's later autobiographical
work, the *Dialogues*, Rousseau indignantly warns away the reader
who would debase any of his autobiographical writings into mere
works of literature, mere performances for aesthetic pleasure:

> Quant à ceux qui ne veulent qu'une lecture agréable et rapide, ceux
> qui n'ont cherché, qui n'ont trouvé que cela dans mes *Confessions*,
> ceux qui ne peuvent souffrir un peu de fatigue ni soutenir une atten-

tion suivie pour l'interest de la justice et de la vérité, ils feront bien de s'épargner l'ennui de cette lecture; ce n'est pas à eux que j'ai voulu parler, et loin de chercher à leur plaire, j'éviterai du moins cette derniére indignité, que le tableau des miséres de ma vie soit pour personne un objet d'amusement. (666)

(As for those who wish only for pleasant and quick reading, those who sought and found only that in my *Confessions*, those who cannot endure a little fatigue or sustain their attention for the sake of justice and truth—they will be well advised to spare themselves the boredom of reading this book. It is not to them that I wished to speak, and far from trying to please them, I shall at least avoid this last indignity: that this picture of the miseries of my life should be to anyone a subject of entertainment.)

By the time of the *Dialogues*, personal vindication had become Rousseau's monomania. To a man tormented by his sense of the world's injustice to him, what could be more intolerable than an audience coolly measuring whether his story is boring or, even worse, entertaining! But Rousseau's outrage at the mere thought of this indignity in the *Dialogues* only takes to the extreme of personal obsession a bias ever-present in his writings. Rousseau's commitment to truth in the *Confessions* draws energy from the deep distrust of art which he expresses so often in both personal and philosophic terms, beginning with the first *Discours*, and then again in *Emile*, in the *Lettre à d'Alembert*, and in many scattered comments all through the autobiographical writings. The progress of the arts reflects the progressive corruption of human nature and social virtue. The Swiss are right to prohibit theater. Emile shall remain pure by reading only *Robinson Crusoe*. Literature is the frivolous and corrupting amusement of the salon.[9]

Rousseau is, paradoxically, a brilliant writer who disapproves of the whole activity of literature, despite his own success even in its conventional forms, as in his novel *La Nouvelle Héloise*. In his autobiography he will show how one can write without being literary, without abandoning the commitment to justice and truth and nature which literature, in his view, characteristically betrays for other more trivial or self-serving aims. Rousseau dissociates his sincerity from the very act of literary composition: "Si je veux faire un ouvrage écrit avec soin comme les autres, je ne me peindrai pas, je me farderai. C'est ici de mon portrait qu'il s'agit et non pas d'un livre" ("Ebauches des Confessions," 1154). (If, like others, I sought to produce a carefully written work, I would not be so much portraying as disguising myself. What is at stake here is my portrait, and not a book.) Books are composed with care and the very act of composing masks the subject. His writing will reveal truth instead of disguising it. He is not writing a book, in the ordinary sense; he is offering an exact portrait of himself.

To earlier writers of portraits, truth and artistry were not opposed. La Bruyère did not consider his commitment to "la vérité" to be threatened by his literary ambition. On the contrary, the moral and psychological truth of his portraits would be the proof of his artistic skill: "C'est un métier de faire un livre, comme de faire une pendule."[10] (It is a craft to make a book, like making a clock.) Only the true portrait would work, like a clock with every piece accurately in place.

Although Montaigne seems closer to Rousseau in distinguishing nature from art, even Montaigne asks us to admire his apparent artlessness for aesthetic reasons. He compares his digressive manner to the art of the Platonic dialogue or to the style of Plutarch; the bold movements of thought and language in those writings command admiration as much for their aesthetic appeal as for their furtherance of truth:

> J'ayme l'alleure poetique, à sauts et à gambades. C'est une art, comme dict Platon, legere, volage, demoniacle. . . . O Dieu, que ces gaillardes escapades, que cette variation a de beauté, et plus lors que plus elle retire au nonchalant et fortuite![11]
>
> (I love the poetic gait, by leaps and gambols. It is an art, as Plato says, light, flighty, daemonic. . . . Lord, what beauty there is in these lusty sallies and this variation, and more so the more casual and accidental they seem.)

In the *Confessions*, as in other of his writings, Rousseau identifies himself as the unique champion of truth against a historical background marked by the habitual compromise of truth for beauty and pleasure. Rousseau's standard of truthfulness may seem narrowly, naïvely literal-minded. But Rousseau is no simple Philistine. His disparagement of art belongs to a systematic and complex criticism of society and to a theory of history. Rousseau urges a greater respect for literal-mindedness than is fashionable in polite or literary society. True judgment of a person's life—and of human life, generally—is at stake in all biographical or autobiographical writing, and Rousseau would make literal-mindedness into respect for the dignity of unadorned human nature. Moreover, the literary tradition which he challenges itself boasts a special commitment to truth. Rousseau claims distinction within a tradition of writing already dedicated, presumably, to the study and judgment of actual human experience. Rousseau's autobiography both challenges and belongs to a literary tradition of a special sort—a tradition of nonfictional writing which invites distinctions between art and truth more directly than would seem pertinent to what we ordinarily call imaginative literature. Histories, biographies, and portraits profess, by tradition as well as by their very character, a relation to literal truth different from novels or plays or epic poems.

In *The Prelude*, Wordsworth brings quite different standards to bear upon his plan to tell "the story of my life." Wordsworth's poem offers a story, not a demonstration of veracity. It is a narrative poem, and we are made aware even before the story begins that the poet aspires to join a traditional company of lofty poets and storytellers.

> O there is blessing in this gentle breeze,
> A visitant that while it fans my cheek
> Doth seem half-conscious of the joy it brings
> From the green fields, and from yon azure sky.
> Whate'er its mission, the soft breeze can come
> To none more grateful than to me; escaped
> From the vast city, where I long had pined
> A discontented sojourner: now free,
> Free as a bird to settle where I will.
> What dwelling shall receive me? in what vale
> Shall be my harbour? underneath what grove
> Shall I take up my home? and what clear stream
> Shall with its murmur lull me into rest?
> The earth is all before me. With a heart
> Joyous, nor scared at its own liberty,
> I look about; and should the chosen guide
> Be nothing better than a wandering cloud,
> I cannot miss my way. I breathe again!
> Trances of thought and mountings of the mind
> Come fast upon me: it is shaken off,
> That burthen of my own unnatural self,
> The heavy weight of many a weary day
> Not mine, and such as were not made for me.
> Long months of peace (if such bold word accord
> With any promises of human life),
> Long months of ease and undisturbed delight

Are mine in prospect; whither shall I turn,
By road or pathway, or through trackless field,
Up hill or down, or shall some floating thing
Upon the river point me out my course?

Dear Liberty! Yet what would it avail
But for a gift that consecrates the joy?
For I, methought, while the sweet breath of heaven
Was blowing on my body, felt within
A correspondent breeze, that gently moved
With quickening virtue, but is now become
A tempest, a redundant energy,
Vexing its own creation. Thanks to both,
And their congenial powers, that, while they join
In breaking up a long-continued frost,
Bring with them vernal promises, the hope
Of active days urged on by flying hours, —
Days of sweet leisure, taxed with patient thought
Abstruse, nor wanting punctual service high,
Matins and vespers of harmonious verse![12]

                                                        (I. 1-45)

Book I of *The Prelude* begins as a lofty song, a prophecy of joy and freedom and high poetic service. The speaker of the opening lines is not directly announcing his intentions to an audience. He speaks only to himself and to the "open fields." We seem to overhear a private meditation, of a particular literary sort. The many epic and specifically Miltonic echoes in the language affiliate the poet's meditation with such earlier inspired musings as Milton's invocations in *Paradise Lost*. This is the meditation of a poet, who speaks even to himself in the words and phrases of high poetic discourse: "visitant," "sojourner," "What dwelling shall receive me?," "taxed with patient thought/Abstruse."

The song of joy ends with an abrupt shift of perspective at line 45. To our surprise, the invocation recedes into an episode in a story that has, in a sense, already begun to be told:

Thus far, O Friend! did I, not used to make
A present joy the matter of a song,
Pour forth that day my soul in measured strains
That would not be forgotten, and are here
Recorded.

                                                        (I. 46-50)

We discover that the confident joy of the invocation belongs to a past time. Since then the poet has discovered more impediments to lofty poetic service than he anticipated. He now meditates about his dejection. Yet the formal poetic decorum of his language never falters. He continues to speak in "measured strains," even while acknowledging his uncertainty to the Friend who now becomes the poem's explicit audience. The Friend is Coleridge, we learn later, but his particular identity hardly matters at first. The title Friend or "honoured Friend" refers as well to any well-disposed reader of the poem, or to a more abstract idea of a poetic audience, following Milton's hope for a "fit audience, though few." The poet's voice shifts direction, back and forth: now he addresses the Friend directly, now he withdraws into further private meditation.

Wordsworth's autobiographical subject emerges out of the seeming meandering of the poetic voice in Book I. The poet moves with apparent spontaneity into the story of his life, before declaring his special interest in that story. First, he invokes the memory of his privileged childhood to rebuke his present low spirits; then he continues on a wave of excitement aroused by the memories themselves. Wordsworth formally announces his plan only at the end of Book I, after the autobiographical narrative is well under way:

> One end at least hath been attained; my mind
> Hath been revived, and if this genial mood
> Desert me not, forthwith shall be brought down
> Through later years the story of my life.
> The road lies plain before me, — 'tis a theme
> Single and of determined bounds; and hence
> I choose it rather at this time, than work
> Of ampler or more varied argument,
> Where I might be discomfited and lost:
> And certain hopes are with me, that to thee
> This labour will be welcome, honoured Friend!
> (I. 636-646)

Wordsworth's formal announcement belongs to a literary design or fiction already in motion by the end of Book I. Even without knowing that Wordsworth wrote many parts of *The Prelude* before the introduction, we do not feel urged to take the movement of Book I as a literal record of how it was composed. The consciously literary and allusive style of the poem from the beginning makes us accept the poet's design as a literary device, and we wait to see what meaning it will assume in relation to the rest of the poem.

The design is already expressive in Book I, for it arouses interest in the regenerative power of memory and in the spontaneous, unpredictable sources of poetic power. There is no prior commitment by the poet to tell the story of his life, nor does he suggest that he regards the study of a man's life to be a supremely interesting or valuable activity. In contrast to Rousseau, who takes the value of that study for granted, Wordsworth presents himself as a poet at the opening of his career, absorbed in contemplating his power and in seeking the best theme for a heroic song.

Before Wordsworth chooses the autobiographical theme, he contemplates other possibilities, "of ampler or more varied argument." As an aspiring epic poet, Wordsworth does not place himself in relation to a tradition that asserts the proper study of mankind to be man. The alternately hopeful and discouraged poet in Book I first considers possible legendary or mythic subjects more obviously appropriate to his ambition:

> . . . some British theme, some old
> Romantic tale by Milton left unsung;
> More often turning to some gentle place
> Within the groves of Chivalry, I pipe
> To shepherd swains . . .
>
> (I. 168-172)

> Sometimes, more sternly moved, I would relate
> How vanquished Mithridates northward passed,
> And, hidden in the cloud of years, became
> Odin, the Father of a race by whom
> Perished the Roman Empire.
>
> (I. 186-190)

By the end of Book I the poet has curbed his heroic and romantic aspirations. By deciding to tell a human story, his own story, he deliberately chooses a relatively "plain" road: "The road lies plain before me, —'tis a theme / Single and of determined bounds; and hence / I choose it rather at this time, than work / Of ampler or more varied argument." The decision has an air of compromise, cautious restraint.

Yet Wordsworth's very measuring of his theme in relation to earlier epics itself follows the example of Milton in *Paradise Lost*: "Sad task, yet argument / Not less but more Heroic than the wrauth / Of stern *Achilles*" (IX. 13-15). Although Wordsworth lacks Milton's righteous certainty, he too is boldly setting out to create a new epic subject. He brings to his purposely limited theme the same quality of ambition voiced earlier in the poem in phrases like "some work of glory," "some arduous work." He describes his enterprise as a "labour," the word traditionally associated with the activity of heroic poets. His argument may at first seem mundane compared to earlier epic themes, but he will prove it to be a heroic argument nonetheless, as high if not higher than the themes put aside by Milton and perhaps worthy of rivaling even Milton himself.

Wordsworth's apparent reticence may be heard then as the traditional formal humility appropriate to the opening of a heroic poem. The epic poet, following Milton, must be humble, for he relies on powers beyond his deliberate control. Thus Milton invokes his "celestial Patroness, who deigns / Her nightly visitation unimplored" (IX. 21-22). Wordsworth's Muse is more personal and terrestrial, yet his "genial mood" is as mysterious as Milton's goddess, and perhaps even less reliable: "and if this genial mood / Desert me not, forthwith shall be brought down / Through later years the story of my life."

The Miltonic poet's special kind of spontaneity, or "unpremeditated verse," depends on inspiration. The spontaneous song at the opening of *The Prelude*, Wordsworth explains, signified a state of holy transport. His spirit was, for a time, reclothed, as in an act of conversion or religious initiation: "poetic numbers came / Spontaneously to clothe in priestly robe / A renovated spirit" (I. 51-53). The poet's inspired spontaneity differs fundamentally from Rousseau's frankness, for Rousseau disdains all costume, priestly or secular. Rousseau regards all literary garb as disguise or mask. His title, the *Confessions*, suggests that to tell the truth is to reveal a hidden, perhaps shameful reality. His portrait will unmask the self by throwing off the rituals of art altogether.

Rousseau does not rely on inspiration. While others have failed to be true because of cowardice or vanity, his strength of deliberate commitment guarantees his success: "Je connois jusqu'ici nul autre homme qui ait osé faire ce que je me propose." (I know no other man until now who has dared do what I propose.) For Rousseau, telling his story is an act more of daring than of inspiration. Spontaneity is a moral achievement, the courage to be sincere, frank, and self-revealing.

Since Rousseau assumes that to judge a man truly we must see him as he sees himself, his autobiography dares to allow the reader into his own most intimate view of himself. Unimpeded by the customary disguises of art, we shall come to understand his life as he does—and therefore we shall apprehend its inner truth. Rousseau thus depends upon his language to create an extraordinary identification between writer and reader. His language encourages, even demands, total participation in Rousseau's own view of his sensibility. His view is trustworthy, Rousseau insists, because he repudiates the artifice of composition. Rousseau vouches for the truth of his portrait by the bravery of his own trust in the spontaneous dictates of memory and feeling.

While the poet in *The Prelude* also speaks from feeling, the self that governs the poetic style is a "renovated spirit," new and higher than the habitual and characteristic self. Spontaneity of style for Wordsworth in *The Prelude* therefore sets the poet apart and above his audience, and even above his own everyday person. The inspired poet performs his art clothed in priestly robes. He does not simply choose his garments; they come to him from sources beyond his deliberate resolve. By the end of Book I, the "genial mood" has spontaneously returned. His trust in his powers revives. But he cannot really guarantee the success of his song, for it depends upon the mysterious and spontaneous grace of his Muse.

The difference between the "spontaneity" invoked by Rousseau and by Wordsworth tends to be glossed over by the familiar generalizations about Romanticism. Meyer Abrams, placing Romantic aesthetic theory in the critical tradition, loosely joins under the rubric "expressive theory" the two attitudes toward style which I have been contrasting:

> In general terms, the central tendency of the expressive theory may be summarized in this way: A work of art is essentially the internal made external, resulting from a creative process operating under the impulse of feeling, and embodying the combined product of the poet's perceptions, thoughts, and feelings. The primary source and subject matter of a poem, therefore, are the attributes and actions of the poet's own mind; or if aspects of the external world, then these only as they are converted from fact to poetry by the feelings and operations of the poet's mind. . . . The paramount cause of poetry is not, as in Aristotle, a formal cause, determined primarily by the human actions and qualities imitated; nor, as in neo-classic criticism, a final cause, the effect intended upon the audience; but instead an efficient cause—the impulse within the poet of feelings

and desires seeking expression, or the compulsion of the "creative" imagination which, like God the creator, has its internal source of motion.[13]

Abrams sounds remarkably like Hazlitt in 1816 explaining the egotism of Rousseau and Wordsworth. The "expressive theory" defines a literature of egotism, rooted in the thoughts and feelings of the writer. Autobiography, in one form or another, is the natural subject of this art, or all subjects become autobiographical, just as Hazlitt described the way Rousseau and Wordsworth "wind their own being round whatever object occurs to them."

Spontaneity and sincerity, Abrams goes on to say, are the important values in the expressive theory of art and also the crucial attributes of style and form. The lyric therefore becomes the paradigm of literary form since it is the type of poetry traditionally associated with personal feeling.[14] Abrams describes the Romantic tendency to lyricize other traditional forms of art, a chief example being Wordsworth's conversion of the epic into a spontaneous overflow of feeling in *The Prelude:*

> Concurrently we discover a tendency to convert the lyric "I" from what Coleridge called the "I-representative" to the poet in his proper person, and to express experiences and states of mind which can be verified from the testimony of the poet's private letters and journals. Even in the contemporary practice of narrative or dramatic forms, the reader is often invited to identify the hero with his author.[15]

Abrams' historical categories help to define Wordsworth's transformation of the epic and also Rousseau's originality in the tradition of portraiture. Yet the idea of a conversion to expressiveness is a misleading simplification too, for it underrates the degree to which individual writers in the Romantic period extend rather than abandon earlier values and conventions. Wordsworth's idea of spontaneity owes more to Milton's epic than Abrams acknowledges. The heroic voice in *The Prelude* is not that of the "poet in his proper person." Wordsworth invites us to identify the hero with the author of the poem only in a very special way. While the style of his poem is freely expressive and personal, it also follows Milton's ideal of unpremeditated inspiration. And like Milton, Wordsworth makes his poetic performance an argument, intended to persuade an audience of new heroic values by the creation of a new epic subject.

What Abrams identifies as neoclassic concern for "a final cause, the effect intended upon the audience," survives undiminished in *The Prelude*, as it does also in the *Confessions*, in another way. The general category of expressiveness blurs Rousseau's purpose too. Rousseau does courageously choose to reveal himself in his proper (and improper) person, even beyond what usually appears in letters and journals. His style will be frank self-expression, and this very frankness is intended to have quite definite effects upon the audience. Rousseau does not write only under the impulse of feelings seeking expression. He expects and is determined to vindicate his character against the calumny of his former friends and, indeed, all Europe. And the correction of the personal injustice done to him will also have further and lasting effects, for it will overturn the false picture of man entrenched in literature through the vanity and the artifice of the past.

2

Rousseau and the Vocabulary of Feeling

If Rousseau is taken at his own word in the Prefaces to the *Confessions*, his attitude toward style seems confident, nonchalant:

Je prends donc mon parti sur le style comme sur les choses. Je ne m'attacherai point à le rendre uniforme; j'aurai toujours celui qui me viendra, j'en changerai selon mon humeur sans scrupule, je dirai chaque chose comme je la sens, comme je la vois, sans recherche, sans gêne, sans m'embarrasser de la bigarrure. ("Ebauches des Confessions," 1154)

(I have made up my mind about style as about content. I shall not strive for uniformity. I shall always have the style that comes to me; I shall change it according to my mood and without scruple; I shall speak of each thing as I feel it, as I see it, without affectation or constraint, and without concern for colorful effects.)

In the actual narrative, however, Rousseau's promise to say exactly what he feels quickly engages him in a scrupulous attention to language after all. In the very effort to reveal the truth of his inner life, Rousseau discovers that he cannot simply commit his feelings to whatever words happen to come to mind. The struggle to find the right word, the uncomfortable sense that most words are not right—this consciousness of style appears to be more than an artifact of composition; it is deep in the movement of Rousseau's thought.

17

Among the many obstacles to saying what he feels, the most formidable, from Rousseau's point of view, is the treachery hidden in the very character of language. Others may suspect conscious (or unconscious) artifice behind Rousseau's apparent frankness. But to Rousseau, the problem goes deeper than judgment of his possibly impure motives. Even his most thorough commitment to free and full expression must contend with the artificiality that seems inherent in language itself.

Rousseau's effort of style—or perhaps more accurately, his struggle against the inevitability of style—arises because, fundamentally, he trusts language much less than his bold autobiographical project suggests, and even requires. Rousseau's ideal of spontaneity requires that language be neutral, or at least flexible enough to take the varying shape of inward experience. Yet Rousseau distrusts literature, even the very act of writing because, in addition to its connection with other social and moral vices, language itself appears to him to be a primary source of the evil he perceives in the world.[1]

Far from being a naïve enthusiast of free expression, Rousseau comes to his autobiography as an experienced philosopher of language. Paul de Man, Jacques Derrida, and a few other recent critics of Rousseau have demonstrated how complex a problem Rousseau understood the very nature of language to pose for any statement of what could be called reality. Derrida observes that in Rousseau's writings about language (especially in L'Essai sur l'origine des langues) diverse efforts to affirm even the conceptual possibility of a free and true language are always accompanied by proof that the ideal language is an illusion.[2] In his philosophic speculations about language, Rousseau proposes many historical and theoretical distinctions—between song and speech, speech and writing, the languages of the north and south —to discriminate forms of expression more or less faithful to an original reality of feeling. The contrast between ordinary composition and the free projection of feeling into words is yet another of these distinctions. Rousseau's theory of language, however, cannot really avoid the suspicion that *all* forms of language inevitably supplant and, in a sense, destroy the reality they are created to re-present.

If language inevitably displaces what it is supposed to preserve, any plan to manifest the full truth of the inner life in autobiography is doomed from the start, no matter how the book is composed. Moreover, further obstacles to free expressiveness arise from Rousseau's special claims for his sensibility. The *Confessions* begin with Rousseau's assertion that he is unique, not just individual but different from

others: "Si je ne vaux pas mieux, au moins je suis autre"(5). (I may be
no better, but at least I am different.) The language of the autobiography must justify this extraordinary claim. Yet words themselves
have common public identities. Rousseau may be unique among
writers in composing a book without artifice, but insofar as he describes himself in the same words used by other men, his unique self is
in danger of being trapped in the meanings other men attach to those
words. Rousseau utterly relies on language to justify himself. Yet both
his view of himself and his attitude toward language make words an
inherently unreliable medium.[3]

Rousseau's paradoxical blend of faith in and distrust of language
has been remarked by Derrida and others. The historical and literary
framework of Rousseau's preoccupation with the problem, however,
tends to be lost in the fascinating theoretical questions of primary
interest to the best recent critics of Rousseau, especially in France. For
my subject, it is crucial to recognize that (in the *Confessions*, though
elsewhere too) Rousseau's theoretical fear of being misrepresented by
words takes the practical form of a protest against particular conventions of language in the French tradition. Indeed, the strength of those
conventions may even account for the direction of Rousseau's theoretical concerns, for he takes the tendencies of the language he knows
best to represent the action of language generally. In the *Confessions*,
Rousseau strains to free his inner life from the language of feeling and
judgment given authority by his great literary predecessors in France.
He sees himself in a struggle against the falsity of all language, but he
is also and more immediately rebelling against certain established uses
of language in the French tradition. The whole enterprise of the *Confessions* protests against the literary portraiture of the past; the protest
goes on at every level of the work, even to the implications of syntax
and the meaning of individual words.

The great prose writers of seventeenth-century France established
an authoritative language of psychological description which drew
strength precisely from the public character of language. By labeling
and defining passions or principles of character and motive, the seventeenth-century portraitist strove to locate the common human core of
apparently diverse individual experiences.[4] Apparent idiosyncrasies
could be referred to the general principles of human nature and named
in clear, precise terms: vanity, greed, sexual appetite, love. The multi-
ple and confusing surfaces of social behavior could be classified into a
smaller number of essential and nameable motives, smaller because

many different surfaces cover a few abiding realities. Thus La Rochefoucauld unmasks the diverse forms of "amour-propre" (self-love) or
Pascal sees distraction from the single need for God through all the
paraphernalia of civilized work and play. Language, then, for La
Rochefoucauld, La Bruyère, and Pascal works to reduce the multiplicity and to transcend the idiosyncracy of appearances. In order to preserve any sense of his uniqueness, Rousseau must resist the generalizing impulse of seventeenth-century portrait-writing and the deep
imprint of this tradition on the French language.

Rousseau's position here, as so often, seems paradoxical, for he
does not systematically oppose general theories of human nature. On
the contrary, a general theory of man unifies Rousseau's own work,
his social and political commentaries particularly, but his other writings too. In one sense, Rousseau's obsession with his uniqueness in the
Confessions seems oddly inconsistent with his other philosophic positions. Rousseau grandly assumes that the idiosyncracies of others are
more conventionally accountable than his own. This is the first prem-
ise of the autobiography at the start. Nature having broken the mold
in which he and only he was formed, it follows that the generalizing
language of portraiture radically breaks down only when it has to
contain *his* inner life. He differs from other people more than they differ from each other. That stubborn conviction partly accounts for the
special stylistic demands which Rousseau saw in the writing of his
autobiography.

From another perspective, however, the apparent discrepancy between Rousseau the autobiographer and Rousseau the social theorist
can be at least partially bridged. Rousseau offers his general idea of
human nature as a theoretical hypothesis, not the description of present or even historical actuality. His portrait of man in the state of
nature is, admittedly, a fiction. In the remote and even hypothetical
past, a few simple and uniform characteristics defined human nature.
But as the state of nature falls into history, the character of man becomes distorted, complicated, individualized. Rousseau's general idea
of human nature refers back to the myth of man's original and now
lost state.[5]

Rousseau's mythical state of nature operates first as an ideal standard by which to criticize the fragmentation of contemporary reality.
Further, Rousseau's historical and developmental perspective explains
the multiplicity of the present, but without explaining it away. Having
established the concept that natural *man* has disintegrated into social
men, Rousseau seems ready to register the many forms of the disinte-

gration. The unifying principles of human nature are pushed back to the hypothetical past rather than discovered beneath the surfaces of life here and now.

The seventeenth-century moralists primarily sought ways of organizing their perceptions of present reality. They analyze, define, and classify the present and, it would seem, permanent structure of human feelings and behavior. They tend to grasp their subjects in full-blown actuality rather than to construct a real or hypothetical development over time. Even though Rousseau's perceptions of men in society often closely resemble what the seventeenth-century moralists called man's permanent nature, Rousseau's historical approach is more than a different way of explaining the same phenomena. The emphasis on development allows more room for individual and idiosyncratic patterns since no two lines of experience in time are exactly parallel, and they may diverge widely. Thus Emile can become different from other men because radically new principles of education will guide his development. Rousseau is unlike other men at least partly because his experience, from the moment of birth, followed a singular path.

In his autobiographical writings, Rousseau uses his historical perspective to ward off the moral and psychological classifications handed down by earlier moralists. The *Lettres à Malesherbes*, four autobiographical essays written a few years before the *Confessions* were begun, show Rousseau appealing to his history for protection against established and (in Rousseau's opinion) misleading labels:

Une ame paresseuse qui s'effraye de tout soin, un temperament ardent, bilieux, facile à s'affecter et sensible à l'excés à tout ce qui l'affecte semblent ne pouvoir s'allier dans le même caractere, et ces deux contraires composent pourtant le fond du mien. Quoique je ne puisse resoudre cette opposition par des principes, elle existe pourtant, je la sens, rien n'est plus certain, et j'en puis du moins donner par les faits une espece d'historique qui peut servir à la concevoir. (1134)

(A lazy soul, afraid of any exertion, and an ardent bilious temper, easily moved and excessively sensitive to anything that might affect it, would seem not to go together in the same character, and yet these two opposites constitute the basis of mine. Although I cannot resolve this opposition theoretically, it is there nevertheless; I feel it; nothing is more certain, and I can at least give a sort of historical account of the facts which may help in the understanding of it.)

Rousseau knows, and he expects his reader to know, the conventional meaning of "une ame paresseuse." The concept of "la paresse" was offered as one principle of human character by the seventeenth-century moralists, especially by La Rochefoucauld who defined it as one of the permanent motives of human action—or inaction.[6] To La Rochefoucauld's cynical eye, "la paresse" is that force of human inertia which keeps men from great excess, either of virtue or of vice: "La modération est la langueur et la paresse de l'âme, comme l'ambition en est l'activité et l'ardeur."[7] (Moderation is the languor and the laziness of the soul, just as ambition is its activity and its ardor.) What others would call the virtue of restraint, La Rochefoucauld reduces to the psychological (or even physiological) motive of laziness.

In the *Lettres à Malesherbes*, Rousseau rebels against a label derived from maxims which simplify the structure of the inner life and the terms of moral judgment. Although he wants to describe something passive and timid in his character, he also defends the delicacy, energy, and therefore the virtue of his affections. Further, he wants to ally rather than oppose these apparently contradictory characteristics. La Rochefoucauld's "la paresse" is a moral and emotional brake. Rousseau's "ame paresseuse" is passive yet painfully, unrestrictedly vulnerable to strong feelings.

Rousseau does not here claim new generalizing or theoretical power. He does not write new maxims. The strength of his argument lies simply in his fidelity to the contradictory facts of his own experience. Although he cannot overturn established principles by new ones, he hopes to escape false labeling by "une espece d'historique." Autobiographical narrative thus offers an alternative and a challenge to psychological and moral principles. The facts—"les faits"—of the inner life, viewed historically, will have explanatory power, even with all their apparent illogic and inconsistency.

We encounter Rousseau's certainty about his own history almost as a refrain in the long narrative of the *Confessions*. But "une espece d'historique" does not in any simple way solve Rousseau's problem of style, for it remains problematic which words can faithfully render inward reality even in the form of a history. Although the history of the inner life may have the incontrovertibility of fact, a language of mere fact can hardly hope to elucidate the subtle motives and responses which are the substance of feeling to Rousseau. What he needs is a language that can register the "facts" of feelings—feelings taken as particular, substantial events in a single life. His language must both trace the development of feelings and also disclose the precise nuances of a particular moment. Most difficult, Rousseau must devise a language that is intelligible, yet not available to the reader as a potential weapon to be turned back against Rousseau's own incontrovertible sense of himself.

The words that Rousseau finds most treacherous, and yet most necessary, for the history of his inner life belong to the vocabulary of love. Rousseau asserts as a fact that he has been the most loving of men. Yet the established vocabulary of love cannot convey that truth; it only distorts his extraordinary sensibility. His feeling for Mme de Warens, to take one of the most difficult and important examples, cannot at all be bound even to the word "amour." Starting with his account of his first meeting with Mme de Warens, and continuing through the many phases of their long and strange liaison, Rousseau works to evoke his true feeling for this woman by freeing it from what he regards as the constraints of the word "amour."

For some readers, this may not seem a unique or even a very interesting problem. English and French alike, we all recognize that nervousness around the word "love," in any language, is one of the most familiar and tedious symptoms of adolescence. As when he insists that he alone is unique, Rousseau often seems most remarkable for his power to sustain common adolescent preoccupations even into old age.[8] It is likely to be especially difficult for any *English* reader to take with full seriousness Rousseau's struggle against one of the most common and various words of ordinary and literary discourse. Even coming from English writings of the eighteenth century, the word "love" does not have the restrictiveness which "amour" has for Rousseau. In Johnson's *Dictionary of the English Language,* we shall go on to see, passion, friendship, and even simply kindness are included in the large, flexible definition of "love." A look at the French *Encyclopédie* shows the different habits of thought and language coming out of the French tradition into eighteenth-century France, and these habits must be seen as at least part of Rousseau's predicament.

The *Encyclopédie* divides the entry *Amour* into a dozen or more distinct, seemingly exclusive categories: "amour des sexes," "amour filiale," "amour de soi," and so on. The effort is to clarify, even at times to prescribe, the exact attributes of essentially different feelings. Further distinctions continue even within the single subcategory, "amour des sexes," where use at the beginning and end of two maxims by La Rochefoucauld sets the restrictive and exclusive tone:

Il n'y a qu'une sorte d'*amour;* mais il y en a mille différentes copies. La plupart des gens prennent pour de l'*amour* le désir de la jouis-

sance. Voulez-vous sonder vos sentimens de bonne foi, et discerner
laquelle de ces deux passions est le principe de votre attachement,
interrogez les yeux de la personne qui vous tient dans ses châines. Si
sa présence intimide vos sens et les contient dans une soumission
respectueuse, vous l'aimez. Le véritable *amour* interdit même à la
pensée toute idée sensuelle, tout essor de l'imagination dont la déli-
catesse de l'objet aimé pourroit être offensée, s'il étoit possible qu'il
en fût instruit: mais si les attraits qui vous charment font plus
d'impression sur vos sens que sur votre âme; ce n'est point de
l'*amour*, c'est un appétit corporel. . . . De tout ce que nous venons de
dire; il s'ensuit que le véritable *amour* est extrêmement rare. Il en est
comme de l'apparition des esprits; tout le monde en parle, peu de
gens en ont vu.[9]

(There is only one kind of *love*; but there are a thousand copies of
it. Most people mistake sensuous longing for *love*. If you want to
test your feelings in good faith and discern which of these two passions is the basis of your attachment, question the eyes of the person
who keeps you in bondage. If her presence daunts your senses and
keeps them respectfully submissive, you love her. True *love* bars
even the mind from any sensuous thought, from any flight of imagination which might offend the delicacy of the beloved object,
should she happen to become aware of it: but if the attractions that
charm you make a stronger impression on your senses than on your
soul, it is not *love*, it is a bodily appetite. . . . From all that we just
said it follows that true *love* is extremely rare. It is the same as with
apparitions; everyone talks about them, few people have seen
them.)

La Rochefoucauld wittily exposed the pretenses of drawing-room
passion in his *Maximes* by withdrawing its right to the name of "love."
What generally passes for love appears to La Rochefoucauld as mere
costume, cheap imitation of a rarity, a miracle.[10] The *Encyclopédie*
changes the spirit of La Rochefoucauld's maxims, reducing his dry
probing of social gesture to a solemn diagnostic test for real love as
distinct from mere appetite. In the *Encyclopédie*, La Rochefoucauld's
maxims become more prudish, or perhaps only more sentimental and
moralistic. But whatever the differences of tone, we may recognize in
the echoing of La Rochefoucauld the style of restrictive definition
which is one legacy of the seventeenth-century moralists. Their wit
was forever manipulating the boundaries around the word "amour."
La Bruyère, less caustic than La Rochefoucauld, exemplifies the same
style, particularly in the service of distinguishing love from friendship:

L'amour naît brusquement sans autre réflexion, par tempérament
ou par faiblesse: un trait de beauté nous fixe, nous détermine.

L'amitié au contraire se forme peu à peu, avec le temps, par la pratique, par un long commerce.

Le temps, qui fortifie les amitiés, affaiblit l'amour.

L'amour et l'amitié s'excluent l'un l'autre.

L'amour qui croit peu à peu et par degrés ressemble trop à l'amitié pour être une passion violente.[11]

(Love is born suddenly and without reflection, from temperament or from weakness: some beautiful feature strikes us and determines our fate. Friendship, on the contrary, is formed little by little, with time, experience, and long interchange.

Time, which fortifies friendship, weakens love.

Love and friendship exclude one another.

The kind of love which grows gradually, little by little, resembles friendship too much to be a violent passion.)

For Rousseau, the aphorisms of the "false" portraitists seem to make both "amour" and "amitié" unusable words for his relationship to Mme de Warens. His feeling for her does not fit any of the moralists' categories. He did not feel intimidated by Mme de Warens, yet he felt more than mere sexual desire. He did adore her immediately, yet his feeling also grew stronger with time. Rousseau could try to dissociate "amour" from its conventional and limited meanings to give it more personal flexibility by his own usage. He could individualize the word through metaphor or suggestive detail or resonant allusion to other writers. But Rousseau continues the moralists' fascination with the abstract definition of feeling, even while he repudiates the definitions themselves:

J'oserai le dire; qui ne sent que l'amour ne sent pas ce qu'il y a de plus doux dans la vie. Je connois un autre sentiment, moins impétueux peutêtre, mais plus délicieux mille fois, qui quelquefois est joint à l'amour et qui souvent en est séparé. Ce sentiment n'est pas non plus l'amitié seule; il est plus voluptueux, plus tendre; je n'imagine pas qu'il puisse agir pour quelqu'un du même séxe; du moins je fus ami si jamais homme le fut, et je ne l'éprouvai jamais près d'aucun de mes amis. Ceci n'est pas clair, mais il le deviendra dans la suite. (104)

(I will venture to say that anyone who feels no more than love misses the sweetest thing in life. For I know another feeling, less impetuous perhaps but a thousand times more delightful, which is sometimes joined with love and sometimes separate from it. This feeling is something other than friendship, something less temperate and more tender. I do not think that it can be felt for anyone of the same sex. I have known friendship, at least, if ever a man has, and I have never had this feeling for any of my friends. This statement is obscure, but it will become clear in the sequel.)

Rousseau plays with the same boundaries as the moralists, even if only to deny that they are binding to him. He relies on the same general words of feeling, if only in negation, for he holds off the established vocabulary of love without replacing it with another. Instead, he seems to be summoning his private inarticulable sense of his own emotions to test the words against. If both "amour" and "amitié" fail the test, Rousseau turns against the words, protecting his sense of his experience from the contamination of language generally. Whereas the *Encyclopédie* follows the moralists in isolating clear and general categories of feeling from the murkiness or fakery of individual experience, Rousseau asserts his private sense of feeling as the unyielding measure of truth, however it may elude the artificial clarity of words.

The play of Rousseau's private certainty of feeling against an inadequate but still authoritative vocabulary is one recurrent drama of style in the *Confessions*. In the history of his liaison with Mme de Warens, the drama begins with Rousseau's account of their first meeting:

Supposons que ce que j'ai senti pour elle fut véritablement de l'amour; ce qui paroitra tout au moins douteux à qui suivra l'histoire de nos liaisons; comment cette passion fut-elle accompagnée dès sa naissance des sentimens qu'elle inspire le moins; la paix du coeur, le calme, la serenité, la sécurité, l'assurance? (52)

(Supposing that what I felt for her was really love—which will appear at least doubtful to anyone who follows the story of our relationship—how could that passion have been accompanied from its birth with the kind of feelings most foreign to love, with peace of heart, calmness, serenity, security, confidence?)

Rousseau makes no effort to loosen the meanings that words of feeling carry. For him , too, "amour" evokes a fixed set of sentiments, gestures and other words. Rousseau leaves the conventional pattern of associations undisturbed while he dissociates his experience from it by asserting the contrary facts of his emotion—sentiments made to seem almost like facts of sensation, even though what he names are still other abstractions: "la paix du coeur, le calme, la serenité, la sécurité, l'assurance." Rousseau creates the impression that he is offering the particularity of his inner life by simply listing states of feeling without ordering them into any principle. His tone is more questioning than explanatory: "Il y eut certainement quelque chose de singulier dans mes sentimens pour cette charmante femme, et l'on y trouvera dans la suite des bizarreries aux-quelles on ne s'attend pas" (52). (There was certainly something peculiar about my feelings for this charming woman, and the reader will find, as he reads on, that strange and unexpected developments attended them.) His deliberately paradoxical voice evades any firm definition, creating instead an air of suspense. We are made to hold judgment about this relationship until we see what happens, for no principle guides us to judge—or even guess—what will happen in a relationship with such "bizarre" beginnings.

As Rousseau continues the story of his liaison with Mme de Warens, he must distinguish his subtle changes of feeling at the same time as he affirms the continuing singularity of the relationship. One particularly demanding episode is his response to the cool and solemn proposition of Mme de Warens that she protect him against other temptations by initiating him to sex herself:

> Comment, par quel prodige dans la fleur de ma jeunesse eus-je si peu d'empressement pour la prémiere jouissance? Comment pus-je en voir approcher l'heure avec plus de peine que de plaisir? Comment au lieu des délices qui devoient m'enivrer sentois-je presque de la répugnance et des craintes? . . . J'ai promis des bizarreries dans l'histoire de mon attachement pour elle; en voila surement une à laquelle on ne s'attendoit pas. (195)

> (How, by what miracle was it that in the flower of my youth I was so little eager for my first experience? How could I see the moment approaching with more pain than pleasure? How was it that instead of the delight which should have intoxicated me I felt almost repugnance and fear? . . . I have promised some singularities in the history of my attachment for her; and here is certainly one feature that must be unexpected.)

While Rousseau measures his first meeting with Mme de Warens against conventions that seem ultimately to derive from courtly love (where the first sight of the lady reduces the lover to fits of "inquietude"), here, Rousseau invokes and disavows a different love convention, the adolescent erotic adventure. Jean-Jacques' confused timidity does not follow the pattern of the conventional licentious tale any more than his first feeling of ease obeyed the conventions of courtly love. A young man, "dans la fleur de la jeunesse," is not expected to

hesitate so peculiarly before "la prémiere jouissance" with an experienced woman. Some awkwardness belongs to the conventional comedy of the situation, but not Rousseau's pain and even repugnance.

Rousseau first tries to explain his "bizarrerie" by discerning its true
cause in his personal history. The pattern of explanation recalls the
advantages of a historical narrative stated in the *Lettres à Malesherbes*. Although his feelings at a particular moment seem contradictory or bizarre, they developed in a personal sequence which he can
reconstruct:

> La longue habitude de vivre ensemble et d'y vivre innocemment,
> loin d'affoibler mes sentimens pour elle les avoit renforcés, mais leur
> avoit en même tems donné une autre tournure qui les rendoit plus
> affectueux, plus tendres peut-être, mais moins sensuels. A force de
> l'appeller maman, à force d'user avec elle de la familiarité d'un fils je
> m'étois accoutumé à me regarder comme tel. Je crois que voila la
> véritable cause du peu d'empressement que j'eus de la posséder,
> quoiqu'elle me fut si chére. (196)

> (The long habit of living with her on terms of innocence, far from
> weakening my feelings for her, had strengthened them, but at the
> same time it had given them a different turn, rendering them more
> affectionate, and more tender perhaps, but less sexual. By calling
> her Mamma and treating her with the familiarity of a son, I had
> grown to look on myself as such; and I think that is the real cause of
> my lack of eagerness to possess her, even though she was so dear to
> me.)

For a moment, Rousseau's history may seem only to replace the
label of adolescent appetite with what the *Encyclopédie* calls "amour
filiale." If Rousseau came to love Mme de Warens as a mother, then
the "bizarrerie" disappears, for in the terms of the *Encyclopédie*, filial
love is as clearly distinct from sexual love as "amour" is distinct from
"le desir de la jouissance." But Rousseau is, after all, unwilling to
reduce his special inward experience to any one of the dozen distinct
classifications of "amour" familiar to his contemporaries: "Elle étoit
pour moi plus qu'une soeur, plus qu'une mere, plus qu'une amie, plus
même qu'une maitresse, et c'étoit pour cela qu'elle n'étoit pas une
maitresse. Enfin je l'aimois trop pour la convoiter; voila ce qu'il y a de
plus clair dans mes idées" (196-197). (She was to me more than a sister, more than a mother, more than a friend, more even than a mistress; and that is why she was not a mistress to me. In short I loved her

too much to desire her; that is the clearest idea I have on the subject.) Rousseau holds jealously to the private nuances of his feeling. No public classification will do.

Rousseau allows no single expression to contain the definition of his love. Comparative phrases, one after another circle the same elusive emotion, suggesting the delicate nuances which finally are not merely nuances but the crucial determinants of behavior. His emotion hovers somewhere among all his approximate articulations. Repeated comparatives, relying on the same few abstract and general words, may seem a kind of verbal impoverishment, but they also give a desired air of mystery to the very activity of psychological definition. Rousseau's intimate, probing tone invites us to share the difficulty (and also the pleasure) of transposing feelings into ideas. If his emotion remains elusive, confusing, paradoxical—well, the style argues, that is the true nature of his inner life, truthfully rendered. The very elusiveness of human feeling becomes the shared concern of writer and audience, if we are willing to follow Rousseau in his patient, loving (and self-loving) quest.

Rousseau's description of feeling thus challenges the clear and easy mastery of another person's experience promised by the seventeenth-century aphorism. While retaining an abstract vocabulary of emotion, he destroys the generalizing power that abstract definitions of feeling were granted by the moralists. He breaks down even the syntax of the aphorism, as seen, for example, in La Rochefoucauld: "S'il y a un amour pur et exempt du mélange de nos autres passions, c'est celui qui est caché au fond du coeur, et que nous ignorons nous-mêmes."[12] (If there is a pure love, exempt from the mixture of other passions, it is that hidden in the depths of the heart, and unknown to ourselves.) Even when La Rochefoucauld defines a feeling that, by definition, eludes consciousness and may not even exist, he retains his characteristic certainty of generalization in his sentence. Rousseau, by contrast, sets in motion the well-known style of the maxim, only to turn his syntax to a statement of certainty about his unutterable uniqueness: "S'il y a dans la vie un sentiment délicieux, c'est celui *que nous eprou-vames d'être rendus l'un à l'autre*" (222). (If there is such a thing in life as a sensation of delight, we felt it on being restored to one another.) In the middle of a sentence, Rousseau narrows the general idea of "un sentiment délicieux" so that it includes only his experience (and perhaps that of Mme de Warens). Rousseau does conceptualize his feeling

—the phrase "un sentiment délicieux" refers to an idea based on whatever he felt. But the meaning of the concept resides in the nuances of
his private, unique inner life which is made to seem separate from any
other, not to be contained in any general category, in any analogy, or
even in any concrete image.

Rousseau shuns both metaphor and direct allusion to other writers
in his analysis of feeling. Nothing is *like* his feeling. No one can help
him define what only he experienced. Yet his own style of abstract
definition takes advantage of devices of his predecessors for battle
against them. We have seen in the *Encyclopédie* and in the seventeenth-century moralists how the abstract definition of feeling serves
to clarify the murky surfaces of experience—whether by unmasking
hypocrisy, or by locating primary motives, or by isolating the general
laws of a passion that in actuality gets mingled with others. The con-
cepts purportedly manifest general truths but they are obviously at
one remove from the concrete feel of truth in experience—that is, they
are abstractions.

The distancing effect of abstractions also serves Rousseau's quite
different purposes. In conceptualizing his emotion, he does not strive
for a more concrete language—that is, he does not try to reduce the
distance between the feeling he wishes to convey and the inherent
abstraction of all language from what it represents. As if convinced
that no language, however ostensibly concrete, could really embody
the deliciousness of "un sentiment délicieux," Rousseau chooses at
least to keep the space clear between what he is talking about and the
nature of the medium he is using:

> Nous commençames, sans y songer, à ne plus nous séparer l'un de
> l'autre, à mettre en quelque sorte toute notre existence en commun,
> et sentant que reciproquement nous nous étions non seulement
> necessaires mais suffisans, nous nous accoutumames à ne plus pen-
> ser à rien d'étranger à nous, à borner absolument notre bonheur et
> tous nos desirs à cette possession mutuelle et peutêtre unique parmi
> les humains, qui n'étoit point, comme je l'ai dit, celle de l'amour;
> mais une possession plus essencielle qui, sans tenir aux sens, au
> sexe, à l'age, à la figure tenoit à tout ce par quoi l'on est soi, et qu'on
> ne peut perdre qu'en cessant d'être. (222)

> (We began imperceptibly to become inseparable and, in a sense, to
> share our whole existence in common. Feeling that we were not only
> necessary but sufficient to one another, we grew accustomed to
> thinking of nothing outside ourselves, completely to confine our

happiness and our desires to our possession of one another, which was perhaps unique among human kind. For it was not, as I have said, a love relationship, but a more real possession, dependent not on the senses, on sex, age, or personal beauty, but on everything by which one is oneself, and which one cannot lose except by ceasing to be.)

Rousseau's philosophic language, with its technical distinctions between the necessary and the sufficient, the primary and secondary attributes of identity, gives a clear and distinct idea of his "sentiment délicieux" but it cannot be mistaken for the actuality of the feeling. The adjective "délicieux" suggests sensory and sensuous richness, but Rousseau's language offers only the abstract attributes of the emotion; there is nothing to see or touch. Although the rhythm of the prose, the long sentences and the repetitions of thought and phrasing, make the activity of conceptualization seem almost a sensuous pleasure in itself, the language evokes nothing more sensory than does a definition in geometry. Rousseau luxuriates in abstract definition almost as one might in the memory of physical sensation, but phrases like "à mettre en quelque sorte toute notre existence en commun" and "une possession plus essencielle qui . . . tenoit à tout ce par quoi l'on est soi" do not name sensations nor do they refer to the concrete world of sensation at all.

Rousseau's abstract analysis of feeling often has an awkward precision, as if he were straining to establish the exact quality of what defies articulation in words. In part, there is an acknowledgment of incapacity in this style, for he cannot through abstractions make us *feel* his emotion. Yet the very clarity of the distance between Rousseau's definition of feeling and feeling itself also has advantages from Rousseau's point of view. While he may fail to gain our full participation in his inner experience, he also manages to hold back the certainty of judgment invited by the aphorisms of the moralists. By naming only the abstract attributes of feeling, rather than pretending to offer their substance, Rousseau keeps his feeling just out of our reach—and, from Rousseau's point of view, that is the next best effect to total sympathy. He has not reneged his promise of frankness. His language of feeling is as full and precise as a language of definition can be. Yet while making his inner life clearly available to our understanding, the full truth of his experience remains remote, unimaginable, unique.

Rousseau's language of feeling has none of the easy directness we would expect from "l'écrivain spontané," entrusting his feelings to whatever words come. Instead, Rousseau may be seen strenuously working to turn an inherited style of psychological definition to his desire for total privacy and public clarification at the same time. Insofar as these goals are incompatible, Rousseau will choose fidelity to his sense of inarticulable uniqueness. Rather than be absorbed in the common denominations of language, he will always choose to postpone the final clarification. Yet Rousseau does reconcile the two goals more effectively than would seem possible. He does achieve remarkable precision—we understand exactly the evolution of his liaison with Mme de Warens—at the same time as his feelings remain forever elusive, always one remove from our palpable grasp. Moreover, he does successfully resist the principles of love established by the moralists, for his analysis of feeling persuades us that feelings, his feelings at least, cannot be fully contained in the words of common speech.

3

"Love" in *The Prelude*

"Love" is one of the most frequently used words in *The Prelude*.[1]
Indeed, a primary aim of Wordsworth's epic endeavor is to revive the
seriousness of "love" in poetry. His heroic song tells the story of his
inner life, the growth of his passions, and the most important passion
in the story is love.

Wordsworth shows none of Rousseau's distrust of the word "love."
Though Wordsworth, at least as much as Rousseau, departs from past
literary conventions of love, he does not behave as though the word
itself were contaminated by customary meanings. Instead of Rousseau's chafing against the deforming action of language, Wordsworth
asserts his poet's power to re-create conventional words so that they
accommodate the particular quality and also the range of his individual feelings:

> Thus were my sympathies enlarged, and thus
> Daily the common range of visible things
> Grew dear to me: already I began
> To love the sun; a boy I loved the sun,
> Not as I since have loved him, as a pledge
> And surety of our earthly life, a light
> Which we behold and feel we are alive;
> Nor for his bounty to so many worlds—
> But for this cause, that I had seen him lay
> His beauty on the morning hills, had seen

> The western mountains touch his setting orb,
> In many a thoughtless hour, when, from excess
> Of happiness, my blood appeared to flow
> For its own pleasure, and I breathed with joy.
>   (II. 175-188)

Throughout *The Prelude*, Wordsworth delights in using and reusing the word "love," mainly for his diverse responses to nature. He loves nature—with the depth and constancy of passion reserved by earlier poets for love of women or friends or God. Wordsworth's repetitions of "love" display the word for serious attention; we are not to slide by it as looseness of diction or as a casual flourish inherited from eighteenth-century descriptive poetry. Wordsworth's usage is more insistent, even argumentative. In stating his feelings for the sun, Wordsworth argues that the word "love" can designate different feelings, ranging from the unconscious joy associated with the landscape of childhood to the adult's rather different faith in a principle of universal vitality. The poet's power to give "love" meanings that are diverse but not contradictory bears specifically on Wordsworth's interpretation of his life, for he shows, indeed he insists, that he can absorb the fundamental changes in his life into a larger idea of constancy rather than contrast. Wordsworth thus argues for the bond between his boyhood feeling for nature and his adult emotions even while he distinguishes between them. As a boy he loved the sun and he still loves the sun—that truth of feeling affirms his constancy through all the other changes he may need to acknowledge.

Instead of multiplying what he calls "puny distinctions," Wordsworth uses the large names of feelings to announce discoveries of continuity and reconciliation between the diverse parts of his experience, and also between his experience and traditional values. His assured tone puts the matter beyond quibble. If we are unaccustomed to take the word "love" seriously in either or both of his uses in Book II, that shows our poverty of feeling and language. The poet confidently sets out to enlarge our sympathies by deepening and modifying our response to familiar words. His capacity to do so is the power of his poetic genius: "Remember, also, that the medium through which, in poetry, the heart is to be affected, is language; a thing subject to endless fluctuations and arbitrary associations. The genius of the poet melts these down for his purpose; but they retain their shape and quality to him who is not capable of exerting, within his own mind, a corresponding energy."[2]

Wordsworth's enthusiasm for the creative power of language is quite different from Rousseau's distrustful reliance on words. Whereas Rousseau manipulates words in relation to feelings as though he were trying to fit together separate but equally firm shapes, Wordsworth celebrates the power of the poet to melt and re-form shapes, whether of language or feeling. Rousseau insists that feelings have their own shape and quality, apart and prior to words, and language has fixed shapes too, if only from established usage. Rousseau seeks not so much to melt language, as to keep his sense of himself from melting into it. He protects his feelings by holding them always at a slight distance from language so that we are aware that the forms of words do not coincide with the actual form of his emotion. To Wordsworth, however, poetic power is the very capacity to reshape feelings through language, as if neither emotions nor words were fixed. Like the sun, poetic genius is a creative power. The poet suffers no inevitable constraints from language; the only obstacle to his freedom is the limit of energy in his own mind.

Wordsworth's statement about poetic language in the "Preface of 1815" proclaims his own high ambition and also his faith in the power of literature generally. He sets himself against arbitrary rules for the diction of poetry in the name of a freedom that rightfully belongs to all poetic genius. He describes the power of all great poets in every period, including the one just past. Wordsworth restates what happens, traditionally, in the language of great writers—especially, one must add, in the language of English writers. For Wordsworth's attitude toward language in the "Preface of 1815" is deeply and especially embedded in the English tradition, even through the eighteenth century.

Johnson's *Dictionary* vividly illustrates the point, for Johnson offers a rich history of English attitudes toward language through his use of literary examples, while he also attempts in the very project of the *Dictionary* a clarification of language like that we have already seen in the French seventeenth-century writers and in the *Encyclopédie*. In the Preface to the *Dictionary*, Johnson ruefully recalls his initial resolve: "to pierce deep into every science, to enquire the nature of every substance of which I inserted the name, to limit every idea by a definition strictly logical, and exhibit every production of art or nature in an accurate description."[3] That dream of perfect clarity was an illusion, Johnson acknowledges, not only because the energy of one lexicographer is limited, but also because the very character of the English language baffles logic. The same "wild exuberance" of language that calls out the need for an English dictionary makes logical clarification more difficult in English, if not impossible. Johnson explains how the failure of his resolve leads, after all, to a faithful picture of the language. He relies in the end more on his examples than on logical definition, for "words must be sought where they are used." The power of individual writers to reshape the meanings of words is shown in the *Dictionary* by the multiplicity of examples, gathered by Johnson with evident delight and fascination:

> There is more danger of censure from the multiplicity than paucity of examples; authorities will sometimes seem to have been accumulated without necessity or use, and perhaps some will be found, which might, without loss, have been omitted. But a work of this kind is not hastily to be charged with superfluities; those quotations, which to careless or unskilful perusers appear only to repeat the same sense, will often exhibit to a more accurate examiner, diversities of signification, or, at least, afford different shades of the same meaning: one will show the word applied to persons, another to things; one will express an ill, another a good, and a third a neutral sense . . . the word, how often soever repeated, appears with new associates and in different combinations, and every quotation contributes something to the stability or enlargement of the language.[4]

The individual word "love," in Johnson's mode of definition, preserves a flexibility quite different from "amour" in eighteenth-century French. Johnson's full definition of "love" is too long to quote here, but selections adequately show the point.[5] The word appears as both verb and noun, a flexibility already lacking in the French "amour":

To Love v.a.
   1. To regard with passionate affection, as that of one sex to
      the other.

       "Good shepherd, tell this youth what 'tis to *love*.
       —It is to be made all of sighs and tears."
                                       Shakespeare

   3. To regard with parental tenderness.

       "He that loveth me shall be *loved* of my father and I will
       love him, and will manifest myself to him."
                                    John xiv.21

Love (noun)
  1. The passion between the sexes.

  "I look'd upon her with a soldier's eye,
  That lik'd, but had a rougher task in hand
  Than to drive liking to the name of *love*."

  Shakespeare

  .   .   .   .   .

  2. Kindness; goodwill; friendship.

  "What love, think'st thou, I sue so much to get?
  My *love* till death, my humble thanks, my prayers;
  That *love* which virtue begs, and virtue grants."

  Shakespeare

  .   .   .   .   .

  "By this shall all men know that ye are my disciples, if ye
  have *love* to one another."

  Rom. [John] xiii.35

  .   .   .   .   .

  9. Fondness; concord.

  "Come, *love* and health to all!—
  Then I'll sit down: give me some wine; fill full."

  Shakespeare

  .   .   .   .   .

  13. Due reverence to God.

  "Love is of two sorts, of friendship and of desire; the one
  betwixt friends, the other betwixt lovers; the one a rational, the other a sensitive love: so our *love* of God con-
  sists of two parts, as esteeming of God, and desiring of
  him."

  Hammond

Although Johnson subdivides the definition, his distinctions are less
definite than those in the *Encyclopédie*. The example from John to
illustrate parental love suggests the shading of familial to divine tenderness rather than a contrast between two distinct emotions. Othel-
lo's language poses love as a degree of liking, rather than a feeling different in kind. Hammond's explanation of religious love starts from
the distinction between passion and friendship so interesting to the
French, but even here, the idea of two distinct feelings yields to Hammond's inclusive concept of religious love as a complex emotion, the
parts of which are only theoretically distinguishable.

Johnson's individual examples in themselves keep flexible boundaries between kinds of love. Moreover, Johnson's desire to include many

examples leads him to multiply the categories of his own definition. If
there is any difference between "kindness; goodwill, friendship" and
"fondness; concord," it is certainly not strictly logical. The examples
in this instance seem interchangeable, yet the total effect is richness of
connotation rather than mere vagueness. The word "love" changes
subtly in each example; it acquires no fixed shape, but rather an evoc-
ative life rooted in the diverse purposes of different writers. No one
writer possesses the authority granted by the *Encyclopédie* to La
Rochefoucauld, whose maxims enclose the definition of "amour des
sexes" as if they were permanent statements of truth.[6]

Wordworth's claim, then, that the individual poet has power to
reshape the forms of language only extends an attitude preserved
through the eighteenth century in English. Yet Johnson's *Dictionary*
does not altogether prepare the reader for Wordsworth's language, for
love of nature does not appear at all in Johnson's definition of love.
Wordsworth's meaning is not obscure when he says he loved the sun.
Eighteenth-century descriptive poetry (not included in Johnson's
examples[7]) had already added love of nature to the repertory of emotions in poetry. Moreover, Wordsworth calls simultaneously upon
other meanings of love: familial, patriotic, religious. Yet to love the
sun as insistently as Wordsworth claims to do still bespeaks a more
unusual inner life by eighteenth-century standards than, for example,
Rousseau's liaison with an older woman.

Wordsworth's claims of passionate feeling for nature stretch the
word "love" beyond its central traditional connotations. Even friendly
contemporaries like Hazlitt and Coleridge note that Wordsworth's use
of important common words often alienates the poet from the values,
if not from the understanding, of his audience. The whole substance of
Wordsworth's experience, characteristically an experience in nature,
can seem incommensurate to the vocabulary of feeling used. There
seems either a disproportion of thought to the occasion—"mental
bombast" in Coleridge's phrase—or, the poet is more peculiar than he
acknowledges.[8] For the poet, unlike Rousseau, does not encourage us
to see his feelings as bizarre. On the contrary, Wordsworth strives to
make his story magnificent, wonderful, but not unique, for he offers
his life as the emblem of the heroic potential in all human experience.

Wordsworth's contemporaries, and even recent critics, often have
difficulty accepting the double purpose in Wordsworth's new uses of
common words of feeling. The strangeness of Wordsworth's language
must be recognized, for it measures the poet's distance from other
men, especially when he is in his priestly robes.[9] But though the poet is

special, in his history and in his power of language, his feelings must also seem normal, natural, sane—and therefore to be cherished by other men as a universal ideal. Wordsworth's effort to transform the poet's life into a new epic subject depends upon this possibility of generalization, in contrast to Rousseau's more private, self-justifying goal. Wordsworth's common vocabulary of emotion is a central poetic device for the poet's double purpose. The simple names of feeling assert the normalcy and naturalness of the poet's story, even while the poet's surprising use of familiar words urges us to enlarge our sense of what the shape and quality of natural feelings may be.

In Johnson's *Dictionary*, as in ordinary usage still, the first meanings of "love" refer to feelings for another person. Wordsworth seems to say little about this kind of love in *The Prelude*. He states his love for Man and, more particularly, for Coleridge and for his sister, Dorothy, but Wordsworth's human love seems shadowy in the poem, especially in contrast to Rousseau's precisely rendered entanglements with other people in the *Confessions*. The difference is not simply the relative importance granted to individual people—in a way, Wordsworth's whole poem unfolds as a tribute of love to the Friend, Coleridge. Our sense of uncertainty about the poet's specifically human love comes more from Wordsworth's style. Wordsworth's way of articulating love for his friends, even when he directly addresses the subject, reshapes the connotations of human affection so that it seems only a part of the more mysterious love celebrated in the poem as a whole.[10]

The style of *The Prelude* makes Wordsworth's love for particular people strangely indistinguishable from his love of nature. In Wordsworth's language of feeling, human affection never emerges as a distinct category of the poet's experience. Not only does Wordsworth love the sun as others love a parent, he also loves his sister as though she were the sun—or a stream, or the spirit of spring or of morning:

> . . . and was blest
> Between these sundry wanderings with a joy
> Above all joys, that seemed another morn
> Risen on mid noon; blest with the presence, Friend!
> Of that sole Sister, her who hath been long
> Dear to thee also, thy true friend and mine,
> Now, after separation desolate,
> Restored to me—such absence that she seemed
> A gift then first bestowed. The varied banks
> Of Emont, hitherto unnamed in song,
> And that monastic castle, 'mid tall trees,

Low-standing by the margin of the stream,
A mansion visited (as fame reports)
By Sidney, where, in sight of our Helvellyn,
Or stormy Cross-fell, snatches he might pen
Of his Arcadia, by fraternal love
Inspired.

(VI. 195-211)

Wordsworth places his reunion with Dorothy, presumably after his winter in Cambridge, in relation to other wonderful events celebrated in literature, events that do not all center on the character of human attachments. Whereas Rousseau seeks to guard his feeling for Mme de Warens from the contaminating touch of even other *human* relationships, Wordsworth delights in gathering many kinds of analogies to his joy in the presence of Dorothy. Just as he offers more than one title for her—"Sister," "true Friend"—he allows different images and literary allusions to have a cumulative effect, as if he welcomed diverse ways to give ever-greater resonance to his feeling.

The image of "another morn / Risen on mid noon" makes Dorothy's presence to Wordsworth a miraculous blessing, even more wonderful for its superfluity, like a new sunrise in the middle of an already bright day, or the arrival of the angel Raphael in Eden, according to Milton in *Paradise Lost*:

. . . what glorious shape
Comes this way moving; seems another Morn
Ris'n on mid-noon; som great behest from Heav'n
To us perhaps he brings . . .

(V. 309-312)

Wordsworth's allusion to Milton transforms Dorothy into a "heavenly stranger" miraculously sent by a generous divinity. Wordsworth depends on our recognition of the allusion, partly to evoke the comparison between himself at this time and Milton's Adam (introduced through other Miltonic allusion from the beginning of Book I). The echo of Milton also serves to deepen the meaning of Wordsworth's word "blest"; it enforces the supernatural dimension of a word which might otherwise carry only the loose connotations of social discourse. Further, by the resonance in the morning image of Wordsworth's own characteristic (and also Miltonic) imagery of nature elsewhere, for instance in the praise to the sun already cited from Book II, Dorothy becomes at once like Milton's Raphael and like the poet's own beloved morning sun.

Wordsworth's tone has the awe appropriate to the record of more-than-human events. An aura of mystery and magic surrounds his image of a family reunion. Insofar as his coming together with Dorothy resembles other human events, it evokes the most miraculous, the most unaccountable in purely human terms, like the wondrous family restorations in Shakespeare's last plays: "Now, after separation desolate / Restored to me—such absence that she seemed / A gift then first bestowed." Old tales of loss and strange return come to mind; the poet's reunion with his sister comes to seem like another event in myth or fairy tale. Finally, the explicit reference to Sidney, also a poet and devoted brother, brings Wordsworth's experience back to historical and local tradition, while at the same time extending even further the aura of high poetry and legend around his feeling.

Wordsworth looks to earlier literature for ennobling perspectives in which to place his feeling of "fraternal love." He is not mainly trying to work out devices of language that can directly define the feeling of one person for another. Indeed, he draws on natural and supernatural analogies in order to dissolve the specifically human boundaries of his experience. He reshapes the feeling of "fraternal love" so that it acquires the more-than-human stature appropriate to his epic form. The main effort of this writing is not to render the nuances of a personal relationship in precise psychological terms, but to persuade us that this seemingly commonplace domestic event deserves to be named in heroic song. Rousseau's boldness is to claim the singularity of his every feeling. Wordsworth's boldness here is different. He is claiming the epic stature of ordinary experience. Like Milton daring things unattempted yet in prose or rhyme, Wordsworth will win new regard for events "hitherto unnamed in song."

The boundary around Wordsworth's feeling of "fraternal love" is, then, immense. It extends beyond the exclusively human world, and within that world, too, Wordsworth is generous, inclusive—even to the point, it may seem, of mere vagueness or bombast. Just as he welcomes many analogies to his experience, he also invokes the presence of the other Friend, Coleridge: "blest with the presence, Friend! / Of that sole Sister, her who hath been long / Dear to thee also, thy true friend and mine." Coleridge was not known to Dorothy and Wordsworth at the time of that summer reunion. Coming from Rousseau's careful chronology of his relationship with Mme de Warens, it is striking to observe Wordsworth's free inclusion of Coleridge in the feeling of "love" commemorated in this passage as a whole:

> O Friend! we had not seen thee at that time,
> And yet a power is on me, and a strong
> Confusion, and I seem to plant thee there.
> Far art thou wandered now in search of health
> And milder breezes,—melancholy lot!
> But thou art with us, with us in the past,
> The present, with us in the times to come.
> There is no grief, no sorrow, no despair,
> No languor, no dejection, no dismay,
> No absence scarcely can there be, for those
> Who love as we do.
>
> (VI. 237-247)

At first glance, the rhetoric of the address to Coleridge seems inflated, a hollow repetition of literary language for love, not really appropriate to this occasion. A poet like Donne designs a whole poem to show how human love can transcend absence, but Wordsworth's confident affirmation seems exaggerated; it goes against the human reality reported in the poem itself. For the poem tells us that Coleridge is not with Dorothy and Wordsworth *now* any more than he was before. In the present time of the poem, Coleridge is wandering in search of health. The image of Coleridge in the passage evokes the "melancholy" human world in which paths separate and intimacy dwindles. Coleridge has departed in search of a strength apparently not to be found in friendship itself. Wordsworth seems to expose the limited power of human love even while affirming its transcendence of ordinary reality. Wordsworth's grand assurance that the love of the three friends precludes all grief and even separation seems only to cover the limitations of friendship with a vague assurance of goodwill.

Wordsworth's language of feeling becomes less vague, however, when we realize that he has already urged us to understand the feelings of "those / Who love as we do" in more than human terms. Although he is, in part, offering a formal profession of traditional friendship, his language has also reshaped the meaning of friendship so that the rhetoric of enduring love acquires new shades of meaning. When he includes Coleridge in the joy of his summer with Dorothy, he means to grant Coleridge the power to share in the quite special feelings established by the description of that summer in the poem:

> —that river and those mouldering towers
> Have seen us side by side, when, having clomb
> The darksome windings of a broken stair,

> And crept along a ridge of fractured wall,
> Not without trembling, we in safety looked
> Forth, through some Gothic window's open space,
> And gathered with one mind a rich reward
> From the far-stretching landscape, by the light
> Of morning beautified, or purple eve;
> Or, not less pleased, lay on some turret's head,
> Catching from tufts of grass and hare-bell flowers
> Their faintest whisper to the passing breeze,
> Given out while mid-day heat oppressed the plains.
>   (VI. 211-223)

Instead of Rousseau's abstract definition of feeling, Wordsworth depends on the detail of his natural description to evoke the feelings of that summer. Wordsworth does not isolate for psychological scrutiny the nuances of his intimacy with his sister. The "rich reward" he recalls came to them individually from the landscape as much as from each other, and it is the detail of those perceptions that Wordsworth above all renders. The detail suggests intimacy, for the final moment of catching the whisper from grass and flowers seems too delicate for any but the best of friends to share. Yet the detail also displaces attention from the personal relationship to the landscape, to their feeling for the landscape even more than for each other.

In the manner of pastoral elegy, Wordsworth invokes the landscape as an active participant in this friendship, the witness and also the source of meaning and pleasure. Like Milton's description of the young shepherds in "Lycidas," Wordsworth's imagery commemorates a friendship in perfect accord with the natural order and beauty of nature. To be sure, Wordsworth's interest is not identical to Milton's. These friends are not even figuratively shepherds and their vacation adventures are more particularized than the duties of a pastoral day. Yet Wordsworth follows Milton's design of a composite or characteristic pastoral day, the hours named according to convention: "morning," "purple eve," and "mid-day heat." The pastoral convention helps to locate the meaning of this friendship in its harmony with the order of the day, rather than in the nuances of human intimacy itself.

Wordsworth's imagery, therefore, not only replaces the abstract definition of feeling with suggestive detail, it also defines the value of human love in relation to a larger natural order. Morning, noon, and evening—even the more specific details of natural perception—do not exist exclusively for these two friends. Indeed, Wordsworth, as a poet, has the power to give even the most delicate perceptions permanent

and public presence in the language of his poem. It is perhaps the same
poetic power that draws him to "plant" Coleridge too in the scene. To
the poet, the perception of nature's beauty and the re-creation of that
perception in poetry matter more than merely human intimacy. Or,
what matters for "those / Who love as we do" is the shared delight in
perceptions like those the poet recalls from his summer with Dorothy.
That delight transcends the chronology and literal facts of human
love.

Wordsworth's feeling for both Dorothy and Coleridge ends by
seeming quite complicated, though it is never directly defined. Wordsworth reassures Coleridge that the love of nature shared by Dorothy
and himself characterizes Coleridge, too, however his worldly lot may
now impede him. Wordsworth calls on his own love for Coleridge as a
source of confidence that Coleridge will recover his power. Yet at the
same time he implies the rather stark conditions of his love, for his
friendship with Coleridge seems contingent on Coleridge's own power
to revive his active devotion to nature. That devotion is the essential
bond of love between these friends. The ideal of friendship that
Wordsworth evokes presupposes more than personal affection and
intimacy; it subordinates human intimacy, or at least reshapes its
meaning to imply the sharing of the same natural and supernatural
devotions:

> Though mutually unknown, yea nursed and reared
> As if in several elements, we were framed
> To bend at last to the same discipline,
> Predestined, if two beings ever were,
> To seek the same delights, and have one health,
> One happiness.
>
> (VI. 254-259)

Insofar as Wordsworth in *The Prelude* addresses the reader also as
Friend, we too are offered the poet's love—on the same stark conditions, but also with the same confidence in our potential power of
devotion. Wordsworth's shaping of love through perceptions of nature allows, even encourages, the reader to "plant" himself in the scene
in a way that Rousseau's abstract definition of feeling prohibits.
Wordsworth's language of feeling is more particular in its details, but
it is also less private, more welcoming to the reader. Like Coleridge,
we may not have been favored in our seedtime, and we may now wan-
der alone in search of strength, but as men we have, at least poten-

tially, the power to share in the love that the poet has known with his best friends.

The Prelude makes no episode of human love ultimately important in itself. The highest expression of love in the poem is the call to renew devotion to nature and to poetry. Wordsworth expresses this love for Coleridge and also for the reader. And in the narrative he pays tribute to Dorothy for performing the same service to him after his return from France: "She, in the midst of all, preserved me still / A Poet" (XI. 345-346). The "true self" of Wordsworth in communion with Dorothy is the poetic self; it is not the private, singular, intimate self that Rousseau shared with Mme de Warens. The value of this human attachment comes from its influence on a development whose goal transcends all particular human bonds and any particular human occasion.

Wordsworth's summary of Dorothy's importance to him, in Book XIV, places Dorothy among the other natural and more than natural forces guiding the growth of the poet:

> Thou didst soften down
> This over-sternness; but for thee, dear Friend!
> My soul, too reckless of mild grace, had stood
> In her original self too confident,
> Retained too long a countenance severe;
> A rock with torrents roaring, with the clouds
> Familiar, and a favourite of the stars:
> But thou didst plant its crevices with flowers,
> Hang it with shrubs that twinkle in the breeze,
> And teach the little birds to build their nests
> And warble in its chambers. At a time
> When Nature, destined to remain so long
> Foremost in my affections, had fallen back
> Into a second place, pleased to become
> A handmaid to a nobler than herself,
> When every day brought with it some new sense
> Of exquisite regard for common things,
> And all the earth was budding with these gifts
> Of more refined humanity, thy breath,
> Dear Sister! was a kind of gentler spring
> That went before my steps.
> (XIV. 246-266)

Although it can be argued that Wordsworth's image of himself as a rock adorned by the gifts of spring suggests something bizarre about his attitude toward Dorothy, Wordsworth shows none of Rousseau's apprehensiveness that his feelings will be misjudged. Instead, Wordsworth's metaphoric language demands that we enlarge the terms for understanding the value of human relationships. The image of the poet as a "rock with torrents roaring" suggests the austere and sublime inclinations of the poet's temperament, heroic, but too bare of earthly and human grace. Dorothy, as a kind of gentler spring, seems to anticipate the movement toward greater mildness in the poet's own natural development. She goes before his steps, as a foretaste of spring, bringing to the rock the influence of nature in its benign rather than sublime form. Without fundamentally altering his character, she has adorned it as a severe Alpine landscape may be adorned but not fundamentally altered by the season.

Dorothy exists in the image as one among other influences on the poet's development and she is granted the mysterious natural and supernatural quality of all the other influences on the poet's life. That the poet has been blest by such a sister is made to seem wonderful, but it is not bizarre. It does not demand more precise explanation. The coming of spring to a high mountain transcends human explanation. The appropriate response to such an event is reverent acceptance and gratitude.

Rousseau's painstaking analysis of his feelings assumes that the nuances of personal relationship constitute human happiness or misery. Moral approval or blame depends on judgment of a man's conduct in human affairs. The lack of metaphoric language in Rousseau's statements of feeling reinforces the clear human boundaries of his world. Human feelings are not comparable to other events or things. They cannot be defined metaphorically. Neither divinity nor nature offers images to elucidate human feeling. Rousseau's battle with the language of the seventeenth-century moralists arises partly because he is always traveling so deep within their domain. The study of man is "la vraie étude," and it must be conducted directly, in a language of definition that remains true to man's distinctive existence, separate alike from gods and things.

Wordsworth uses his metaphoric and allusive language to locate himself primarily in relation to sky and earth, divinity and humanity in general rather than in particular human ties. That his feeling for Dorothy does not belong to a separate area of merely human relationship is one reason why she warrants a place in the heroic song, as Annette Vallon, for instance, does not. In the story of the poet's growth, to the poetic imagination guiding that story, Dorothy is like the sun, a divine messenger, the breath of spring. The poet does not worry about the inevitable distance of language from what might be called the anterior reality of his feeling for his sister. On the contrary, it is his poetic language which discovers and creates the significance of that feeling. It is only in the figurative language of his song that the manifold forms of his love acquire their true value, their harmony in relation to each other, and their enduring, substantial form.

Part Two

Rousseau and Wordsworth
Imagination and Memory

4
The Sources of Imagination

At the end of *The Prelude*, Wordsworth explains that the high love celebrated in his poem depends upon the activity of imagination. The imagination raises human affection "from earth to heaven, from human to divine." In tracing the story of his imaginative growth, the poet has shown the meaning of spiritual love. The poem has followed the development in the poet's own life of the capacity to transcend merely human affections by a vision of man's natural and divine affinities. The writing of the poem culminates the growth of imagination which it traces. Wordsworth invites us to see his reshaping of experience in *The Prelude* as the sign of his spiritual love. The view of the past created through the language of the poem testifies to the love that is generated by the poetic imagination.

Rousseau's autobiography also traces the history of his imagination. In his own way, Rousseau also sees his imagination as the creative power in his life and work. But there is no counterpart in the *Confessions* to Wordsworth's heroic conclusion to *The Prelude*. Nowhere in Rousseau's autobiography does he envision the Wordsworthian bond between the imagination and spiritual love. There is, we shall see, a deep connection between love and imagination for Rousseau, but the secular, erotic character of love in the *Confessions* keeps this connection remote from the Wordsworthian sublime. Rousseau's perception of his life does not lead him to Wordsworthian reverence

51

for his own or any other faculty of imagination. As remarked in Chapter 1, Rousseau dissociates his truthful confession from the deceptions of imaginative art. Although we may regard the *Confessions* as well as *The Prelude* to be the reshaping of a life by the power of imagination, it is important to remember that Rousseau himself makes a sharp distinction between a fiction like his novel, *La Nouvelle Héloise,* and the scrupulous memory of exact personal truth found in his autobiography.

The distinction between imagination and the activity of mind at work in the autobiography matters to Rousseau partly because he wants his *Confessions* to extricate him from the personal predicament caused, as he sees it, by the liveliness of his imagination at earlier times in his life. Whereas Wordsworth cherishes the memory of those experiences which have brought him the power of writing his heroic poem, Rousseau looks back at his life from a point of disappointment and disgrace. Past episodes of imaginative exaltation for Rousseau, therefore, bear a different relationship to the spirit of the autobiography than for Wordsworth. Rousseau wants to show the character of his baffling inner life so that we will be more generous and just in our judgment of him in his present misfortune. Like Wordsworth, Rousseau also tries to explain, through his history, how he has come to his present position. But Rousseau views the past with the consciousness of personal failure, not with Wordsworth's mixture of hope, gratitude, and self-encouragement. Although Rousseau remembers some of the troublemaking experiences in his past with delight, his nostalgia feeds on a present sense of irremediable misfortune. Nostalgia in the *Confessions* is always tempered by reminders that even the most rapturous experiences of the past have led him, step by step, to his present plight.

The very idea of Imagination in *The Prelude* seems to preclude Rousseau's kind of irremediable predicament, for Wordsworth regards the Imagination as a form of power, the power of the mind in its most exalted state:

> This spiritual Love acts not nor can exist
> Without Imagination, which, in truth,
> Is but another name for absolute power
> And clearest insight, amplitude of mind,
> And Reason in her most exalted mood.
> This faculty hath been the feeding source
> Of our long labour; we have traced the stream
> From the blind cavern whence is faintly heard

> Its natal murmur; followed it to light
> And open day; accompanied its course
> Among the ways of Nature, for a time
> Lost sight of it bewildered and engulphed:
> Then given it greeting as it rose once more
> In strength, reflecting from its placid breast
> The works of man and face of human life.
>   (XIV. 188-202)

In a general philosophic statement full of Miltonic grandeur, Wordsworth announces the heroic power of the human mind to flow beyond the boundaries of private experience. His own poem exemplifies this power in that it shows not only the bent of his individual mind but the highest attributes of Man in general. Thus the generic "Imagination," "Love," "Reason," "Nature." The poet's philosophic language rises above any mere personal adversity, and even above the sense of general irremediable conflicts, as between the faculties of the mind. Imagination is not the foe of Reason, but the superlative form of that traditional ideal of mental power. Nature is not opposed to spiritual Love; the power of Imagination flows among the ways of Nature as it regenerates the spirit. The poet's life is not in conflict with the larger world. His history is one manifestation of a power beyond any individual life. Wordsworth's metaphoric language locates the stream of Imagination within his own history but not exclusively there. The stream flows from the blind cavern, then to light and open day, among the ways of Nature, until it finally becomes a mighty river flowing past all of life, which it reflects.

Wordsworth dissociates the stream of Imagination from his unique, private history both in its goal and in its genesis. The origin of the stream is "the blind cavern," a source as gratuitous or, rather, as providential as the source of life itself. We have already observed, in Wordsworth's recollection of his feeling for Dorothy, how Wordsworthian metaphor displaces moral and psychological analysis by accounting for human events in nonhuman terms. When Wordsworth invokes the coming of spring to a mountain, the phases of human friendship are made to seem as varied and as inexplicable as the motions of nature. Wordsworth's metaphoric language for the growth of imagination creates the same effect with an even greater air of mystery. The image of the stream separates the origin and the course of imagination from the ordinary psychology of human passions and motives. Words with common psychological and moral meanings, like "bewildered" or "engulphed," become more literal descriptive

terms in Wordsworth's metaphor. *Human* bewilderment may call for
psychic or moral explanation. The disappearance of a stream in a
pathless wood goes back to the literal, root meaning of "bewilderment"[1] and it arouses a different kind of wonder. The stream of Imagination appears to move by a mysterious natural law of its own. The
growth of imagination cannot therefore really be *analyzed*. The
course of the stream can only be described and celebrated, or to repeat
Wordsworth's words, "traced," "followed," "accompanied," and finally "given greeting."

Wordsworth's language throughout *The Prelude* encourages the
reverent rather than analytic attitude toward imagination most directly stated in Book XIV. When, for example, Wordsworth recalls the
way he saw shepherds as a boy, he does not at all suggest that his
imaginative vision was rooted in any personal, psychological cause:

> A rambling school-boy, thus
> I felt his presence in his own domain,
> As of a lord and master, or a power,
> Or genius, under Nature, under God,
> Presiding; and severest solitude
> Had more commanding looks when he was there.
>   (VIII. 256-261)

Wordsworth calls attention to his *response* to the shepherd rather
than to his desire or need to see commanding presences in the landscape. Geoffrey Hartman observes this characteristic emphasis of
Wordsworth's poetry in relation to "The Solitary Reaper." That
poem, Hartman remarks, "is not a brooding analytic inquiry into the
source of an emotion. The poet does not explain why he responded so
strongly to the Highland girl but takes advantage of the strength of his
response. . . . The question why the poet is moved is subordinated to
the fact *that* he is moved."[2] Just as Wordsworth does not probe the
possible personal, psychological reasons why he responded to Dorothy
as if she were an archangel or a breath of spring, in Book VIII he does
not analyze the psychological sources of his boyhood awe before the
stern form of the shepherd:

> . . . suddenly mine eyes
> Have glanced upon him distant a few steps,
> In size a giant, stalking through thick fog,
> His sheep like Greenland bears: or, as he stepped
> Beyond the boundary line of some hill-shadow,
> His form hath flashed upon me, glorified

By the deep radiance of the setting sun:
Or him have I descried in distant sky,
A solitary object and sublime,
Above all height! like an aerial cross
Stationed alone upon a spiry rock
Of the Chartreuse, for worship.
                    (VIII. 264-275)

Wordsworth emphasizes how suddenly the visions "flashed" upon him, as if given by some power, natural or divine. Psychoanalytic criticism of *The Prelude* has portrayed Wordsworth driven to seek spiritual grandeur in nature by unconscious personal need.[3] But Wordsworth's version of his experience presents the boy, in one psychological sense, as passive, merely receptive. He did not, the language implies, especially want or need to see giants stalking around him. We are persuaded that shepherds did exist in the visible world outside his imagination, that they were sometimes lost in fog, and that sometimes their forms were "glorified" by a light that existed apart from what may or may not have been his desire, "By the deep radiance of the setting sun." Consequently, the boy's imaginative perception—his transformation of a shepherd into a giant—appears to be more than the refashioning of reality to accord with need or desire. His vision is made to seem an inspired and valid response to the reality that presented itself to his eye. His *response* was, of course, active. The boy's imagination shaped the visible objects into the most sublime forms known to him, giants and Greenland bears.

One might expect the adult poet to recall nostalgically the naïveté of his childish associations, or to measure now how a child's eye distorts and exaggerates. But Wordsworth's poetic language confirms the boy's perception, as if to insist that it remains an inspired and valid shaping of the scene. The poet explains the boy's feeling in stately Miltonic diction and rhythm, giving philosophic dignity to the chance perceptions of a "rambling school-boy." What he felt then was the true position of the shepherd, "in his own domain," not simply in the domain of the boy's inner life.

Wordsworth lifts the shepherd and the act of perceiving him outside of time and outside the boy's individual psychology. He recollects the experience of imaginative perception in the continuous past tense: "have glanced," "hath flashed," "have I descried." The tense of the verbs allows the past of boyhood an indefinite continuing life. The act of perceiving shepherds as giants does not belong to a strictly circumscribed past. By the end of the passage we almost forget that the perception of a child is being recollected. The image of the "aerial cross" endows the boy's perception with new, more sophisticated implications, drawn from literature and from the poet's own later experience, specifically his visit to the convent of the Chartreuse narrated in Book VI.

The figure of the shepherd appears still or at least again to the more literate and experienced adult who glorifies the remembered object further by the light of his mature imagination. The poetic imagination reshapes the image of memory as the boy's imagination, working in accord with the radiant sun, formerly shaped the visual object. In the mind's eye now, the shepherd of childhood has a twofold glory. He is still the heroic giant stalking before the child's vision and, in addition, he takes on the Christian (and specifically Miltonic) stature of the shepherd as spiritual guide, as in *Paradise Lost:* "That Shepherd, who first taught the chosen Seed, / In the Beginning how the Heav'ns and Earth / Rose out of *Chaos*" (I. 8-10).

In an unstated and unorthodox way, the local shepherd had been the boy's spiritual guide, teaching him the true place of Man in the order of earth and heaven. That shepherd seems even more worthy of worship to the poet now than he seemed to the boy in the past. The poet understands the spiritual significance of the solitary and sublime figure in terms beyond what could have flashed upon the boy's consciousness. His new images augment his childhood perception. The memory of imaginative vision thus becomes the means to new spiritual insight, new perceptions of relationship between earlier and later parts of his own experience, and new recognition of his kinship to other poets and worshippers in the past. It is the memory of his childhood perception that makes the shepherd available to the poet now as an image of spiritual presence in nature, like the Chartreuse cross or the figure of Christ himself. For the poet, the shepherd seems an even more enduring symbol of spiritual presence than the Cross, for in his own experience, it has been less shaken by the revolution of time than even the cross of Jesus in the Alps, "Memorial reverenced by a thousand storms" (VI. 486).

Wordsworth's vision of shepherds is one among the many flashings of imaginative power commemorated in *The Prelude.* The idea of imaginative perception that emerges from the poem draws, it has often been observed, upon the long study of the mind's encounter with the external world pursued by the English empirical psychologists through the eighteenth century. Wordsworth's debt to them and his departure from them have been much discussed by critics who have variously noted "the indigenous tendency toward the concept of creative perception which developed within the confines of the English empirical tradition."[4] Most commentaries on the subject remark how the eighteenth-century psychologists established the active role of the mind in the experience of perception. It is, however, equally important to understand how the English psychologists' interest in perception turned away from the moral and psychological analysis of imagination that, we shall see, continued to dominate Rousseau and later French writers as it did some English writers in the eighteenth century, like Samuel Johnson. English empiricism did not simply increase respect for the mind's active contribution to what we call knowledge; it also, and perhaps more fundamentally, shifted the moral and psychological terms for understanding mental activity.

The shift can be observed in a curious passage from Addison's *Pleasures of Imagination* where two quite different modes of psychology appear somewhat awkwardly mingled. In his popularization of Locke, Addison tries to adjust the vocabulary of an older moral tradition to the framework of the new empirical psychology:

> We are everywhere entertained with pleasing shows and apparitions, we discover imaginary glories in the heavens, and in the earth, and see some of this visionary beauty poured out upon the whole creation; but what a rough, unsightly sketch of nature should we be entertained with, did all her colouring disappear, and the several distinctions of light and shade vanish? In short, our souls are at present delightfully lost and bewildered in a pleasant delusion, and we walk about like the enchanted hero of a romance, who sees beautiful castles, woods, and meadows; and at the same time hears the warbling of birds, and the purling of streams; but upon the finishing of some secret spell, the fantastic scene breaks up, and the disconsolate knight finds himself on a barren heath, or in a solitary desert.[5]

Addison's diction seems to make moral and psychological distinctions like those an earlier or even a later moralist like Johnson makes between "luscious falsehood" and the "bitterness of truth."[6] The "enchanted hero" of Addison's little allegory, like a Spenserian knight, seems lost in the wood of "pleasant delusion," and the "barren heath" or "solitary desert" may seem to represent the moral reality of the actual world, so much less delightful than the fantastic scenery of romance. Read in this way, Addison seems to exemplify neoclassic distrust of the imagination, taken as the faculty that caters to the human desire for pleasure, lusciousness, and romance. Addison's diction, "lost and bewildered in a pleasant delusion," suggests the moral confusion generated by the imagination. We seem far from Wordsworth's use of "bewildered" to signify a phase of imaginative decline in Book XIV of *The Prelude*. The difference between Addison and Wordsworth is obvious. But Addison also foreshadows Wordsworthian Romanticism in this allegory in odd ways.

Addison uses the vocabulary of moral allegory to describe the fundamental conditions of all human perception. The moral language, in effect, asks us to recognize delusion as the basic, inevitable human condition. But unlike Johnson in "The Vanity of Human Wishes," Addison is not primarily making a moral statement of this theme:

> It is not improbable that something like this may be the state of the soul after its first separation [from the body after death], in respect of the images it will receive from matter, though indeed the ideas of colours are so pleasing and beautiful in the imagination, that it is possible the soul will not be deprived of them, but perhaps find them excited by some other occasional cause, as they are at present by the different impressions of the subtle matter on the organ of sight.
> I have here supposed that my reader is acquainted with that great modern discovery, which is at present universally acknowledged by all the inquirers into natural philosophy: namely, that light and colours, as apprehended by the imagination, are only ideas in the mind, and not qualities that have any existence in matter . . . if the English reader would see the notion explained at large, he may find it in the eighth chapter of the second book of Mr. Locke's *Essay on Human Understanding.*[7]

Addison's allegory of the deluded knight does not probe the moral and psychological dangers of man's effort to evade truth. Addison tries, rather, to explain a principle of "natural philosophy," concerning the way the mind perceives objects and "the several distinctions of light and shade." Addison sends his reader to Locke rather than to a moralist. The "pleasant delusion" he describes is not the consequence of human wishes, but simply the way we perceive objects in the external world. We respond to colors with delight, but we do not create the illusion of color out of personal repugnance for bare truth. Addison, in this essay, does not suggest possible personal motives—individual passions or desires—which may stimulate imagination. He is talking about a general natural law and he limits his subject to "only such pleasures as arise originally from sight."

Visual experience can seem devoid of personal motive; it is to be explained by a psychology of perception rather than by a psychology of motive and desire. The study of perception calls attention to the character of natural responses rather than scrutinizing individual, personal psychodynamics. The final cause of imaginative pleasure, Addison admits, is unknown to man, but it must reflect some fundamental harmony between the human mind and the universe arranged by the "first contriver," the "Supreme Author of our being."

Addison is, of course, still far from Wordsworth's Imagination. Although he grants the pleasures of imagination a divine source, Addison's language everywhere limits the moral and spiritual value of the spectacle which is perceived. The commonplace about neoclassic distrust of imagination still pertains to Addison even as he discusses natural philosophy. That the universe should appear to have the visionary beauty of romance may be part of the natural and even the divine order, but the perception of this beauty does not constitute the discovery of what Addison would call "truth." To relish the "pleasing shows and apparitions" of the visible world is even made to seem slightly frivolous, although Addison is only talking about the perception of color. A "pleasant delusion" may be all of reality visible to human perception, but it remains a "delusion" nonetheless.

Wordsworth, in contrast, does claim the title of "truth" for the visionary beauty perceived in the visible world by his imagination:

> Call ye these appearances—
> Which I beheld of shepherds in my youth,
> This sanctity of Nature given to man—
> A shadow, a delusion, ye who pore
> On the dead letter, miss the spirit of things;
> Whose truth is not a motion or a shape
> Instinct with vital functions, but a block
> Or waxen image which yourselves have made,
> And ye adore!
>
> (VIII. 294-301)

Wordsworth's claim depends on a distinction in value between kinds of truth. Addison had relegated to "pleasant delusion" all perceptions that add to objects qualities which cannot be said to "have any existence in matter." The field of true perception is thus pitifully vacant, a "barren heath" or "solitary desert." Wordsworth sharply repudiates such idolatry of material truth. Obeisance to the dead letter of matter is itself made to seem delusion, a false idea of truth created by part of the mind against the full living truth of experience. Wordsworth invokes the authority of traditional religious language in which matter has no special value, and the relationship between "truth" and "vision" is different from what it is in natural philosophy.

Religious vision traditionally implies "insight," the power of apprehending spiritual truth shadowed forth in appearances or even hidden by them. It is this kind of truth which Wordsworth claims for his boyhood way of seeing shepherds. The visual impression became a "vision" of spiritual truth. To add qualities to matter by the mind—in the language of natural philosophy—extends the vital and holy processes in nature itself, as in the spectacular effects of sunrise or sunset, moon or fog or mountain shapes in darkness. The poetic mind, in response to such effects, even adds to their magnificence, but the poetic mind is not deluded. The vital spirit of the human mind reaches out in response to the vital spirit at the heart of all life.

Religious tradition grants "seers" more than natural powers of perception. Yet the concept of inspired vision also, in a sense, refers to an idea of perception—the response to realities outside the mind rather than the projection of individual motive.[8] Wordsworth ennobles the English empiricists' interest in perception by extending it to include the mind's power of spiritual vision and spiritual love. Yet he also continues the empiricists' turn away from the motivating passions behind mental events. Spiritual love is itself a passion, but it is the consequence of acts that are as motiveless as the registering of light and color. Those who pore on the dead letter of the physical world are made to seem driven by peculiar motives, misled by the vanity of self-made idols. By contrast, the apparent impartiality of the imagination —that is, the freedom of the imaginative eye from the motive to distort or evade—comes to seem yet further proof of true insight. Imaginative perception transcends the delusions of vanity. It is a natural, and further, an inspired way to see beyond appearances to the very "spirit of things."

Sacred experiences of imaginative perception mark all the phases of the poet's growth, from boyhood visions of shepherds to the vision of the moon through the fog at Snowdon. The number of visions in the poem testifies to the richness and the constancy of the poet's imaginative eye. It is important to see, however, that Wordsworth's language of vision also sanctifies experiences less clearly related to visual perception. In Book III, for instance, the poet recalls his withdrawal from the "dazzling show" of Cambridge life to a world created rather than perceived by his mind:

> Unknown, unthought of, yet I was most rich—
> I had a world about me—'twas my own;
> I made it, for it only lived to me,
> And to the God who sees into the heart.
>
> (III. 143-146)

Wordsworth's retreat from the world of Cambridge differs from the imaginative experiences of childhood. Before, he "saw" the sublimity of the universe; at Cambridge he seems to have "made it" altogether in his own mind. The adolescent at the university lost some of the natural harmony and openness to his surroundings that he formerly had. This change is part of Wordsworth's story. Yet Wordsworth absorbs the impression of contrast into his larger sense of a stream that is continuous, though winding. Wordsworth complicates the simple contrasts between childhood and adolescence or between perception and invention to suggest the deeper continuity between two forms of imaginative vision:

> Some called it madness—so indeed it was,
> If child-like fruitfulness in passing joy,
> If steady moods of thoughtfulness matured
> To inspiration, sort with such a name;
> If prophecy be madness; if things viewed
> By poets in old time, and higher up
> By the first men, earth's first inhabitants,
> May in these tutored days no more be seen
> With undisordered sight.
>
> (III. 149-157)

With rising insistence, Wordsworth asserts that his private, inward experience was another form of vision. Not only did God see *his* pure and holy feeling, but he, too, saw beyond appearances to the heart of truth. Wordsworth proudly claims the heroic and divine ancestry of his visionary power. He withdrew from the "dazzling show" of Cambridge to an inner world which, though private, was like the world as viewed by God, or at least by the poets and prophets in "old time." The noble genealogy, the general names of established modes of knowing: "steady moods of thoughtfulness," "inspiration," "prophecy,"

work together with metaphors of "sight" to ennoble, generalize, vali-
date Wordsworth's private withdrawal. Wordsworth in boyhood saw
shepherds the way poets in old time saw heroes or demigods. He actually saw those shepherds, but when he beheld a world of his own
invention at Cambridge, his vision had the same traditional heroic
stature and the same spiritual validity as his perceptions of nature in
childhood.

Retreat from the external world, in Wordsworth's language, seems
oddly like a version of imaginative perception rather than its opposite.
In Book III there is more of a glance to personal motive than before as
Wordsworth recalls "a strangeness in the mind": "A feeling that I was
not for that hour, / Nor for that place" (III. 81-82). But Wordsworth
moves above and past that hint of psychological cause and effect as
smoothly here as when he talks about visual perception. His syntax
avoids the kind of explanation that would state: Cambridge oppressed
me (or bored me or frightened me) so I withdrew into a private world.
Wordsworth's language preserves the "I" from the indignity of psychic
stress: "I was not for that hour . . ." Hours and places do not weigh
heavily enough upon the Wordsworthian "I" to force a reaction. Instead, Wordsworth shows his true self, "endowed with holy powers /
And faculties," continuing the deeper life that had been set in motion
before.

Wordsworth passes by the chance to analyze in personal terms *why*
he responded to Cambridge as he did, calling attention instead to the
strength of his response:

> And as I paced alone the level fields
> Far from those lovely sights and sounds sublime
> With which I had been conversant, the mind
> Drooped not; but there into herself returning,
> With prompt rebound seemed fresh as heretofore.
>   (III. 93-97)

Phrases like "drooped not," "prompt rebound," "fresh as heretofore"
make movement away from external reality seem like a phase of natural growth, not a retreat so much as a way of renewing vital energy
for new encounters with the universe.

Wordsworth insists, moreover, that his earlier receptivity to the
influence of nature continued unabated all during this time:

To every natural form, rock, fruit or flower,
Even the loose stones that cover the high-way,
I gave a moral life: I saw them feel,
Or linked them to some feeling: the great mass
Lay bedded in a quickening soul, and all
That I beheld respired with inward meaning.
Add that whate'er of Terror or of Love
Or Beauty, Nature's daily face put on
From transitory passion, unto this
I was as sensitive as waters are
To the sky's influence in a kindred mood
Of passion; was obedient as a lute
That waits upon the touches of the wind.
                                        (III. 130-143)

This may be one of those instances in *The Prelude* where Wordsworth
protests too much that all the aspects of his experience are harmonious, continuous, reconciled. He seems perhaps too eager to put off the
charge of "madness" by allying mysterious intuitions of spirit with
sensory experience. There is an air of the merely dutiful in his "adding" mention of continuing obedience to nature's influence while recalling his strange inner feeling. The impulse to subdue impressions of the
bizarre can lead Wordsworth to what seems like rhetorical sleight-of-
hand. The beautiful metaphor of the Aeolian harp and the different
verbs of "seeing" sweep past a difficult transition. To have "seen" living spirit even in the loose stones of the road implies a significantly
different relation between mind and nature than sensitivity to the
changing passions of "Nature's daily face." We may feel more strain in
the transitions of the passage than Wordsworth acknowledges. We
continue to remark contrasts, even though he urges us to see harmony
and continuity. Wordsworth's assurance of tone does not quite carry
the argument here, yet one sees that the poetic structure of that argument is the same as for the more persuasive parts of the poem.

Just as the diverse meanings of Wordsworth's "love" subdue impressions of contrast, the flexibility of "sight," "sees," "beheld," "viewed"
aids, if it cannot altogether support, Wordsworth's effort toward in-
clusiveness and reconciliation in this part of Book III. That he "gave"
moral life to natural forms may mean only that he loosely associated
or "linked" things to feelings. Or it may mean that he strangely be-
lieved even the stones on the road to be alive. At the center of the imag-

inative experience are the statements: "I saw them feel" and "all /
That I beheld respired with inward meaning." Wordsworth's language
of vision joins intuition to simple association and then connects both
these possibilities to the actual perception of Nature's daily face.

Metaphors of vision are a central poetic device in Wordsworth's
effort to draw together the mental processes of association, natural
sight, and obscure intuitions, while retaining a sense of the range and
degree of experience at the same time. Perhaps Wordsworth's difficulty in the passage from Book III comes from introducing more precise philosophic distinctions than the figurative language of vision can
then control. Whatever the cause of the problem, if there is a problem,
one still recognizes that Wordsworth is trying to sanctify both his
withdrawal from the external world and his perception of it. Withdrawal and perception, the poet argues, lead to different but unop-
posed modes of creative imagination. Both forms of vision are private, individual experiences and they are also forms of general, traditional, and even holy insight.

To understand Wordsworth's idea of the imagination in *The Prelude*, we are urged by the poet to move as freely as possible between
his general theoretical statements and the character of mental power
displayed directly in the poetry. We are urged also to perceive the continuity between the imaginative experiences of the poet's past and the
immediate performance of imaginative power made possible by that
past. The poem invites and celebrates a flexible conception of the poetic mind—sometimes responsiveness to the visible life of Nature
seems most important, sometimes spiritual Love, sometimes the
power to re-create the past in memory and in poetic language.

Insofar as we are interested in Rousseau's own conception of his
imagination, the *Confessions* call for more precise distinctions between the different faculties of the mind, and also between the different times of life. It is important to be clear about what we are trying to
understand, for it is tempting to argue that Rousseau shows a richer
power of imagination in the writing of the *Confessions* than he knows
or acknowledges. We can call Rousseau's reconstruction of his life a
work of imagination, in the same way that we call the book a work of
art, despite Rousseau's protestations to the contrary. In Chapter 1, I
argue that the antiaesthetic bias of the *Confessions* makes certain aspects of Rousseau's art of stating emotion more comprehensible. Here,

I suggest that Rousseau's refusal to call his autobiography a work of imagination is similarly revealing. We shall see that Rousseau maintains a critical distance from his own memories of imaginative rapture. Instead of riding a wave of power set in motion by the past, Rousseau scrutinizes his memory in order to explicate and even free himself from the pattern he discerns. The idea of the imagination that emerges from this scrutiny is different from Wordsworth's idea of holy insight. The autobiographer offers his psychological insight into the structure of his character. The history of imagination in Rousseau takes on a different shape than in *The Prelude*. It unfolds in an altogether different style and from basically different philosophic and psychological interests.

The pervasive sense in Rousseau's autobiography of a problem or predicament in need of explanation in itself invites an analytic attitude toward the imagination rather than the reverentially descriptive stance taken by Wordsworth. Since Wordsworth regards all his imaginative activity as one or another form of power, richness, and insight, there is no incentive within Wordsworth's argument for inspecting the personal motives behind the activity of imagination. Perhaps that is why psychoanalytic studies of Wordsworth tend to begin from the least persuasive parts of the poetry, points where the discrepancy between what is stated and what seems (unintentionally) expressed suggests problems and motives unacknowledged by the poet himself.[9]

In the *Confessions*, the sense of a problem accompanies Rousseau's own history of his imagination from the start. His first picture of himself is at age five or six, a motherless child up all night reading novels aloud with his father. The bizarre quality of his inner life seems already set in this first account of the somewhat illicit pleasures of the imagination. His apprenticeship in adolescence to a clock-engraver is the next crucial episode. Looking back to that unhappy time, Rousseau sees the full pattern of experience that has brought him to his present predicament:

> Dégouté de tout ce qui étoit à ma portée, et sentant trop loin de moi tout ce qui m'auroit tenté, je ne voyois rien de possible qui put flater mon coeur. Mes sens émus depuis longtems me demandoient une jouissance dont je ne savois pas même imaginer l'objet. J'étois aussi loin du véritable que si je n'avois point eu de sexe, et déjà pubere et sensible, je pensois quelquefois à mes folies, mais je ne voyois rien au delà. Dans cette étrange situation mon inquiete imagination prit

un parti qui me sauva de moi-même et calma ma naissante sensual-
ité. Ce fut de se nourrir des situations qui m'avoient intéressé dans
mes lectures, de les rappeller, de les varier, de les combiner, de me
les approprier tellement que je devinsse un des personnages que
j'imaginois, que je me visse toujours dans les positions les plus agréables selon mon gout, enfin que l'état fictif où je venois à bout de me
mettre me fit oublier mon état réel dont j'étois si mécontent. Cet
amour des objets imaginaires et cette facilité de m'en occuper acheverent de me dégouter de tout ce qui m'entouroit, et déterminerent ce
gout pour la solitude, qui m'est toujours resté depuis ce tems-là. On
verra plus d'une fois dans la suite les bizarres effets de cette disposi-
tion si misantrope et si sombre en apparence, mais qui vient en effet
d'un coeur trop affectueux, trop aimant, trop tendre, qui, faute d'en
trouver d'éxistans qui lui ressemblent est forcé de s'alimenter de fictions. Il me suffit, quant à présent, d'avoir marqué l'origine et la
prémiére cause d'un penchant qui a modifié toutes mes passions, et
qui, les contenant par elles-mêmes, m'a toujours rendu paresseux à
faire, par trop d'ardeur à desirer. (40-41)

(Revolted by everything within my reach, and feeling that anything
which might have attracted me was too far away, I saw nothing that
could possibly stir my heart. My senses, which had been roused
long ago, demanded delights of which I could not even guess the
nature. I was as far from the reality as if I had been entirely lacking
in sexuality. My senses were already mature, and I sometimes
thought of my past eccentricities, but I could not see beyond them.
In this strange situation my restless imagination took a hand which
saved me from myself and calmed my growing sensuality. What it
did was to nourish itself on situations that had interested me in my
reading, recalling them, varying them, combining them, and giving
me so great a part in them, that I became one of the characters I
imagined, and saw myself always in the pleasantest situations of my
own choosing. So, in the end, the fictions I succeeded in building up
made me forget my real condition, which so dissatisfied me. My
love for imaginary objects and my facility in lending myself to them
ended by disillusioning me with everything around me, and determined that love of solitude which I have retained ever since that
time. There will be more than one example in what follows of the
strange effects of that trait in my character which seems so gloomy
and misanthropic. In fact, however, it arises from my too loving
heart, from my too tender and affectionate nature, which find no
living creatures akin to them, and so are forced to feed upon fictions. I am satisfied for the moment to have indicated the origin and
prime cause of an inclination which has modified all my passions,
and restrained them by making use of those very passions to curb
themselves. So it is that I have been slow in accomplishment
through excess of desire.)

Rousseau's inward withdrawal from his apprenticeship belongs to no holy tradition of inspired vision. Rousseau recalls a past colored by obscure intimations of sexuality rather than by the radiance of the setting sun. He isolates his imaginative activity within the private space of his personal history. His sensibility found no satisfaction in the circumstances of his apprenticeship, so he retreated to daydream. In contrast to Wordsworth, moving through Cambridge with his "I" sustaining its vitality from within, Rousseau shows the distortion of his sensibility under the pressure of outward circumstance. Disgusted with all that surrounded him, he withdrew, and his tendency to withdraw from the disappointments of reality lasted throughout his life.

Rousseau casts no doubt on the substantial reality of the drearily ordinary world of his apprenticeship. The world outside him was as mean and restricted as it seemed. And this actual ordinary world was no mere "show" like Wordsworth's Cambridge. The stingy, tyrannical master, the bookseller, the room where he read and daydreamed—all this constituted, unfortunately, the truth of his "état réel." Rousseau recalls how he fled from the lonely tedium of this reality to the richer, more loving world of fantasy.

Rousseau's language opposes "l'état fictif" to "mon état réel" as clearly as Johnson characteristically opposes "luscious falsehood" to the "bitterness of truth." Rousseau suggests no way for his imagination to have perceived reality anew, at least no way that could still be called "true." No question about the nature of perception clouds Rousseau's distinction here between truth and fiction. The images created by his desire were only "des objets imaginaires." No matter how immediate and palpable they seemed, they were clearly distinct and separate from the real objects of his actual life. To have become preoccupied with the imaginary was, finally, to *forget* the real world altogether: "enfin que l'état fictif où je venois à bout de me mettre me fit oublier mon état réel dont j'étois si mécontent." Nothing could be less like Wordsworth than the style of this sentence from the *Confessions*. Wordsworth's language draws together seemingly opposed terms. Rousseau enforces distinctions and insists upon contrasts. We have seen Rousseau try to protect his *feelings* from reductive, restrictive categories of language. But when Rousseau talks about his imagination, he perpetuates the limiting definitions and antitheses characteristic of classical French prose. No Wordsworthian sunset glorifies the shape of objects; nor does any fog obscure them. Reason and imagination *are* opposed, withdrawal from reality cannot be transformed into a version of perception. Antithetical categories break down as soon as one begins to explain the *feelings* involved in imaginative retreat, but the contrast between fiction and reality is as clear as a clear day.

Rousseau's distinction between what he wanted and what he actually had brings to mind the tradition of moral observation and judgment that goes back through seventeenth-century France to the precepts of Epicurus:

> The wealth demanded by nature is both limited and easily procured; that demanded by idle imaginings stretches on to infinity.

> For of the fools none is satisfied with what he has, but is grieved for what he has not. Just as men with fever through the malignance of their disease are always thirsty and desire the most injurious things, so too those whose mind is in an evil state are always poor in everything and in their greed are plunged into ever-changing desires.[10]

Samuel Johnson is the notable bearer of this tradition in eighteenth-century England, while some other writers—Addison, for example—were becoming diverted by "natural philosophy." Johnson, like Epicurus, poses the problem of imagination in the context of a moral and psychological consideration of man's dissatisfaction with ordinary reality:

> He who has nothing external that can divert him must find pleasure in his own thoughts and must conceive himself what he is not; for who is pleased with what he is? He then expatiates in boundless futurity, and culls from all imaginable conditions that which for the present moment he should most desire, amuses his desires with impossible enjoyments, and confers upon his pride unattainable dominion. The mind dances from scene to scene, unites all pleasures in all combinations, and riots in delights, which nature and fortune, with all their bounty, cannot bestow.[11]

In *Rasselas*, the moral problem posed by imagination has little to do with inquiry into the nature of perception. The thirst or what Johnson elsewhere calls the "hunger" of imagination arises from desires unsatisfied within the limits of an all too clearly perceived reality—what a man "has" and what he "is."

With varying degrees of severity and compassion, the moralists—Johnson as well as Epicurus—offer precepts about the dangers of imaginative escape from reality. In the *Confessions*, of course, Rousseau is not trying to define the proper relationship between desire and reality; his aim is not to offer moral precepts, but to unravel the labyrinth of his own complex experience, to explain and, finally, to defend it. But it is useful to recall that earlier, in *Emile*, Rousseau was writing as a preceptor. There he speaks of imagination in language even more clearly derived from an older moral tradition: "Le monde réel a ses bornes, le monde imaginaire est infini, ne pouvant élargir l'un, retrécissons l'autre."[12] (The real world has its limits; the imaginary world is infinite; since we cannot enlarge the one, let us contract the other.) In *Emile* Rousseau poses the antithesis even more sharply than in the *Confessions*. The real world and the imaginary world are distinct and opposed; Rousseau's language offers no bridge between them, nor any way of perceiving one in terms of the other. Of the two, "le monde réel" is the less flexible so that the imaginary world must be surrendered, or at least restricted.

Moral precepts gain their force from an assumption that man is morally and psychologically free to choose the wisdom they offer. According to Epicurus, only "fools" indulge in "idle imaginings" and his precept is intended to educate fools into wise men. But Rousseau's precepts in *Emile* are for the tutor rather than the pupil, as if education were a strategy to keep wise babes from the irresistible temptation of turning into fools. It is the tutor who must understand the dangers of imagination and who must prevent the child from developing the desire for "un monde imaginaire." Emile would not be allowed to read romantic fiction, for instance, as the child Rousseau did. Emile's tutor would keep him too busy for idle fantasy. Control of any tendency toward imagination is a central strategy of Rousseau's supposedly "free" pedagogy, for once desire for the imaginary is aroused, Rousseau warns, a fatal psychological sequence begins which no moral precept can reverse.

There is a kind of determinism in Wordsworth's comparison of imagination to a stream, following its own natural course. But the metaphor of the stream itself suggests the mysterious, apparently free and meandering movement of the inner life in *The Prelude*. There is no sense of compulsion or even urgency to the movement of the stream which Wordsworth describes. Its course was determined, in the sense that—in retrospect at least—the triumph of the power seems guaranteed. There is no determinism in the sense of psychological helplessness, partly of course because Wordsworth never tried, or wanted to try, to resist the expansive movement of his imagination. Its continuous growth, a kind of manifest destiny, can be perceived now as he traces the whole pattern of his life, as on a large map. But the individual experiences of imagination are remembered for their seeming suddenness as they "flashed" upon him. He recollects "visitings of imaginative power," as though they were bestowed upon him unpredictably from outside. Those moments at the time seemed determined only in the sense that some hidden guardian in the universe seemed to be showering extravagant and unasked for gifts upon him.

Rousseau has a quite different idea of psychological determinism. Whether he describes man in society at large, as in the *Discours*, or a child's education in *Emile*, or his own history in the *Confessions*, Rousseau orders human development into a chain of strict causes and consequences. In his recollection of adolescence, Rousseau does emphasize the movement and energy of his creative imagination—choosing, combining, and appropriating "des objets imaginaires" with apparently infinite abandon. But Rousseau at the same time binds his creativity into a seemingly rigid and involuntary psychological sequence.

Rousseau's "inquiete imagination" does not have the autonomous vitality of Wordsworth's Imagination. The initial energy in the inner drama comes from his agitated sensuality. Imagination intervenes only after the drama is in motion. Rousseau understands very well the psychodynamics of fantasy, the way fantasy may protect the "real," that is, the acting, everyday self from disturbing desires. He understands too the way fantasy has its own momentum, generating further desire and eventually influencing the whole personality. What began as a motion to protect a precarious psychic equilibrium becomes, in turn, an active force with its own disruptive consequences. Rousseau's erotic fantasies at first "saved" him from his confused sexual desire, but they ended, he explains, by turning his sensibility inward to the point of apparent misanthropy.

Rousseau organizes the phases of experience into a sequence of progressive causes and consequences. Events are linked to each other through causal words and phrasing: "enfin," "acheverent de," "déterminerent," "qui m'est toujours resté depuis ce tems-là," "qui vient en effet de," "est forcé de." Each consequence answers to a need, and in a sense, solves a problem, but only in turn to generate a further phase of deterioration.[13] The *Confessions* stretch before the reader innumerable chains of development, whole in themselves and intricately bound to each other. The ends of the chains always reach to Rousseau's present experience and to one of those fundamental traits of character which it is the task of the autobiography to analyze and defend.

Rousseau defends what he acknowledges to be his bizarre character by explicating the personal causes and origins of his peculiarities. The historical reconstruction of his development explains his apparent contradictions of character: the paradoxical joining of laziness and ardor, the impression of misanthropy made by a sensibility that is, at heart, all too loving and tender. By analyzing the sources of his character and by showing how, in a quite literal way, one thing led to another, Rousseau hopes to make the singular reality of his self known and justified.

Rousseau seeks no holy precedent for seeming "madness" as Wordsworth does. He is more eager to be acquitted by his contemporaries than to join a company of outcasts, however hallowed by tradition. Where Wordsworth celebrates a deeper vision than is conventional "in these tutored days," Rousseau protests that it is unfair to convict him of misanthropy. The term "misanthropy" is pejorative. It suggests callousness, arrogant toughness. But the chain of his experience reveals different, more complex feelings. He traces his "appearance" of misanthropy back to feelings which are conventionally the very opposite: "affectueux," "aimant," "tendre." The psychological chain shows, first, that he could not help what he became and, second, that the admittedly bizarre appearances of his behavior really derive from more admirable or at least innocent feelings than has been realized. We are all experts now in this double mode of self-defense which Rousseau inaugurated in literature: My history will show you that I could not help becoming this way and you will also see from my past how totally different I am from your conventional notion of the person who behaves the way I involuntarily do!

Rousseau's defense of his character does not at all challenge the reality of appearances in the universe outside his own mind. As Starobinski has justly remarked, the nature of Rousseau's own activity of perception is not at stake.[14] Rousseau challenges only the false judgments made of him by others on the basis of *his* appearance. The analysis of inward experience will bridge the disparity between incriminating moral appearances and the reality of his emotional need and desire.

Rousseau's great departure from the moralists before him comes, of course, in the tolerance and even respect which he demands for his emotional needs. The force of psychic need in the *Confessions* establishes personal desire as one ineradicable form of reality itself, forever opposed to the rest of the actual world but equal in strength to it. Rousseau thus ends by complicating the initially straightforward distinction between "le monde réel" and "le monde imaginaire." The unreal world created by imagination reflects and projects the private reality of feeling. This purely inward reality proves to be at least as unyielding as the world outside the self. In the *Confessions* two kinds of reality are pitted against each other in an endless combat which no precept can resolve. In the moral tradition, the style of antithesis defines clear, permanent, and general truths. Rousseau preserves this kind of distinction in his contrast between truth and fiction, but he goes on to absorb it into the more varied and baffling structure of his narrative. The force of moral precept is dissipated through Rousseau's progressive and intimate story of desire, withdrawal, failure, restless accommodation, renewed desire, new retreat, new failure.

The key episode in this story forms Book IX of the *Confessions*, the sequence of experiences at l'Hermitage beginning with a seemingly idyllic rural retreat and ending in exile after the scandal of Rousseau's infatuation with Mme d'Houdetot. This sequence too begins with unsatisfied desire and ends in personal calamity. The initial disparity between desire and reality at l'Hermitage is even more fundamental and irremediable than during Rousseau's apprenticeship, for l'Hermitage was already a privileged world, designed in apparent accord with what Rousseau had thought to be his desire. But the equilibrium between desire and reality for Rousseau is never stable. Even though he was the welcome guest of an aristocratic lady at l'Hermitage and was living there in peace with Thérèse whom he presumably loved, Rousseau was not satisfied: "Il me sembloit que la destinée me devoit quelque chose qu'elle ne m'avoit pas donné" (426). (It seemed to me that fate owed me something she had never given me.) Characteristically, his mind answers the vague demands of desire by veering away to the image of some superior happiness. At l'Hermitage, he first retreats to nostalgia for the lost pleasures of les Charmettes with Mme de Warens and then luxuriates in the memory of all the other idyllic moments in the past. Nostalgia leads quickly to fantasy. Once more imagination creates a fictitious world, more gratifying than any actual experience present or past. The delights of fantasy end abruptly, however, as a severe urinary attack ignominiously brings him back to "le monde réel." But a new cycle begins upon his recovery, a new retreat to fantasy, leading this time to the plan of the novel, *La Nouvelle Héloise*. Deep in this project, he meets Mme d'Houdetot and transfers to her the ideal qualities of his fictional characters. The infatuation ends in a public scandal.

In *The Prelude*, the very presence of the poem we are reading testifies, as it were, to the virtue of the poet's past. Since his past has brought him to the power of this achievement, there is no need to regret any turn in the course of events. When Rousseau, however, recalls writing *La Nouvelle Héloise*, he reduces the novel to just an episode in his personal history. The creation of the novel in no way seems to justify or govern the shape of that complicated period in his life, as in many biographies of artists, great imaginative achievements blot out the personal disasters originally associated with them. Rousseau recalls the intense pleasure he felt in writing *La Nouvelle Héloise*, but in a defensive, embarrassed tone. In retrospect, the novel was "le meilleur parti qui se put tirer de mes folies" (435) (the best use I could have put my follies to), but the novel does not seem to redeem the personal disaster which it precipitated. Rousseau contains *La Nouvelle Héloise* in a larger and still continuing sequence of personal catastrophes. Rousseau's work of art forms only one link in an intricate chain of experience reaching back to childhood and forward to disgrace and to his need to vindicate himself in the autobiography we are reading.

Perhaps at the height of what Rousseau calls his delirium at l'Hermitage, he transcended the conflict between desire and reality, since he moved totally into "le pays des chiméres." But as the more sober narrator of the *Confessions*, Rousseau exposes this rapture to have been only a dangerous though ecstatic illusion:

L'impossibilité d'atteindre aux êtres réels me jetta dans le pays des chiméres, et ne voyant rien d'existant qui fut digne de mon délire, je le nourris dans un monde idéal que mon imagination créatrice eut bientot peuplé d'êtres selon mon coeur. Jamais cette ressource ne vint plus à propos et ne se trouva si féconde. Dans mes continuelles extases je m'enivrois à torrens des plus délicieux sentimens qui jamais soient entrés dans un coeur d'homme. Oubliant tout à fait la race humaine, je me fis des societés de créatures parfaites aussi celestes par leurs vertus que par leurs beautés, d'amis sûrs, tendres, fidelles, tels que je n'en trouvai jamais ici bas. Je pris un tel goût à plâner ainsi dans l'empyrée au milieu des objets charmans dont je m'étois entouré que j'y passois les heures, les jours sans compter, et perdant le souvenir de toute autre chose, à peine avois-je mangé un morceau à la hâte que je brulois de m'échaper pour courir retrouver mes bosquets. (427-428)

(The impossibility of attaining the real persons precipitated me into the land of chimeras; and seeing nothing that existed worthy of my exalted feelings, I fostered them in an ideal world which my creative imagination soon peopled with beings after my own heart. Never was this resource more opportune, and never did it prove more fertile. In my continual ecstasies I intoxicated myself with draughts of the most exquisite sentiments that have ever entered the heart of a man. Altogether ignoring the human race, I created for myself societies of perfect creatures celestial in their virtue and in their beauty, and of reliable, tender, and faithful friends such as I had never found here below. I took such pleasure in thus soaring into the empyrean in the midst of all the charms that surrounded me, that I spent countless hours and days at it, losing all memory of anything else. No sooner had I eaten a hasty morsel than I was impatient to escape and run into my woods once more.)

Rousseau's language repeatedly, insistently, forces a contrast between distinct and opposing terms: "êtres réels"—"le pays des chiméres," "rien d'existant"—"un monde idéal," "la race humaine"—"des societés de créatures parfaites," "l'empyrée"—"le souvenir de toute autre chose." Apparent transcendence was achieved only by managing to expunge one set of terms from his mind altogether. The narrator in retrospect, however, must recall the reality which was at that time ignored, because it eventually reasserted its implacable power over him and he is still living out the consequences.

The opposition between desire and reality assumes radical implications by Book IX of the *Confessions*. In his recollection of adolescence Rousseau defined his "état réel" in terms of a specific situation, his apprenticeship with its particular and perhaps unusual constraints. In Book IX the unsatisfactory reality seems to include the very condition of human life on earth. His desire demands an ideal world beyond actual possibility, unlike any world that exists apart from his desire. Although words like "l'empyrée," "idéal," "celeste" connote divinity, Rousseau does not affirm any correspondence between his fantasy and a "real" supernatural realm. There is no Wordsworthian claim that the world created by the imagination corresponds to the divine creation, nor is private invention affiliated with the sacred and inspired vision of holy seers in the past.

Although Descartes deduced divinity from the clear presence in his mind of the conception of God, Rousseau has a more plaintive recognition that his conceptions of ideal creatures prove only the character of his own sensibility: "J'ai souvent regretté qu'il n'existât pas des Dryades; c'eut infailliblement été parmi elles que j'aurois fixé mon attachement" (428). (I have often regretted that dryads do not exist; for among them I should assuredly have found an object for my love.)

Rousseau's feeling for dryads or other ideal figures of the imagination does not at all prove or even suggest that they exist. At most his feelings show that he is by sensibility too fine for the actual world. His feelings constitute a reproach to reality rather than a redefinition of it. Characteristically for Rousseau, self-examination has a slippery way of turning around into criticism of the world, but without any change of metaphysical assumptions. His chronic dissatisfaction shows his incurable maladjustment; turning that around, it also reveals his distinguished sensibility doomed to suffer in the mean actual world. He had to escape to fictions because the real world could offer "rien d'existant qui fut *digne* de mon délire" (italics mine). Rousseau boasts of his sensibility without ever losing sight of the fact that it chronically leads him away from what he himself regards as reality.

In *Rousseau et la réalité de l'imaginaire*, Marc Eigeldinger describes Rousseau's writing as "*irréaliste*, that is to say that it turns away from real experience to rely on the imaginary."[15] The characterization seems appropriate to *La Nouvelle Héloise* and perhaps even to the social and political writings, but it ignores the careful distinction between truth and fiction which Rousseau insists upon in the *Confessions*. The temptation of the imaginary is, to be sure, one of the recurrent themes of Rousseau's autobiography, but the voice describing this temptation keeps reminding us of the reality which he formerly tried to evade. In the *Confessions*, the raptures of imagination belong to a social and domestic tableau which Rousseau reviews, at least in part, with the eye of an ironic observer. Social details and colloquial phrases keep imaginative exaltation rooted in the familiar world of human conversation and gesture. From this perspective, Jean-Jacques was carrying on in an absurd way and Rousseau sees himself in retrospect in part as a foolish figure: "et voila le grave Citoyen de Genève, voila l'austére Jean Jaques à près de quarante cinq ans redevenu tout à coup le berger extravagant" (427) (and there was the grave citizen of Geneva, the austere Jean-Jacques at almost forty-five, suddenly become once more the love-sick swain).

Instead of Wordsworth's reverence, Rousseau expresses only tenderness toward his past flights of imagination.[16] He indulges his sensibility, yet he stays within an analytic and ironic perspective, closer to the stance of novelists like Stendhal or Flaubert in the nineteenth century. Irony controls the story of his inglorious collapse from an imaginary paradise to the sickbed:

> Au fort de ma plus grande exaltation je fus retiré tout d'un coup par le cordon comme un Cerf-volant et remis à ma place par la nature à l'aide d'une attaque assez vive de mon mal. J'employai le seul remède qui m'eut soulagé savoir les bougies, et cela fit trève à mes angéliques amours: car outre qu'on n'est guére amoureux quand on souffre, mon imagination qui s'anime à la campagne et sous les arbres, languit et meurt dans la chambre et sous les solives d'un plancher. (428)

> (At the supreme height of my exaltation I was suddenly pulled down, like a kite on a string, and restored to my place by Nature by the agency of a fairly sharp attack of my complaint. I used the only remedy which afforded me any relief, the catheters, and they put a stop to my celestial amours. For not only is one seldom in love when in pain, but my imagination, which only thrives in the country and under trees, languishes and dies in a room beneath the rafters of a ceiling.)

Rousseau swiftly descends in the narrative from "mes angéliques amours" to the human ignominy of his urinary disease. The fall represents a descent from "un monde idéal" to the order of "la nature." Rousseau is famous for his idealization of the term "la nature," but it is important to see that, among other meanings, nature for Rousseau is the force of destiny—here, in its most concrete form of physical disease. Nature puts man back in his limited human place: a domestic scene where one suffers physically from disease and mentally from all kinds of social harassment. Escape to the ideal world demanded by desire and created by imagination is only a temporary holiday from the ordinary routine of pain.

When Wordsworth, in Book I of *The Prelude*, recalls watching kites, the kite becomes, like the boy himself at other moments, mysteriously free from any tie to the ground. The kite falls because of the storm rather than the pull of the string:

—Unfading recollections! at this hour
The heart is almost mine with which I felt,
From some hill-top on sunny afternoons,
The paper kite high among fleecy clouds
Pull at her rein like an impetuous courser;
Or, from the meadows sent on gusty days,
Beheld her breast the wind, then suddenly
Dashed headlong, and rejected by the storm.
(I. 491-498)

Wordsworth's kite has heroic, almost supernatural energy, like Pegasus breasting the wind, restlessly straining at the bit. When Rousseau, describing his illness, compares himself to a kite, the center of the image is the string which reveals the kite's only illusory freedom: "je fus retiré tout d'un coup par le cordon comme un Cerf-volant et remis à ma place." In the *Confessions*, Rousseau never loses hold of the string which binds even the highest flights of his imagination to the ground. The illusion of freedom is the activity of imagination; the perception of the string, or, from another point of view, the chain, comes after the event, in memory. Thus Rousseau refuses to call his autobiography a work of imaginative literature. He wishes to distinguish the power of memory which allows him to reconstruct the full chain of his experience from the power of imagination which flies in the face of the reality to which it is nevertheless bound.

5

The Charm of Memory

To the moralist, memory is the instrument of conscience; it summons the past for moral judgment as well as rational analysis. "It is, indeed," explains Samuel Johnson, "the faculty of remembrance, which may be said to place us in the class of moral agents."[1] Even Coleridge continues to respect the traditional moral value of memory. His objection to Wordsworth's word "bliss" for the memory of daffodils in "I Wandered Lonely as a Cloud" reflects more loyalty to eighteenth-century moral priorities than Coleridge himself quite acknowledges. He is ostensibly listing the few instances of bombast in Wordsworth's poetry, but his objection really goes to the heart of Wordsworth's loosening of memory from its traditional and relatively straightforward moral function:

It is a well-known fact, that bright colors in motion both make and leave the strongest impressions on the eye. Nothing is more likely too, than that a vivid image or visual spectrum, thus originated, may become the link of association in recalling the feelings and images that had accompanied the original impression. But if we describe this in such lines as
> "They flash upon that inward eye,
> Which is the bliss of solitude!"
in what words shall we describe the joy of retrospection, when the images and virtuous actions of a whole well-spent life, pass before

that conscience which is indeed the *inward* eye: which is indeed *"the bliss of solitude?"* Assuredly we seem to sink most abruptly, not to say burlesquely, and almost as in a *medly*, from this couplet to—
"And then my heart with pleasure fills,
And dances with the daffodills."[2]

Although Coleridge is interested in the psychology of perception, the only kind of memory that he accords the serious religious title of "bliss" is a moral faculty almost synonymous with conscience. "Bliss" is attainable through memory, but only when the inward eye reviews a virtuous life, not a show of dancing flowers.

Coleridge's criticism of Wordsworth reflects the continuing force of eighteenth-century moral values in the Romantic period. He often sounds more like Samuel Johnson than like Wordsworth, not least by observing bad conscience to be more common than good among men. Memory, as viewed by both Coleridge and Johnson, tends therefore to bring more pain than joy, and though good resolves may be strengthened through honest review of the past, both Coleridge and Johnson measure with compassion the limits of the good to be gained through painful retrospection. The guilty conscience of the Ancient Mariner engenders despair; he needs to be healed. Johnson, also speaking as a healer, contemplates the value of forgetting:

> We suffer equal pain from the pertinacious adhesion of unwelcome images, as from the evanescence of those which are pleasing and useful; and it may be doubted whether we should be more benefited by the art of memory or the art of forgetfulness. . . .
> Regret is indeed useful and virtuous, and not only allowable but necessary, when it tends to the amendment of life, or to admonition of error which we may be again in danger of committing. But a very small part of the moments spent in meditation on the past, produce any reasonable caution or salutary sorrow. . . .
> It would add much to human happiness, if an art could be taught of forgetting all of which the remembrance is at once useless and afflictive, if that pain which never can end in pleasure could be driven totally away, that the mind might perform its functions without incumbrance, and the past might no longer encroach upon the present.[3]

Of course the art of forgetfulness cannot take Wordsworth or Rousseau (or any autobiographer) very far in his project. Rousseau, writing in the spirit of the eighteenth century's moral conception of memory, deliberately commits himself to remember, partly because he wants to show that his conscience is clear, clearer at least than his reputation. Still, moral vindication does not account for the charm of memory to Rousseau. At key moments in the *Confessions*, the moral significance of the past recedes, as Rousseau indulges the sheer joy of reliving his own remembered feelings. He does not share Johnson's fear of the useless and painful encroachment of the past, partly because he claims to possess, by a happy gift of temperament, the very art of selective forgetfulness which Johnson wistfully recommends:

> Il est étonnant avec quelle facilité j'oublie le mal passé, quelque récent qu'il puisse être. . . . J'épuise en quelque façon mon malheur d'avance; plus j'ai souffert à le prévoir, plus j'ai de facilité à l'oublier; tandis qu'au contraire sans cesse occupé de mon bonheur passé, je le rappelle et le rumine, pour ainsi dire, au point d'en jouir derechef quand je veux. (585)

> (It is astonishing how easily I forget past ills, however recent they may be. . . . In a way I exhaust my misfortunes in advance. The more I suffer in anticipation, the easier I find it to forget. Whereas, on the other hand, I am continuously preoccupied with my past happiness. I remember it and chew it over, so to speak, in such a way that I can enjoy it afresh at will.)

Rousseau's delight in his power to revive the happiness of his past brings him closer to Wordsworth and to what is generally understood as the Romantic conception of memory.[4] Perhaps even more boldly than Rousseau, Wordsworth also reinterprets memory to signify the freedom of the mind rather than the burden portrayed by Johnson and even by Coleridge. Regret need not dominate the experience of memory, partly because the mind can freely choose where in the past to dwell, and partly because the renewal of feeling comes to matter as much as the verdict pronounced upon the past by moral judgment. The review of a well-spent life does not constitute the main charm of memory for either Rousseau or Wordsworth. Nor do they seek in the past Johnsonian cautions and salutary sorrows. The deeper, more mysterious appeal of memory for Rousseau and Wordsworth resides in their sense of the mind's power to repossess the past as if it still existed in the inner life: "And then my heart with pleasure fills, / And dances with the daffodills."

In the *Confessions*, the desire to fill the heart with pleasure again governs Rousseau's narrative as strongly as the deliberate moral commitment to review the past. Rousseau's attitude toward his memory is therefore complex, if not contradictory. He wants to have his memory both ways. He guarantees the truth of his portrait because his memory does not lie, yet memory consoles him because he has the gift of discarding "le mal passé." His memory is a discipline of desire because he reconstructs the far from desirable chain of causes and consequences in the past. But memory is also a new indulgence of desire, because, like the imagination, it carries him away from present pain to a world of feeling controlled by his own mind.

Rousseau's absorption in the happy past blurs his own distinction between reality and fantasy, and between memory and imagination. Rousseau seems to come closer to Wordsworth, both writers cherishing the deeply affiliated sources of joy in the mind. Yet the analogy between Rousseau and Wordsworth still does not go very far, for even when Rousseau's nostalgia resembles the imagination, it functions like the imagination in Rousseau's own sense of the term, not in Wordsworth's. Rousseau turns to memory at certain moments in the autobiography very much the way he had, at earlier times in his life, turned to fantasy. Rousseau, writing autobiography to lose himself in the vivid inner world of past happiness resembles, psychologically, Rousseau's own earlier self retreating to the pleasures of imagination. And although Rousseau releases these pleasures from ordinary moral strictures, he still does not claim for them the stature of Wordsworthian "bliss."

Idyllic memory in Rousseau's experience has the appeal but also the moral ambiguity of the imagination. Though the feelings evoked by the mind may be innocent, Rousseau shows that thorough absorption in them actively undermines moral strength. In the past, for example at l'Hermitage, the pleasures of memory and imagination went together, or rather, one led to the other. Rousseau describes how, before he escaped to fiction at l'Hermitage, he first lost himself in the charm of the happy past:

Bientôt je vis rassemblés autour de moi tous les objets qui m'avoient donné de l'émotion dans ma jeunesse, Mlle Galey, Mlle de Graffenried, Mlle de Breil, Made Basile, Made de Larnage, mes jolies écoliéres et jusqu'á la piquante Zulietta, que mon coeur ne peut oublier. Je me vis entouré d'un serrail d'Houris de mes anciennes connoissances, pour qui le goût le plus vif ne m'étoit pas un sentiment nouveau. (426-427)

(Soon I saw all around me the persons I had felt emotion for in my youth: Mlle Galley, Mlle de Graffenried, Mlle de Breil, Mme Basile, Mme de Larnage, my pretty music pupils, and even the enchanting Giulietta, whom my heart can never forget. I saw myself surrounded by a seraglio of houris, by my old acquaintances, a strong desire for whom was no new sensation to me.)

Memory was almost as thorough a distraction from the reality of l'Hermitage as the imaginative revery which it stimulated. And it was equally debilitating. Writing the autobiography, Rousseau describes the intoxication of nostalgia as though he were tracing the first phase of an illness: "L'ivresse dont je fus saisi, quoique si prompte et si folle, fut si durable et si forte, qu'il n'a pas moins fallu pour m'en guérir que la crise imprévue et terrible des malheurs où elle m'a précipité" (427). (The intoxication that seized me, although so sudden and so foolish, was so strong and lasting that it took nothing less than the unforeseen and terrible crisis it brought upon me to cure me of it.) Even while he evokes all the precious names of the past in the narrative, yielding to their charm again just as he had done at l'Hermitage, he interprets his vulnerability to nostalgia as a fatal weakness of character.

Irony cuts across the lyricism in Rousseau's account of his tender mood at l'Hermitage. He exposes the incongruity between the delights of conjuring the sweet past and the severe program of personal reform he was supposedly following at that time of his life. Rousseau the autobiographer still admires the austere rational principles by which he had tried to live and think during the six-year period before the visit to l'Hermitage, the time during which he wrote Le Contrat social and other essays of social criticism and theory. He regrets the return of his old regime of sensibility, even while he shows himself still under its sway.

Rousseau's critical evaluation of his nostalgia is in direct contrast to Wordsworth's view of his decline and revival of power during the French Revolution. In The Prelude, Wordsworth traces the darkest phase of his development to his infatuation in France with just the kind of rational principle which Rousseau was developing during his period of reform:

> In such strange passion, if I may once more
> Review the past, I warred against myself—
> A bigot to a new idolatry—
> Like a cowled monk who hath forsworn the world,
> Zealously laboured to cut off my heart
> From all the sources of her former strength.
>   (XII. 75-80)

Wordsworth's temporary confusion in France exemplifies the deadly zeal of revolutionary ideology: a worship of rational principle isolated from the sources of strength in the past. Wordsworth interprets his revolutionary enthusiasm as a betrayal of memory in both social and personal terms:

> Dare I avow that wish was mine to see,
> And hope that future times *would* surely see,
> The man to come, parted, as by a gulph,
> From him who had been.
>
> (XII. 57-60)

Echoing Burke's criticism of the French Revolution, Wordsworth asserts that social and personal vitality disappears in the void of abstract principle. The gulf separating present from past must be closed, in Wordsworth's terms, through "the reanimating influence" of memory. *The Prelude* is the record of the poet's early strength, his lapse, and his recovery. Moreover, the style of the poem affirms new ties to the past, the past of literature and myth as well as childhood. Fidelity to the sources of strength in the past becomes in *The Prelude* a new moral value, quite apart from the morality of that past judged according to rational principle alone.

Rousseau records the revival of his sensibility at l'Hermitage with more indulgence than approval. He observes that his program of personal reform had not severed his heart from his earlier self as thoroughly as he had imagined. But there is no ennobling lesson to be learned from his experience at l'Hermitage, only the personal fact that nostalgia proved to be irresistibly seductive to him. The chain of feeling to the past could not be broken; Rousseau shows himself involuntarily fixed in the bias of his sensibility. Nostalgia caters to the unchanging reality of emotional need, always at odds with actual current possibilities of experience. Rousseau's memory thus resembles imagination in seducing his mind to an inner world fashioned more perfectly in accord with desire. He shows his mind always ready to devise different kinds of refuge from a world which no power of mind seems able either to change or to accept.

Rousseau the autobiographer tells us that his imagination no longer tempts him, but he seeks the solace of memory now almost without compunction:

Je ne vois plus rien dans l'avenir qui me tente; les seuls retours du passé peuvent me flatter, et ces retours si vifs et si vrais dans l'époque dont je parle me font souvent vivre heureux malgré mes malheurs. (226)

(I no longer see anything in the future to attract me; only a return
into the past can please me, and these vivid and precise returns into
the period of which I am speaking often give me moments of happiness in spite of my misfortunes.)

Although the psychology of his memory is no different than it was at
l'Hermitage, the utter hopelessness of his present position gives new
legitimacy to his nostalgia now. Forcibly deprived of all present satisfaction or hope for the future, he must be allowed to pursue his only
source of consolation. Rousseau the autobiographer no longer strives
for austere personal reform. Without devaluing that earlier effort, he
cares more to establish his identity as a complex and tender sensibility.
It is only within this limited personal framework that Rousseau claims
a kind of moral value for his nostalgia. Love for the happy past indirectly becomes a part of Rousseau's apologia as it demonstrates the
helpless but essentially innocent bondage of "une âme sensible."

Memory in the *Confessions* is, paradoxically, both bondage and
liberty. While memory frees the mind from the present, it binds the
self to one's own former desires and also to the shape and texture of
experience as it was. Rousseau's delight in memory comes from his
sense that he can revive past feeling without essentially changing its
substance. Although he may not be able to devise language that can
fully contain the emotions of his past, those feelings still survive intact
within him. The debilitating consequences of memory, however, also
derive from the same durability of past feeling, for Rousseau's
memory directs him only inward and backward. Wordsworth's sense
of power—sources of power in the past, new power for the future—is
missing from Rousseau's concern for the sheer revival of feeling. The
"charm" of memory for Wordsworth implies the almost magical
release of new energy. To remember the past is to be "nourished,"
"repaired," "revived"; memories "penetrate" the mind, "enable" it to
rise by means of their "invigorating virtue." Instead of Wordsworth's
active verbs, Rousseau's key words are usually nouns and adjectives
which identify the quality of a past feeling with the mood induced by
recollecting it. "Le charme" and "la force" of his happy memories
come from their vivid presence in his mind. His memories are strong,
without being strengthening. The past feelings were "douces,"
"tendres," "délicieux"; to remember them is to experience again the
same "douceur," "plaisir," "jouissance."

Rousseau's memory of a night spent outdoors near Lyons illustrates the contrast to Wordsworthian memory clearly, especially since the episode itself resembles some of Wordsworth's own cherished moments in nature:

> Je me souviens même d'avoir passé une nuit délicieuse hors de la ville dans un chemin qui cotoyoit le Rhône ou la Saone, car je ne me rappelle pas lequel des deux. Des jardins elevés en terrasse bordoient le chemin du côté opposé. Il avoit fait très chaud ce jour-là; la soirée étoit charmante; la rosée humectoit l'herbe flétrie; point de vent, une nuit tranquille; l'air étoit frais sans être froid; le soleil après son coucher avoit laissé dans le ciel des vapeurs rouges dont la réfléxion rendoit l'eau couleur de rose; les arbres des terrasses étoient chargés de rossignols qui se répondoient de l'un à l'autre. Je me promenois dans une sorte d'extase livrant mes sens et mon coeur à la joüissance de tout cela, et soupirant seulement un peu du regret d'en joüir seul. Absorbé dans ma douce rêverie je prolongeai fort avant dans la nuit ma promenade sans m'appercevoir que j'étois las. Je m'en apperçus enfin. Je me couchai voluptueusement sur la tablette d'une espéce de niche ou de fausse porte enfoncée dans un mur de terrasse: le ciel de mon lit étoit formé par les têtes des arbres, un rossignol étoit précisément au dessus de moi; je m'endormis à son chant: mon sommeil fut doux, mon réveil le fut davantage. Il étoit grand jour: mes yeux en s'ouvrant virent l'eau, la verdure, un paysage admirable. Je me levai, me secouai, la faim me prit, je m'acheminai gaiment vers la ville resolu de mettre à un bon déjeuné deux piéces de six blancs qui me restoient encore. J'étois de si bonne humeur que j'allois chantant tout le long du chemin, et je me souviens même que je chantois une Cantate de Batistin intitulée *les Bains de Thoméry* que je savois par coeur. (168-169)

(I even remember spending one delightful night outside the town, on a road that ran beside the Rhône or the Saône—I cannot remember which. On the other side of this road were some gardens built up on a terrace. The day had been very hot. The evening was most pleasant, and the dew was falling on the parched grass. There was no wind, the night was still, and the air was fresh without being cold. The sunken sun had left red wisps of vapour in the sky, and their reflection stained the water a rosy red. The trees on the terrace were full of nightingales which answered one another's song. I moved in a kind of ecstacy, surrendering my senses and my heart to the enjoyment of it all, and only occasionally sighing with regret that I was enjoying all this alone. Deep in my sweet reverie, I walked on late into the night without noticing that I was tired. I was aware of it at last, and lay down voluptuously upon the step of a kind of niche or false door let into the terrace wall. The canopy of my bed was formed by the tops of the trees. One nightingale was perched

exactly above me, and sang me to sleep. My sleep was sweet and my
awaking sweeter still. It was broad day; and as my eyes opened I
saw the water, the greenery, and a lovely countryside. I got up and
shook myself. I felt the pangs of hunger, and walked cheerfully
towards the city, determined to spend the two small coins I still had
left on a good breakfast. I was in such fine spirits that I sang the
whole way; and I even remember what I sang. It was one of Batistin's cantatas, called 'At the Baths of Thomery', which I knew by
heart.)

Rousseau recollects the feeling of "une nuit délicieuse." The emotion,
rather than any visual perception of the landscape, forms the center of
the memory. Rousseau does not retain a group of perceptions, but a
distinctive feeling and mood, a particular mildness of air and voluptuous softness. Though at first glance the night may seem to be an object
of perception, very little is actually described. The successive phrases
of description do not move toward a fuller painting of the scene, nor
does Rousseau elaborate a perception through metaphor. The phrase
"une nuit tranquille" repeats the quality of feeling in "la soirée étoit
charmante"; the phrase "l'air étoit frais sans être froid" only restates
the beginning, "Il avoit fait très chaud ce jour-là." The sentences do not
progress to greater precision or larger significance. The only forward
movement is from evening to night to morning, but even this movement in time is subordinate to the folding of the phrases back upon
each other. The effect is of a voice lingering, almost caressing a
remembered feeling of mild ease.

Rousseau mentions some specific details in the scene: terraced
gardens bordered the road, the water of the river reflected the sunset,
he slept upon the step of a kind of niche or false door in the terrace
wall, a nightingale sang directly over his head as he fell asleep. The
details of what will become the standard idyllic landscape of Romanticism are here. The details make what Rousseau calls "un paysage
admirable." But he shows no Wordsworthian eagerness to elaborate
his remembered perception of the landscape; its elements are merely
listed, almost like facts that keep the recollected emotion anchored in
that specific experience. *That* was the night he slept on the step; *that*
was the morning he sang the cantata by Batistin. The rather vague
emotion gains specificity by such particular details, but it does not
depend on them. The mood of Rousseau's night seems to survive in
memory by its own strength, separable from the "collateral objects
and appearances," in Wordsworth's phrase. As when he recalls his

feeling for Mme de Warens, Rousseau expresses the quality of his emotion directly, through rhythmic evocation and words which name moods: "extase," "joüissance," "doux," "voluptueusement." The charm of the memory is the still continuing presence of that mood in the inner life, even now that the specific facts of the scene belong to the past.

Wordsworth's analogous night spent outdoors at Lake Como has an altogether different charm:

>   We left the town
>   Of Gravedona with this hope; but soon
>   Were lost, bewildered among woods immense,
>   And on a rock sate down, to wait for day.
>   An open place it was, and overlooked,
>   From high, the sullen water far beneath,
>   On which a dull red image of the moon
>   Lay bedded, changing oftentimes its form
>   Like an uneasy snake. From hour to hour
>   We sate and sate, wondering, as if the night
>   Had been ensnared by witchcraft. On the rock
>   At last we stretched our weary limbs for sleep,
>   But *could not* sleep, tormented by the stings
>   Of insects, which, with noise like that of noon,
>   Filled all the woods; the cry of unknown birds;
>   The mountains more by blackness visible
>   And their own size, than any outward light;
>   The breathless wilderness of clouds; the clock
>   That told, with unintelligible voice,
>   The widely parted hours; the noise of streams,
>   And sometimes rustling motions nigh at hand,
>   That did not leave us free from personal fear;
>   And, lastly, the withdrawing moon, that set
>   Before us, while she still was high in heaven;—
>   These were our food; and such a summer's night
>   Followed that pair of golden days that shed
>   On Como's Lake, and all that round it lay,
>   Their fairest, softest, happiest influence.
>   (VI. 699-726)

The episode is superficially similar to Rousseau's: a summer night in adolescence spent outdoors. The first contrast to Rousseau is, of course, in the mood of the occasion. Wordsworth's preference for the sublime over the idyllic is explicit in *The Prelude* and can be understood in various ways. It is a personal bias from the moors, mountains, and headlands loved by the poet since childhood, and it is part of Wordsworth's deliberate effort to challenge and revise pastoral conventions. Without diminishing these basic themes in the poem, I would add that the Wordsworthian sublime also presupposes and argues for a different conception of memory than Rousseau's revival of past feeling.

From Rousseau's point of view, a sharp line separates happy memory from "le mal passé." Since memory retains the exact texture of past feeling, the idyllic past is of course to be preferred, for the pain of the past remains pain, pleasure remains pleasure. Wordsworth's sublime memories celebrate Nature in its fearsome aspect, not simply because the poet learned from fear nor because he now enjoys experiencing fear again, but more fundamentally, because memory transforms the specific emotions of the past. Most wonderfully, the poet's memory has the power to transform fear to awe, personal anxiety to a more lofty sense of mystery and wonder.

Wordsworth, recalling his summer night, tells surprisingly little about his feelings at the time. He says only enough to indicate that he and his friend passed an exceedingly uncomfortable night. The impression emerges more from the narration of events than from the reserved statement of emotion. They left the town, then became lost and sat down. They were tired but could not sleep because of insects, so they continued to sit there all night not altogether "free from personal fear." The insects "tormented" them but Wordsworth does not say whether this was the predominant feeling they had at the time. What matters most to the poet now is the way the experience survives in memory.

Wordsworth's emphasis is quite the reverse of Rousseau's. The feelings—of personal fear, discomfort, torment—are mentioned, but only to be removed to the background of circumstance. What survives most vividly is a marvelous spectacle for the eye and ear. The look of the scene does not belong to the realm of fact. The details are present as still vivid perceptions, revitalized now in the descriptive language of the poem:

> . . . the sullen water far beneath,
> On which a dull red image of the moon
> Lay bedded, changing oftentimes its form
> Like an uneasy snake.

To be sure, the "image" and changing "form" of the moon and

water do suggest feelings of confusion and helplessness. The simile of the snake and the traditional connotations of "bewildered among woods immense" suggest the frightening aspect of the landscape. But Wordsworth never specifies the emotion felt during that night, nor do we believe that Wordsworth the poet re-experiences the same anxiety in recalling the event. In memory, the feeling of the experience shifts, or at least the sense of what is important about it becomes transformed.

What remains alive in memory from the summer night is a set of perceptions, images of sound or sight associated in a flexible way with feelings of awe and wonder. The distinctive emotion of the actual occasion recedes, for the surviving perceptions are only loosely tied to the feelings of the original experience:

> But *could not* sleep, tormented by the stings
> Of insects, which with noise like that of noon,
> Filled all the woods; the cry of unknown birds;
> The mountains more by blackness visible . . .

Wordsworth *begins* to recall the feeling of torment, but in the middle of a line he shifts to the noise of the insects as the first in a series of increasingly mysterious perceptions. The sound made midnight resemble noon. Strange noises filled the woods. Blackness was visible in the night. In memory, the awesome perceptions with their connotation of some more than natural power in the scene displace the original feeling of torment, even though the intensity of that original feeling may be what first opened the mind to deep impressions. In retrospect, however, Wordsworth re-views the scary night with pleasurable excitement. It nourished the mind perhaps even more than the two golden days on Lake Como that came before. The power of images to live and grow in the mind comes to seem the most important charm of memory, and the darkness of the past possesses this charm for Wordsworth at least as richly as any golden day.

The details that live in Rousseau's memory are different; they are not perceptions, in Wordsworth's sense, but circumstantial facts of personal history which ground elusive emotions in the particulars of time and place.[5] The strange bed of the night near Lyons, the name of the song he sang in the morning are characteristic kinds of detail in Rousseau's *Confessions*; they locate feeling in relation to the everyday world of things. Perhaps that is why Rousseau's use of detail appears most richly in his recollections of social and domestic occasions where the distinct identity of things made a clearer impression on Rousseau's mind than the more anonymous landscape of nature could do. The contrast to Wordsworthian detail seems especially sharp in Rousseau's memory of such experiences as his winter at age seventeen in pension with the music teacher at Annecy:

> Cet intervalle est un de ceux où j'ai vécu dans le plus grand calme, et que je me suis rappellés avec le plus de plaisir. Dans les situations diverses où je me suis trouvé, quelques uns ont été marqués par un tel sentiment de bien être qu'en les rememorant j'en suis affecté comme si j'y étois encore. Non seulement je me rappelle les tems, les lieux, les personnes, mais tous les objets environnans, la temperature de l'air, son odeur, sa couleur, une certaine impression locale qui ne s'est fait sentir que là, et dont le souvenir vif m'y transporte de nouveau. Par exemple . . . un vieux charpentier boiteux qui jouoit de la contrebasse, un petit abbé blondin qui jouoit du violon, le lambeau de soutane qu'après avoir posé son épée, M. Le Maître endossoit par dessus son habit laïque, et le beau surplis fin dont il en couvroit les loques pour aller au choeur: l'orgueil avec lequel j'allois, tenant ma petite flute à bec m'établir dans l'orchestre à la tribune, pour un petit bout de récit que M. le Maître avoit fait exprès pour moi . . . ce concours d'objets vivement retracé m'a cent fois charmé dans ma mémoire, autant et plus que dans la réalité.
>
> (122)

(This period is one of those in which I enjoyed the greatest calm, and which I have remembered ever since with the utmost pleasure. Of the various situations in which I have found myself some have been marked by such a feeling of well-being that when I remember them I am as much moved as if I were in them still. Not only do I recall times and places and persons but all the objects surrounding them, the temperature of the air, the smells and colours, and a certain local impression only to be felt there, the sharp recollection of which carries me back there again. For instance . . . one old lame carpenter who played the bassviol; a fair little priest who played the violin; the ragged cassock which M. le Maître threw over his lay clothes, having first unbuckled his sword, and the grand, fine surplice which hid his rags when he was going into the choir; the pride with which I went, with my little flageolet in my hand, to take my place with the orchestra in the gallery and play a little solo piece that M. le Maître had composed especially for me . . . all these things, sharply outlined in my memory, have charmed me countless times in retrospect, as much and even more than they did in reality.)

Rousseau explains as well as illustrates how his memory of certain occasions retains the detail of people, objects, textures, what he calls "une certaine impression locale." His quick deft sketches of life with the music teacher of the cathedral are offered only as examples, selections from what is made to seem an endless store of remembered things. We believe that he could give more details about the little blond abbé who played the violin. Rousseau almost teases us with his limited selection of detail. He lets us know that he possesses more then he gives. He does not care to share his total memory; he is not using his memory to create for our entertainment a full picture of a characteristic provincial scene. As when he defines states of feeling directly, Rousseau beckons the reader to his inner world and at the same time marks off the boundary of privacy. The reader will never possess all that Rousseau retains from this experience; we are told only enough to show that he himself can repossess it fully whenever he pleases.

Rousseau gives only enough detail to particularize the feeling of certain occasions—at Annecy, his childlike delight in his own musical precocity and in the easy blend of the theatrical, the sacred, and the familial at the cathedral. Rousseau is intent to preserve the particular feeling of each interlude of time. He does not therefore grant separate details the autonomous life that they have for Wordsworth. That is to say, individual things do not break free from their places in an original experience. Rousseau does not want remembered detail to have that kind of freedom. Perhaps that is why he is no more drawn to metaphor when describing the objects in his memory than when directly recalling feeling. Whereas Wordsworth's metaphoric comparisons— the moon to a snake, the shepherd to an aerial cross—shift and enlarge the significance of past perceptions, Rousseau wants to reconstitute "une certaine impression locale" of a past time. Memory displays this restorative power precisely by keeping all the details in place.

From Rousseau's point of view, the more trivial the detail, the more faithful he shows his memory to be. Thus Rousseau describes himself (in one of the most famous passages of the *Confessions*) coming upon a periwinkle nearly thirty years after his stay with Mme de Warens at les Charmettes. By an extraordinary process of association, the sight of the flower arouses a "transport" of emotion. He recalls his first day at les Charmettes, when Mme de Warens had shown him a periwinkle. He had barely glanced at it at the time and had not seen another for thirty years.

Modern critics like to regard this episode as an early example of "la mémoire affective," later celebrated by Bergson and Proust, in the episode of the "madeleine," for example.[6] But in Proust's novel, whole blocks of the narrator's past are lost; the past has only a potential life in memory until reawakened by the magical touch of a present sensation. Although Rousseau's response to the periwinkle may, in fact, have been an example of such a psychological process, Rousseau in his own narrative makes a rather different point: "Le lecteur peut juger par l'impression d'un si petit objet de celle que m'ont fait tous ceux qui se rapportent à la même époque" (226). (The reader can judge by the effect on me of something so small, the degree to which I have been moved by everything which relates to that stage in my life.) Rousseau's flower does not release an otherwise lost past. The miracle for Rousseau is the way this most cherished part of his past is not lost at all.

Rousseau boasts of the actual rather than the potential life of the idyllic past for him. He needs no talismans to awaken his first feelings for Mme de Warens. The periwinkle is important because of its triviality; it is "un si petit objet," hardly noticed at the time, and yet even it has not *escaped:* "Rien de tout ce qui m'est arrivé durant cette époque chérie, rien de ce que j'ai fait dit et pensé tout le tems qu'elle a duré n'est échappé de ma mémoire. . . . je me rappelle celui-là tout entier comme s'il duroit encore" (226). (Nothing that happened to me during that delightful time, nothing that I did, said, or thought all the while it lasted, has slipped from my memory. . . . I recall that time in its entirety, as if it existed still.)

Rousseau's details testify to the presence in his inner world of total occasions which he has not let escape. The details remain, as it were, fastened to the original experience and to its all-important emotion. They do not become metaphors for other experiences. They are not buried in his unconscious. Their significance is not changed by the retrospective eye. We scarcely believe Rousseau's claim, I suppose. We feel sure that the happiness of the past, if not its misery, is being idealized and exaggerated, and that certain details (like the nightingale directly over his head during the night near Lyons) are inventions for expressive purposes. Idyllic memory in the *Confessions* often seems closer to fiction than Rousseau cares to acknowledge. Yet his insistence on the minute fidelity of his memories is part of their peculiar power for the reader. We are interested in the detail itself, and we are also fascinated by the certainty of his conviction: This is exactly the way it was; I remember every detail. . .

Wordsworth's pride in his memory implies different, though no less bold convictions. To some twentieth-century readers, Wordsworth's apparent evasion of past feelings seems even more remarkable than Rousseau's boast of exactitude. Why does Wordsworth not probe the "torment" of the night at Como? More centrally, why doesn't he inspect his despair at his mother's death? Or his guilt and anxiety when his father died? Some recent critics see Wordsworth always moving to deny disturbing feelings which he will not or cannot bring to full consciousness. It is possible to discern patterns of unresolved personal conflict beneath the surface of Wordsworth's design, so that the shepherd in Book VIII, for instance, resembles a threatening father more than Wordsworth's own image of an aerial cross. The many ominous, almost punitive forms in the poem may suggest dark feelings which haunt the poet in memory even though he refuses to acknowledge continuing anxiety. In some of the boldest turns in *The Prelude*, Wordsworth evokes past feeling and then turns emphatically away to celebrate some different, even incongruous emotion. In the famous rowboat episode, for example, he evokes a terror so great that he had felt a mountain to be a grim and alien thing in pursuit of him. When he concludes the episode in a grateful hymn to the "Wisdom and Spirit of the universe," the celebratory invocation seems flagrantly to deny the feelings of desolation just suggested by the narrative.[7]

Yet Wordsworth never seems eager to disguise the fear or anxiety that he felt in his past. The rowboat episode has provoked comment precisely because the child's terror is made so vivid. Memory, for Wordsworth, does not idealize the past by denying its pain. That charge seems more pertinent to the idyllic interludes in Rousseau's *Confessions*. Wordsworth does not interpret his anxiety in psychological terms and undoubtedly he is, in a Freudian sense, "unconscious" of its exact meaning. But the crucial point for Wordsworth is that memory does not confine the mind to the already finished round of emotional experience. The poet, according to Wordsworth, is able to accept even the pain of his past with a generosity alien to lesser minds precisely because images from the past are not tightly bound to their original emotional associations. Memory can be a continuous source of new imaginative power because of the new, more flexible life which the past assumes in the poetic mind.

Wordsworth re-creates painful experiences but then moves beyond them as if to display the difference between what such experiences *felt like* at the time and where the memory of them can lead the mind. What most often remains alive in his mind is the vision of a landscape transformed by the pressure of deep feeling. By some mysterious activity of mind, the vision retains a vitality independent of the obscure emotion at its source. The same separation appears in lines describing the Wanderer's youth in *The Excursion*: "and deep feelings had impressed / So vividly great objects that they lay / Upon his mind like substances" (I. 136-138). The tie seems almost severed between the precise feelings and the "great objects" which all deep feelings impress upon the mind.

Johnson longs for an art of forgetting so that the mind may perform its functions without encumbrance. "The business of life is to go forwards," Johnson advises.[8] The memory of sorrows gone by only allows the past to undermine the new tasks of the day. But to Wordsworth, memory itself is a healing power, transforming the pain of the past into a source of creative energy and therefore of joy. Poetry comes from the mind's power to keep alive diverse images, drawn from all kinds of experience, and to re-form those images in relation to other perceptions, memories, feelings, or ideas. Even the poet's memory of his father's death is inspiring, mainly because the vision of a landscape impressed upon his mind at that time has remained alive. In the famous "spots of time" passage in Book XII of *The Prelude*, that vision leads the poet to intuitions about the mind's control over "outward sense." His celebratory statement of the mind's power in itself shows how memory leads to new feelings, for the poet has absorbed the pain of his father's death into his new sense of wonder at the mysterious processes of the mind.

The English empirical psychologists in the eighteenth century taught that experience remains "stored" in memory in its original form. Locke explains that images and ideas may disappear or fade from memory, but this "decay of sense" (to go back to Hobbes's term for the same process) seems the primary change which memories undergo: "The pictures in our minds are laid in fading colors; and if not sometimes refreshed, vanish and disappear."[9] The metaphor of a "picture" (like the other common metaphors of this theory—a "storehouse" or a "repository") implies the fixed character of memory. Indeed, the power of the mind to revive past ideas and perceptions without distorting them was seen in the eighteenth century as fundamental to learning as well as to the exercise of conscience.

The limited pleasure of memory, however, follows from the same assumption of fixity. Samuel Johnson echoes the terms of contemporary psychology to explain why the past offers so little amusement to the mind:

> It is, therefore, I believe, much more common for the solitary and thoughtful, to amuse themselves with schemes of the future, than reviews of the past. For the future is pliant and ductile, and will be easily moulded by a strong fancy into any form. But the images which memory presents are of a stubborn and untractable nature, the objects of remembrance have already existed, and left their signature behind them impressed upon the mind, so as to defy all attempts of rasure or of change.[10]

If Wordsworth thoroughly overturns Johnson's common truth, explicitly making his scheme for the future a review of his past, that is not only because he regards his past as peculiarly favored. Beyond that, Wordsworth attributes a more flexible life to "the objects of remembrance" than eighteenth-century psychology implies. The images of the past are, by their very nature, pliant. The mind—at least the poetic mind—does not need to attempt erasure or change by dogged effort. Images remain alive in the mind, changing and growing. The activity of memory is a new act of imaginative perception. The poetic mind remolds the forms of the past, as it remolds the objects of perception in all acts of vision. Thus in *The Prelude*, Wordsworth compares himself to "one who hangs down-bending from the side / Of a slow-moving boat" (IV. 256-257). What he sees blends object and reflection, what is materially there under the water and what his gaze adds to it, just as in all forms of imaginative vision.

When Johnson describes the signature of the past impressed upon the mind, he locates the true identity of an event in its original form, in the initial configuration of motives, passions, and consequences still discernible in memory. Wordsworth's view of memory as a form of creative perception frees the mind from the moral as well as the emotional bondage implicit in Johnson's view. The poet recalls, for example, the plunder of birds' nests in childhood without dwelling on either the motive for the child's violence or the nuances of guilty pleasure in such an adventure: "though mean / Our object and inglorious, yet the end / Was not ignoble" (I. 329-330). Wordsworth glances past the moral and emotional complexity of the child's violent attack on nature. The end of the experience transcends both the original motive and the particular emotion associated with it. The end is what eventually came from the excitement and what remains most vividly of it in memory: the sublime perception of loud dry wind and unearthly sky:

> While on the perilous ridge I hung alone,
> With what strange utterance did the loud dry wind
> Blow through my ear! the sky seemed not a sky
> Of earth—and with what motion moved the clouds!
>   (I. 336-339)

Wordsworth characteristically comes up to painful or morally suspect experiences of the past and then transforms the "virtue" or "end" of the memories before our eyes. The repeated pattern of transformation may seem perverse, neurotic, even willfully blind. Yet the power of *The Prelude* cannot really be separated from Wordsworth's sublime mastery over the laments, regrets, and self-reproaches that Johnson saw as the ordinary accompaniments to memory. Wordsworth's transformations of the past are not at all nonchalant. The poet displays with wonder the extraordinary, almost miraculous power and freedom of the mind to re-create itself anew. The original shape and import of a past experience is no more inviolate than the "dead letter" of the physical world. To kneel before the past as if it were a fully formed object is to Wordsworth another idolatrous worship of waxen images.

Wordsworth's memory therefore need not morbidly retrace past feelings of guilt or fear or anxiety. For a poet, the images impressed upon the mind at all times of deep feeling live a rich and autonomous life. They constitute now the sometimes beautiful, sometimes fearful, but most important, the *living* spectacle which flashes upon his imaginative eye. No single meaning of an image is fixed. Like nature itself, the mind is continuously growing and changing, becoming something other than it was without ceasing to be itself.

Rousseau, by his emphasis on the fixed reality of his memories, seems to remain closer than Wordsworth to the premises of eighteenth-century psychology. He probes the emotional nuances of his experiences and he explains his character by the lasting imprint of past feelings on his sensibility. But Rousseau, in a certain historical sense, is relatively unpsychological in comparison to Wordsworth. His interest in states of feeling keeps him only at the edge of that area of eighteenth-century psychology concerned not with passions but with the individual components of mental experience. As we have already seen in relation to the imagination, Wordsworth learned from the empirical psychologists to attend to the fate in the mind of individual images, ideas, and perceptions. His originality proceeds along the line of the eighteenth-century English interest in the components of normal mental life, especially as they bear upon the encounter between the mind and the outside world.

Memory for Rousseau, by contrast, is not so much an act of perception as a renewed contact with passions still alive within him. Rousseau's scrutiny of his memory in the *Confessions* does not therefore reevaluate the formal role of memory in mental growth or in the perception of external reality. Rousseau continues to refer memory as well as imagination to the states of feeling that are to him the most important reality in his life. By the end of the *Confessions*, Rousseau's external reality has become so dire that he embraces memory for its very power to obliterate perception. Instead of enlarging insight into the true spirit of the outside world, Rousseau's memory offers him the only durable refuge from a world clearly intent upon reducing his personal spirit to nothing but pain and despair.

In the *Confessions*, Rousseau's concern for a "true" portrait keeps him from withdrawing exclusively to the idyllic past. By the time of the later autobiographical work, *Les Rêveries du promeneur solitaire*, Rousseau shows no further hope or even desire to make his past exactly understood. At that point, Rousseau's memory becomes even more thoroughly like his imagination. In the "Cinquiéme promenade," after lamenting his forced departure from the Ile de Saint Pierre, Rousseau aggressively asserts the inviolability of the island as an inner refuge: "Les hommes se garderont, je le sais, de me rendre un si doux azyle où ils n'ont pas voulu me laisser. Mais ils ne m'empêcheront pas du moins de m'y transporter chaque jour sur les ailes de l'imagination, et d'y gouter durant quelques heures le même plaisir que si je l'habitois encor" (1049). (Mankind will take care, I know, not to give me back that sweet refuge where they would not let me stay. But they will not prevent me at least from transporting myself there every day on the wings of imagination, and from tasting, for those hours, the same pleasure as if I were living there still.) Memory and imagination have

become synonymous; they are the wings of the mind which can transport the self to islands of pleasure separate and safe from the hostile
outside world.

Rousseau no longer cares whether or not we believe in the exact
fidelity of his memory. He insists only that we realize that his happy
states of feeling are beyond our power to destroy. Memory or
imagination interchangeably name the liberty of the mind which
Rousseau is most eager to assert in the autobiographical writings after
the *Confessions*. In the *Dialogues*, memory and imagination have a
defensive, protective value. The imaginative man possesses a fortress
no enemy can destroy:

> Malgré tous les complots des hommes, tous les succés des méchans
> il ne peut être absolument misérable. Depouillé par des mains
> cruelles de tous les biens de cette vie, l'espérance l'en dédomage dans
> l'avenir, l'imagination les lui rend dans l'instant même: d'heureuses
> fictions lui tiennent lieu d'un bonheur réel; et que dis-je? Lui seul est
> solidement heureux, puisque les biens terrestres peuvent à chaque
> instant échapper en mille maniéres à celui qui croit les tenir: mais
> rien ne peut ôter ceux de l'imagination à quiconque sait en jouir. Il
> les possede sans risque et sans crainte; la fortune et les hommes ne
> sauroient l'en dépouiller.
>   Foible ressource, allez-vous dire, que des visions contre une
> grande adversité! Eh Monsieur, ces visions ont plus de réalité peut-
> être que tous ces biens apparens dont les hommes font tant de cas,
> puisqu'ils ne portent jamais dans l'ame un vrai sentiment de bon-
> heur, et que ceux qui les possedent sont egalement forcés de se jetter
> dans l'avenir faute de trouver dans le présent des jouissances qui les
> satisfassent. (813-814)

(Despite all the schemes of men and all the good fortune of the
wicked, he cannot be totally miserable. Stripped by cruel hands of
all earthly goods, hope nevertheless compensates him for them in
the future, and imagination returns them to him even in the present
moment. Happy fictions serve him in place of real happiness; but
what am I saying? He alone is solidly happy, since, at any moment
and in a thousand ways, earthly goods may elude the man who
thinks he has them in his hold: nothing, however, can take away the
possessions of the imagination from the man who knows how to
take advantage of them. He owns them without risk or fear; fate
and men cannot strip him of them.
     A feeble resource, you would say—nothing but visions against a
great adversity! Well sir, these visions may have more reality to
them than all the apparent goods which men hold in such esteem

and which never bring the soul a true feeling of happiness; for those who have them must nevertheless throw themselves into the future for lack of finding in the present any delight which can satisfy them.)

Although in the *Dialogues* Rousseau manipulates the term "réalité" to deny the value of the world, his metaphysical assumptions remain the same as before. He still does not claim his inner world of feeling as a form of true perception. His happy fictions—whether they replace external reality with memories or fantasies—are true only within the private realm of feeling. In Rousseau's phrase, "un vrai sentiment de bonheur," the word "vrai" specifies only the texture and vividness of feelings. The feeling of happiness, whatever its source or metaphysical status, is finally the only solid achievement in a world of dire and un-relenting threat. The desire for happiness overrides the value of what is ordinarily called truth and reality. Rousseau separates happiness from the perception of truth—by the time of the *Dialogues*, that may be the only kind of happiness that he can even imagine.[11]

Rousseau defiantly announces his withdrawal into the citadel of feeling in the *Dialogues*. One can see how his position takes almost to the point of willful madness the attitude toward memory and imagina-tion presented in more complex relation to other values in the *Confes-sions*. All through the autobiographical writings, Rousseau circles back from every direction to the ineradicable need of his heart for sat-isfactions that his present reality never provides. Epicurus had called ever-changing desire "greed," and Johnson associated the unbridled indulgence of desire with "pride." It is Rousseau's disturbing achieve-ment to hold with utmost intensity to his experience of desire and, ultimately, to his exclusively inward resources of satisfaction. Rous-seau ends by releasing memory from the rule of conscience not through Wordsworth's new "virtue" of creative vision but through his refusal to bend his private resources for happiness to the traditional strictures of morality. That his imagination and memory invented torments at least as bad as those inflicted upon him by the real world is a dark irony Rousseau never fully confronts. In the midst of his despair, he retains an oddly optimistic conviction that his own mind, at least, will not become an enemy.

It is interesting to note a curious passage in the *Encyclopédie* which measures the relationship of feeling to reality with a cooler, clinical eye, while suggesting how Rousseau was elaborating a conception of the inner life already "official" by the middle of the eighteenth century in France. The passage appears, significantly, under the heading *Imaginaire*:

> IMAGINAIRE, . . . qui n'est que dans l'imagination; ainsi l'on dit en ce sens un *bonheur imaginaire*, une *peine imaginaire*. Sous ce point de vue, *imaginaire* ne s'oppose point à réel; car un bonheur *imaginaire* est un bonheur réel, une peine *imaginaire*, est une peine réelle. Que la chose soit ou ne soit pas comme je l'imagine, je souffre ou je suis heureux; ainsi *l'imaginaire* peut être dans le motif, dans l'objet; mais la réalité est toujours dans la sensation. Le malade *imaginaire* est vraiment malade; d'esprit au moins, sinon de corps. Nous serions trop malheureux, si nous n'avions beaucoup de biens imaginaires.[12]

> (IMAGINARY, . . . that which exists only in the imagination; thus one speaks of an *imaginary happiness*, an *imaginary pain*. From this point of view, *imaginary* is not opposed to real; for an *imaginary* happiness is a real happiness, an *imaginary* pain, a real pain. Whether the thing be or not as I imagine it, I suffer or I am happy; thus *imaginary* can be in the cause, in the object; but reality is always in the sensation. The hypochondriac is really sick; in his mind at least, if not in his body. We would be too unhappy if we did not possess many imaginary goods.)

In the view of the *Encyclopédie*, the mind is as likely to create pain as pleasure. The inwardness of feeling is no guarantee of benevolence. Yet the "cri de coeur" that Rousseau bequeaths to French Romanticism is already sounded here in a matter-of-fact tone. No claim is made about the relation of feeling to objective or transcendent truth. The article supersedes the conventional opposition between "imaginaire" and "réel" in the same way that Rousseau does, by granting the term "réel" to inward feeling while at the same time preserving the clear distinction between illusion and fact. "Que la chose soit ou ne soit pas" remains an objective and apparently simple distinction, uncomplicated by theories of knowledge or perception. Imaginary experience is honored, at best, as a psychological resource, valued precisely because the real world is inadequate to human desire.

The history of French Romantic poetry suggests that the withdrawal to feeling elaborated by Rousseau had only limited value as a thematic and rhetorical source for lyric poetry, at least until Baudelaire added to it a more complex idea of artistic truth. Rousseau's turn to idyllic memory as a refuge from external reality was fervently imitated at the beginning of the nineteenth century in France, but nostalgic lyricism generated no poetic renaissance comparable to the achievement of English Romantic poetry.

Rousseau's attitude toward imagination and memory had its most successful issue in nineteenth-century France in those great prose studies of the maladjusted sensibility—René, Adolphe, Julien Sorel, Emma Bovary—that now seem the best and most distinctive achievement of French literature in the period. The novelists developed further Rousseau's way of using detail to particularize the emotional nuances of situations. And they continued Rousseau's interest in imagination and memory as part of the psychology of everyday life, the painful and sometimes comic social and personal life that goes on within our commonsense world.

The line of development from Rousseau to this mode of nineteenth-century French prose is suggested by Mme de Staël's portrait of Rousseau:

Je crois que l'imagination étoit la première de ses facultés, et qu'elle absorboit même toutes les autres. Il rêvoit plutôt qu'il n'existoit, et les événemens de sa vie se passoient dans sa tête plutôt qu'au dehors de lui. Cette manière d'être sembloit devoir éloigner de la défiance, puisqu'elle ne permettoit pas même l'observation; mais elle ne l'empêchoit pas de regarder, et faisoit seulement qu'il voyoit mal. Il avoit une âme tendre: comment en douter, lorsqu'on a lu ses ouvrages? Mais son imagination se plaçoit quelquefois entre ses affections et sa raison, et détruisoit leur puissance; s'il paraissoit quelquefois insensible, c'est qu'il n'apercevoit pas les objets tels qu'ils étoient; et son coeur eût été plus ému que le nôtre, s'il avoit eu les mêmes yeux que nous.[13]

(I think that imagination was the first of his faculties and that indeed it absorbed all the others. He dreamed more than he existed, and the events of his life took place more in his head than outside of him. This mode of being seems as though it should have kept him from suspiciousness, since it did not even allow for observation; but it did not keep him from looking, and so only made him see badly. He had a tender soul; how can one doubt it when one has read his works? But his imagination would sometimes insert itself between his affections and his reason and destroy their power; if at times he appeared insensitive, it is because he did not perceive things as they were; and his heart would have been more moved than ours, had he had our eyes.)

Mme de Staël enjoys analyzing the character of "une âme tendre," a character she sympathetically criticizes as dominated by imagination. She gives Rousseau the indulgence demanded by him, but her sympathy never blurs her commonsense distinctions between the real and the imaginary, observations and feelings, objects as they are and as they appear within the self. Rousseau has given her the terms for probing his character, and the character of the human mind generally, yet without in the least tampering with a clear and firm distinction between what goes on in the private space of the inner life and what goes on in the world before our eyes.

6

The Sentiment of Being

Memory and imagination comfort Rousseau for the disappointments of experience. But his experience finally becomes much worse than disappointing. When he sees the world turn aggressive, persecuting, conspiratorial, Rousseau goes further to seek protection in more extreme resources of his consciousness. Although he affirms the solace of memory in *Les Rêveries du promeneur solitaire*, the most satisfying experience he remembers from the Ile de Saint Pierre is a state of feeling in itself different from either memory or imagination. Rousseau claims to have enjoyed on the Ile de Saint Pierre a new happiness more impervious to the external world than any ordinary state of consciousness. In the "Cinquiéme promenade" of the *Rêveries*, he calls the feeling "le sentiment de l'existence."

The phrase has fascinated later writers and critics, partly because Rousseau himself liked it so much. "Le sentiment de l'existence" occurs, not only in the *Rêveries* but also in Rousseau's earlier writings, and always to carry a significant weight of argument. Another reason for fascination is that an almost identical phrase in English appears at a crucial point in *The Prelude*. In Book II, Wordsworth celebrates his version of absolute happiness, also distinct from both memory and imagination, the "bliss ineffable" of his youth:

> I was only then
> Contented, when with bliss ineffable

I felt the sentiment of Being spread
O'er all that moves and all that seemeth still.

(II. 399-402)

"The sentiment of Being," "le sentiment de l'existence"—the rhetorical grandeur (as well as the remarkable similarity) of the phrasing has evoked so much veneration that the secret of Romanticism in general has been thought to lie hidden there, even if that secret may be only a vague exaltation of tone.[1] What seems especially fascinating to me, however, is the difference between "le sentiment de l'existence" and Wordsworth's "sentiment of Being." The words of Rousseau and Wordsworth are not as vague as the interpretations that try to make the phrases interchangeable. Though it is true that Rousseau and Wordsworth both celebrate mysterious feelings, different from the habitual experiences of the mind, they differ in their ideal extremity of consciousness as much as in the more natural range. Even if Wordsworth actually adapted his phrase from Rousseau, he changes its significance in translation.[2] Not only do Rousseau and Wordsworth use the phrase in different personal contexts, they also guide us to think in different ways about the meaning of their rhetoric and about its relation to their other experiences and to ours.

To understand Rousseau's "le sentiment de l'existence" in the Rêveries, one needs to trace the phrase from his earlier theoretical writing. He does not devise a strange new locution in the "Cinquiéme promenade" as we feel Wordsworth to do in Book II of The Prelude. Even for his own most mysterious experience, Rousseau stays with the vocabulary developed in his social and moral essays. The meaning of Rousseau's language in the "Cinquiéme promenade" draws upon a theoretical vocabulary of extraordinary continuity and coherence in his career.

The crucial first example comes from the Discours sur l'origine de l'inégalité (the second Discours). This is the famous essay where Rousseau develops the myth of natural man in the state of nature. Rousseau argues that inequality is not the condition of nature; it is the consequence of a long development, a simultaneous progress and decline of man starting from the simple and equal attributes of his original state: "Le premier sentiment de l'homme fut celui de son existence, son premier soin, celui de sa conservation."[3] (The first sentiment of man was that of his existence, his first care, that of his preservation.)

In Rousseau's myth of natural man, "le sentiment de l'existence" refers to conscious, though not intellectual, self-awareness. The feeling is intuitive and as sure and private as a physical sensation. Rousseau argues that in the devolution of history, this natural foundation of consciousness has disintegrated. The process (in some sense a progress) seems inevitable. Yet Rousseau laments it. His whole myth expresses his lament for his own sense of inner contradiction and for the factitious self everywhere generated by society. Social inequality, competition, restlessness—all the vices of contemporary life—follow upon man's loss of his natural intuitive certainty about his own existence: "Le Sauvage vit en lui-même; l'homme sociable, toûjours hors de lui ne sait vivre que dans l'opinion des autres, et c'est, pour ainsi dire, de leur seul jugement qu'il tire le sentiment de sa propre existence."[4] (The Savage lives within himself; the social man, always outside of himself, knows how to live only in the opinion of others, and it is, so to speak, from their judgment alone that he draws the sentiment of his own existence.)

By endowing natural man with an innate "sentiment de l'existence," Rousseau ignores the Lockian concept of mental structure and development. Hume argues this point in his *Treatise*, explaining that empirical psychology provides no basis for a distinct and continuous feeling of personal existence. Hume rejects the idea altogether—he, at least, can locate no such feeling in himself.[5] Yet Rousseau's myth, in a way, remains untouched by the empirical argument, for Rousseau does not care primarily to establish a model of individual mental organization in the second *Discours*. He does not, for example, try to explain the origins of "le sentiment de l'existence" in the childhood of natural man, nor does he identify particular faculties of the mind that can be said to generate it. Rousseau's thesis has a moral and social aim and it keeps moral judgment separate from empirical psychology. Self-preservation and the feeling of existence are axioms to Rousseau, or, rather, they are hypotheses introduced for the purpose of a social thesis. Beginning from a revulsion against current social values, Rousseau constructs a myth of history that measures the human cost of civilization. The attributes of so-called natural man name the qualities that civilized men least possess. That Hume feels no "sentiment de l'existence" confirms Rousseau's point, and Hume's apparent complacency about his lack only shows how alienated man has become from his own nature. Rousseau is less alienated because he at least desires "le sentiment de l'existence." Rousseau's conception of man's natural state derives from his own consciousness of what he lacks. The purpose of Rousseau's myth is to elucidate the reality of deprivation rather than to describe the actual structure of the individual mind.

Rousseau sees men in society driven to construct a self from the opinion of others; they lack the sure instinctive consciousness that Rousseau imagines natural man to have had independently and without exertion. Yet he does not picture natural man sitting idly through the day absorbed in his "sentiment de l'existence." Though indolent compared to competitive, restless men in society, natural man was nevertheless robust and energetic:

> Accoutumés des l'enfance aux intempéries de l'air, et à la rigueur des saisons, exercés à la fatigue, et forcés de défendre nuds et sans armes leur vie et leur Proye contre les autres Bêtes féroces, ou de leur échapper à la course, les Hommes se forment un temperament robuste et presque inaltérable. . . . [ils] acquiérent ainsi toute la vigueur dont l'espèce humaine est capable.[6]

> (Accustomed from infancy to extremities of weather and to the rigor of the seasons, trained in fatigue, and forced, naked and without arms, to defend their lives and their prey against other wild beasts, or to escape by outrunning them, men develop a robust and almost unalterable temperament. . . . [they] thus acquire all the vigor of which the human species is capable.)

As in his autobiography, Rousseau wants to break down the artificial distinction between lazy and energetic, active and passive. The crucial point about natural man is not the quantity of his activity or idleness. Whatever natural man did or did not do in his free and simple life, he perpetually experienced the essential integrity and security of his sense of self.

To some extent, Rousseau makes the course of human history run parallel to the chain of development repeated in every individual life. That is why he can explain the disorder of his own life by the same historical method that he uses for man generally. But Rousseau's analogy between individual and general history is not strict. First, the contemporary child arrives directly into society. Moreover, the hypothetical childhood of natural man does not especially further the most important values affirmed by Rousseau's myth. Rousseau's praise of the natural state centers on the value of individual autonomy. Since the prolonged dependency of the human child seems an incontrovertible fact of nature, Rousseau's historical myth gives relatively little attention to childhood. The first, that is, the most basic, feeling of *man* in the state of nature is the palpable and sure feeling of his own existence.

The pedagogical treatise, *Emile*, however, directly concerns childhood and it is interesting to see how Rousseau's values in the second

Discours reappear in the form of educational theory. At the beginning of *Emile*, Rousseau again sets his theme in terms of "le sentiment de l'existence":

> Vivre, ce n'est pas respirer, c'est agir; c'est faire usage de nos organes, de nos sens, de nos facultés, de toutes les parties de nous-mêmes que nous donnent le sentiment de nôtre existence. L'homme qui a le plus vécu n'est pas celui qui a compté le plus d'années; mais celui qui a le plus senti la vie.[7]
>
> (To live is not simply to breathe, it is to act; it is to make use of our organs, our senses, our faculties, of all the parts of ourselves which give us the sentiment of our existence. The man who has lived the most is not he who can count up the most years, but he who has felt life the most.)

As in the second *Discours*, Rousseau envisions an ideal of whole identity different from the artificial and fragmented character of men in actual society. Emile will develop into a man in harmony with himself, more complex in his faculties than the original man of nature, but without complexity disintegrating the self. On the contrary, the education designed by Rousseau for Emile will intensify his sense of identity. All forms of action, thought, and feeling will confirm Emile's "sentiment de l'existence," for all his faculties will be in harmony and they will all be directed by and for himself.

Rousseau's ideal in *Emile* presupposes a particular development from childhood, but childhood does not epitomize the ideal. He cares more for the life Emile will be enabled to live because of his childhood than for the quality of childhood itself. Rousseau invents a pedagogy that promises to develop human capacities while preserving, even enlarging, the sense of self that historical man has sacrificed in his actual development. In the second *Discours*, "le sentiment de l'existence" was a simple feeling, almost a sensation. In *Emile*, Rousseau uses the same language to absorb that feeling into a more complex idea of identity. What was the simple bedrock of human consciousness in the state of nature evolves into the ideal goal of the ideal education.

Rousseau has his eye on principles of psychological, social, and moral well-being. "Le sentiment de l'existence" has only peripheral reference to the nonhuman natural universe or to divinity. *Emile*, like the second *Discours*, directs attention to man's relation to himself and to other men. The ideal therefore differs from the strange consciousness of such Wordsworthian figures as the leechgatherer or the child asleep in Abraham's bosom. Those figures, like the poet's image of himself at certain moments of childhood, are wonderful because they resemble nonhuman beings, either natural or divine. Rousseau, by contrast, envisions a unified, self-sufficient, individual *human* consciousness: "l'unité numérique, l'entier absolu qui n'a de rapport qu'à lui-même ou à son semblable"[8] (the numerical unity, the absolute totality, which relates only to itself or to its own likeness).

Undaunted by the distance of his ideal from ordinary reality, or even from what he believes to be the utmost possibilities in the actual world, Rousseau's ideas are frankly visionary. Yet they also partially derive from his best memories of his own life. Some of the autobiographical asides in *Emile* connect Rousseau's theoretical vision to the idyllic memories of the autobiographer. The feelings he enjoyed on his walking trips, for example, point to the ideal of natural man. On his "voyages à pied" (especially as a young man), Rousseau temporarily approached the freedom and harmony that natural man enjoyed as a steady possession. The pleasure of the walker represents, figuratively, the ideal human state in which the distant purpose of an action yields to the immediate satisfaction of an activity. Instead of zeal to arrive at a destination, the walker fully enjoys the trip itself: "Nous ne voyageons donc point en courriers mais en voyageurs. Nous ne songeons pas seulement aux deux termes, mais à l'intervalle qui les sépare. Le voyage même est un plaisir pour nous."[9] (We do not then travel as couriers, but as travelers. We do not think only of the two ends, but of the interval which separates them. The trip itself is a pleasure for us.) Rousseau's trips took him into nature, that is, they freed him to experience his own nature and to revive the natural man in himself. He did what he wished. Nothing constrained his free movement of mind and body. He was independent, self-sufficient, free to follow his own road.

In the *Confessions*, Rousseau expands his account of his walking trips to evoke even more clearly the ideal of "le sentiment de l'existence." On these holidays, he did not revert to the primitive beginnings of consciousness, but he experienced the active harmony of his faculties that presupposes the presence of that foundation:

> Jamais je n'ai tant pensé, tant existé, tant vécu, tant été moi, si j'ose ainsi dire, que dans ceux que j'ai faits seul et à pied. La marche a quelque chose qui anime et avive mes idées: je ne puis presque penser quand je reste en place; il faut que mon corps soit en branle pour y mettre mon esprit. La vue de la campagne, la succession des aspects agréables, le grand air, le grand appétit, la bonne santé que je gagne

en marchant, la liberté du cabaret, l'éloignement de tout ce qui me fait sentir ma dépendance, de tout ce qui me rappelle à ma situation, tout cela dégage mon ame, me donne une plus grande audace de penser, me jette en quelque sorte dans l'immensité des êtres pour les combiner, les choisir, me les approprier à mon gré sans gêne et sans crainte. Je dispose en maitre de la nature entiére; mon coeur errant d'objet en objet s'unit, s'identifie à ceux qui le flatent, s'entoure d'images charmantes, s'enivre de sentimens délicieux. Si pour les fixer je m'amuse à les décrire en moi-même, quelle vigueur de pinceau, quelle fraicheur de coloris, quelle énergie d'expression je leur donne! . . . Dix volumes par jour n'auroient pas suffi. Où prendre du tems pour les écrire? En arrivant je ne songeois qu'à bien diner. En partant je ne songeois qu'à bien marcher. Je sentois qu'un nouveau paradis m'attendoit à la porte; je ne songeois qu'à l'aller chercher. (162-163)

(Never did I think so much, exist so vividly, and experience so much, never have I been so much myself—if I may use that expression—as in the journeys I have taken alone and on foot. There is something about walking which stimulates and enlivens my thoughts. When I stay in one place I can hardly think at all; my body has to be on the move to set my mind going. The sight of the countryside, the succession of pleasant views, the open air, a sound appetite, and the good health I gain by walking, the easy atmosphere of an inn, the absence of everything that makes me feel my dependence, of everything that recalls me to my situation—all these serve to free my spirit, to lend a greater boldness to my thinking, to throw me, so to speak, into the vastness of things, so that I can combine them, select them, and make them mine as I will, without fear or restraint. I dispose of all Nature as its master. My heart, as it strays from one object to another, unites and identifies itself with those which soothe it, wraps itself in pleasant imaginings, and grows drunk on feelings of delight. If, in order to hold them, I amuse myself by describing them to myself, what vigorous brushstrokes, what freshness of colour, what energy of expression I bring to them! . . . Ten volumes a day would not have been enough. How could I have found time to write them? When I arrived, my only thought was for a good dinner. When I set out, I thought only of a good walk. I felt that a fresh paradise was waiting for me at the inn door. I thought only of going out to find it.)

As in his theoretical writings, Rousseau criticizes the deadness of life in society by reviving the force of the words "vivre," "exister," "existence." *To be* is not an empty verb. *Existence* has only deteriorated to an abstraction because the actual experience of being alive has lost concrete reality for most men. Rousseau invokes the self as a palpable entity—"moi"—which can and should be felt almost with the distinctiveness of a physical sensation. The more surely one feels that self, the more one exists. In recollecting his walking trips, Rousseau asserts his recovery of self through a few rather simple devices of style—the rapid exclamatory phrases, for example, or the rush of active, parallel verbs. The writing conveys exhilaration, an almost manic euphoria. At the same time the experience follows the simplest of natural rhythms: "En arrivant je ne songeois qu'à bien diner. En partant je ne songeois qu'à bien marcher."

Rousseau's walking trips revive the natural rhythm of human life. Although his itinerary goes through landscape, the nonhuman meaning of nature remains peripheral, as in *Emile* or the second *Discours*. Phrases like "tout cela dégage mon ame" or "me jette . . . dans l'immensité des êtres" create a vague exaltation of response to the landscape, but not the sense of either natural or mystical communion that some critics claim to discern there.[10] Rousseau barely notices the landscape itself as a living presence, for he is busy rediscovering the buried presence of his own life. This landscape may or may not embody divine spirit. What matters more to Rousseau is that nothing opposes the vitality of his own spirit. He mentions no specific natural detail except the air. Nor does the absence of perception signify mystic transcendence. He simply moves so fast and so excitedly that no particular object stays in view for long. The landscape is only "la succession des aspects agréables." The mild wording claims no spiritual presence in or behind nature, only a general pleasurable impression.

Rousseau's fresh air—"le grand air"—stimulates physical well-being and mental energy without any hint of divine revelation. Rousseau celebrates his own human energy and power: "Je dispose en maitre de la nature entiére." He moves freely through a space, exhilarating mainly for what it does *not* evoke: "l'éloignement de tout ce qui me fait sentir ma dépendance, de tout ce qui me rappelle à ma situation." Liberated from social reminders, the traveler enters the open space of nature as if it were paradise. For an interlude he leaves social reality to experience the paradise of his own nature; that is, he feels alive, whole, and himself.

By the time of Rousseau's stay on the Ile de Saint Pierre, the free excursions of youth were as remote an idyll as the mythical state of nature. Book XII of the *Confessions*, Rousseau's first account of the island, surrounds the experience with nightmarish voyages of flight through landscapes crowded with real or imagined enemies. Perhaps because Rousseau is still living that nightmare while writing Book XII, the island refuge does not fully emerge as a coherent image of a new paradise. Only from the greater distance of the *Rêveries*, written ten years later, did Rousseau discover how to view his happiness on the Ile de Saint Pierre as a solace for lost possibilities and even a new version of them.[11]

In the "Cinquiéme promenade," Rousseau's long worship of "le sentiment de l'existence" resonates through his account of final peace and resignation. On the Ile de Saint Pierre, Rousseau explains, he returned, through the ordeal of persecution and exile, to a feeling akin to the best moments of his youth and even more similar to the security of natural man. Yet the last form of Rousseau's happiness also has different, more poignant connotations. It releases Rousseau's consciousness from years of pain. The feeling resembles sleep more than a hike through the country or the robust ease of natural man. A magical, even artificial quality recalls the enchanted idleness of lotus-eaters. In the *Confessions*, Rousseau compares the island to the legendary Papinamia: "ce bienheureux pays où l'on dort: 'où l'on fait plus, où l'on fait nulle chose' " (640)[12] (the happy land of sleep: 'But one does more than that there, one does nothing').

In Book XII of the *Confessions* Rousseau seems unsure what value or significance to attach to his more than natural passivity on the Ile de Saint Pierre. He recalls "des reveries sans objet," but in the *Confessions* he immediately conventionalizes the idea of formless consciousness by the image of himself in tender prayer to Mother Nature. Prayer does focus the consciousness on an object. So does the act of metaphoric reflection, the next form Rousseau gives to his revery in the *Confessions*, as he shows himself contemplating worldly instability in the movement of the waves in the lake.

In the "Cinquiéme promenade" of the *Rêveries* Rousseau stays more rigorously with the elusive conception of "des reveries sans objet." That blankness of consciousness was the essence of his experience. Rousseau's later description discards the prayer along with all other deliberate mental activity. The discovery of metaphor in the landscape fades to a mere ripple on the surface of the mind. In retrospect, Rousseau discovers that the blank revery of the Ile de Saint Pierre can itself become an object of thought, only he must avoid the distortion of adding conventional objects to it in the act of definition. In memory, the experience of revery clarifies itself. The feeling of that experience survives in the self. It can be revived and analyzed. Though the experience itself was without thought, that very thoughtlessness can be conveyed in language as precisely as other elusive states of feeling:

> Mais s'il est un état où l'ame trouve une assiete assez solide pour s'y reposer tout entiére et rassembler là tout son être, sans avoir besoin de rappeller le passé ni d'enjamber sur l'avenir; où le tems ne soit rien pour elle, où le présent dure toujours sans neanmoins marquer sa durée et sans aucune trace de succession, sans aucun autre sentiment de privation ni de jouissance, de plaisir ni de peine, de desir ni de crainte que celui seul de notre existence, et que ce sentiment seul puisse la remplir tout entiere; tant que cet état dure celui qui s'y trouve peut s'appeller heureux, non d'un bonheur imparfait, pauvre et rélatif tel que celui qu'on trouve dans les plaisirs de la vie mais d'un bonheur suffisant, parfait et plein, qui ne laisse dans l'ame aucun vuide qu'elle sente le besoin de remplir. Tel est l'état où je me suis trouvé souvent à l'Isle de St Pierre dans mes reveries solitaires, soit couché dans mon bateau que je laissois dériver au gré de l'eau, soit assis sur les rives du lac agité, soit ailleurs au bord d'une belle riviére ou d'un ruisseau murmurant sur le gravier.
>
> De quoi jouit-on dans une pareille situation? De rien d'extérieur à soi, de rien sinon de soi-même et de sa propre existence, tant que cet état dure on se suffit à soi-même comme Dieu. Le sentiment de l'existence depouillé de toute autre affection est par lui-même un sentiment précieux de contentement et de paix qui suffiroit seul pour rendre cette existence chére et douce à qui sauroit écarter de soi toutes les impressions sensuelles et terrestres qui viennent sans cesse nous en distraire et en troubler ici bas la douceur. (1046-1047)

(But if there is a state where the soul finds a place solid enough to rest on entirely, and where it can gather together its whole being, without needing to recall the past or leap into the future; where time counts for nothing, where the present lasts forever, but with no mark of duration and without any trace of succession, without any sentiment of deprivation or of enjoyment, of pleasure or of pain, of desire or of fear, other than this one sentiment of our existence, a sentiment which alone can fill it completely; as long as this state lasts, he who finds it can call himself happy, not with an imperfect happiness, poor and relative, like that found in the pleasures of life, but with a sufficing happiness, perfect and full, which leaves in the soul no void which it feels the need to fill. Such is the state in which I often found myself in my reveries on the island of Saint Pierre, whether stretched out in my boat which I let drift with the water, or sitting on the shore of the wavy lake, or elsewhere, on the bank of a lovely river, or by a brook murmuring on the sand.

What is it that one enjoys in such a situation? Nothing external to the self, nothing except oneself and one's own existence. As long as this state lasts, one suffices to oneself, like God. The sentiment of existence, stripped of every other feeling, is in itself a precious sentiment of contentment and of peace, which alone is enough to make existence sweet and dear to anyone who knows how to put aside all those sensual and earthly impressions which keep coming to distract us and to trouble the sweetness of life on earth.)

Rousseau's style in the "Cinquiéme promenade" has a confident precision, often disregarded in mystical interpretations of "le sentiment de l'existence." Rousseau's evident satisfaction with his own language of analysis reduces the aura of the ineffable traditionally associated with accounts of mystical transcendence. Rousseau does not rely on the traditional mystic lament for "the sad incompetence of speech," as Wordsworth does at times for the extreme reach of his experience. Although Rousseau always retains some margin between his language and the full reality of an inner state, the margin here actually diminishes. There is less hedging around the crucial words of definition than in the Confessions. Rousseau directly poses the question of definition—"De quoi jouit-on dans une pareille situation?"—and he answers it with clarity. The general form of the question even puts aside the claim to personal uniqueness, as if the individual nuances of experience had become less important, or else somehow safe from the distorting conventions of language.

Rousseau commits himself to his definition of feeling more freely in the *Rêveries* than in the *Confessions*. Perhaps he cares less now about the judgment of his experience by others. Even more important, he has at hand a theoretical vocabulary firmly established in his own earlier writing. The word "sentiment," for example, has precision from Rousseau's earlier usage. It implies, as it did in the second *Discours*, both sensation and emotion, emotion reduced to the simplicity of sensation, and sensation as diffuse and pervasive as emotion.

The relation of feeling to the external world also relies on Rousseau's earlier efforts of definition. In the "Cinquiéme promenade," he clarifies further the vocabulary and syntax developed to describe the inner life in the *Confessions*. Rousseau's word "où" designates an inner, psychological place, "un état d'âme." Although his revery occurred in the natural scenery of the Ile de Saint Pierre, the important location is inward and the significant events are feelings. As in the *Confessions*, his inner state does not really depend on response to nature as a place. The scene participates merely as a source of sensation and as a *displacement* of other realities:

> Le bruit des vagues et l'agitation de l'eau fixant mes sens et chassant de mon ame toute autre agitation la plongeoient dans une rêverie delicieuse où la nuit me surprenoit souvent sans que je m'en fusse appercue. Le flux et reflux de cette eau, son bruit continu mais renflé par intervalles frappant sans relache mon oreille et mes yeux suppléoient aux mouvemens internes que la rêverie éteignoit en moi et suffisoient pour me faire sentir avec plaisir mon existence, sans prendre la peine de penser. (1045)
>
> (The sound of the waves and the movement of the water, fixing my senses and ridding my soul of all other agitation, plunged me into a delicious revery where the night often surprised me without my having noticed it. The flux and reflux of the water, its continuous but intermittently swelling sound striking my ears and my eyes without cease, replaced the inner movements that revery had extinguished in me and was enough to make me feel my existence with pleasure, without taking the trouble to think.)

The psychological technicality of Rousseau's language theoretically allows other combinations of motion and sound to encourage revery as well as the movement of water in a lake. Indeed, Rousseau goes on to claim that he can artificially induce the state of revery even now, at the time of his writing; he boasts that he could manage it even in the Bastille. States of feeling obey laws of sensation that are independent of place: "Il n'y faut ni un repos absolu ni trop d'agitation, mais un mouvement uniforme et modéré qui n'ait ni secousses ni intervalles" (1047). (What is necessary is neither absolute stillness nor too much movement, but a uniform and moderate movement which has neither shocks nor pauses.)

In the *Rêveries*, Rousseau thus continues to abstract "le sentiment de l'existence" from direct perceptions of nature, as he does consistently beginning with the second *Discours*. The total inwardness does not imply omnipresent divinity, nor does it depend on viewing the mind as a mansion for all beauteous forms, in the sense of Wordsworthian memory. Rousseau separates the inner life from external reality more sharply. Although he enjoys the scenery of the island, its value for revery derives mainly from the absence there of other reminders and associations. As on the walking trips, nature offers the negation of other realities rather than a significant presence of its own.

In Rousseau's hypothetical state of nature, all experience takes place in nature, but the idea of place is fundamentally neutral. The simple, nomadic life of natural man generated no complex relationship to places. In the *Rêveries*, Rousseau's image of the island radically circumscribes the possible location of happiness in the actual world. Only an island can separate the self from the oppressiveness of real places. All places on the mainland of experience generate conflict and the disintegrating feelings of fear, regret, and desire. Rousseau goes so far as to suggest that the very self must become like an island, circumscribed and separate from the causes of discord outside.

From the perspective of earlier Rousseau, a sense of loss and limitation accompanies the withdrawal celebrated in the "Cinquiéme promenade." When Rousseau compares the isolated self to God, the analogy does not suggest communion between the self *and* God, only godlike self-sufficiency. The claim of absolute satisfaction may sound mystical, but Rousseau describes no spiritual ecstasy. Instead, the very idea of satisfaction shrinks. The repeated word "suffire" carries a reduced demand; it probes the limits of reduction: how little will suffice for a feeling of happiness: "on se suffit à soi-même," "et suffisoient pour me faire sentir avec plaisir mon existence," "un sentiment . . . qui suffiroit seul."

The sufficiency of the Ile de Saint Pierre represents reduced expectations rather than the recovery of lost perfection. In both the second *Discours* and *Emile*, Rousseau argues that a sure sense of self frees human energy. Its disintegration produces the weak and helpless men of the social world: "Ainsi combatus et flotans durant tout le cours de nôtre vie, nous la terminons sans avoir pu nous accorder avec nous, et sans avoir été bons pour nous ni pour les autres."[13] (Thus beaten and adrift through the whole course of our lives, we end without having been able to settle with ourselves and without having been good either for ourselves or for others.) In the *Rêveries*, Rousseau reverses his earlier reasoning: prevented by a malevolent society from any active usefulness, he may legitimately retreat to passivity and isolation, retreat to a circumscribed part of the self that is secure, at least, from attack:

Mais un infortuné qu'on a retranché de la societé humaine et qui ne peut plus rien faire ici bas d'utile et de bon pour autrui ni pour soi, peut trouver dans cet état à toutes les félicités humaines des dédomagemens que la fortune et les hommes ne lui sauroient ôter.

(1047)

(But an unfortunate, who has been removed from human society and who can no longer do anything here that is useful or good, either for others or for himself, can find in this state compensation for all human enjoyments, compensation that neither fortune nor men can take away from him.)

Pressed by the extremity of his situation, Rousseau sheds his responsibility for action and even his earlier commitment to the inward action of self-analysis. In the *Confessions*, Rousseau worked to reconstruct a coherent self out of the apparent contradictions in his character. That activity, however, had no power to protect him from the enmity of the world. The autobiography ends with his flight to and then away from the Ile de Saint Pierre. Driven from society and even from peaceful exile by other men, he recognizes no further obligation to justify himself. His ordeal has earned him the right to enjoy the passive harmony of revery. Instead of trying to analyze the sources of conflict in his character, he now detaches the essence of his self from the very experience of discord. He discovers that even the feeling of conflict can be sloughed off, like an external object. Painful emotion is extrinsic; it can be obliterated by total withdrawal from external reality, from all consciousness of all reality, except the mechanical sources of sensation. Rousseau thus transforms the grounding of human consciousness into a refuge from the pain that he now associates with any active exercise of consciousness at all. Rousseau retreats to a minimal form of experience—"depouillé"— stripped voluntarily of the little that has not been forcibly taken away.

The defensive undertone in the "Cinquiéme promenade" suggests how Rousseau's radical final image of happiness requires the sacrifice of social and moral values formerly cherished by Rousseau himself. Nostalgia for the possibility of action, for the free exercise of his human energy, shades the perfection of the happiness Rousseau claims. At the same time, his ideal of absolute withdrawal has a traditional sanction which Rousseau also invokes. His disdain for the world's merely illusory satisfactions carries forward one traditional Christian feeling. Echoes of Pascal, particularly, ennoble Rousseau's turnaway from the futility of worldly pleasure and action. Pascal's sense of ordinary life's profound insufficiency reappears in Rousseau's vision of what revery offers. Rousseau, however, opposes Pascal's theology so directly that one may almost feel them in direct debate. For Pascal, the hollowness of the world is exceeded only by the misery of idleness. It is, indeed, the utter insufficiency of the isolated passive self that ultimately generates religious faith, according to Pascal:

> Rien n'est si insupportable à l'homme que d'être dans un plein repos, sans passions, sans affaire, sans divertissement, sans application. Il sent alors son néant, son abandon, son insuffisance, sa dépendance, son impuissance, son vide.[14]

> (Nothing is so unbearable to man as to be fully at rest, without passion, business, distraction, or application. He then feels his nothingness, his abandonment, his insufficiency, his dependence, his impotence, his emptiness.)

Rousseau turns sharply aside from Pascal's view of "la misère de l'homme sans Dieu." He answers that the individual human consciousness can suffice by its own fullness of being. The single self does not need God, for it can be as self-sufficient *as* God.

Jean Wahl calls Rousseau's final happiness "a sort of existential mysticism."[15] Robert Osmont calls it "the mystic realization of the self."[16] Although I am not sure exactly what these phrases mean, I like them insofar as they register the extreme and paradoxical quality of "le sentiment de l'existence" in the *Rêveries*. Rousseau's inner state has many of the attributes of mysticism—apparent release from time, suspension of thought and ordinary perception, a sense of fullness and harmony—but devoid of any claim to divine communion. Insofar as the outer world ceases to exist as a cause of distress, or even as an object of perception or thought, "le sentiment de l'existence" obliterates all discord between the self and the universe. The impression of harmony, however, results only from eliminating one term of a still unchangeable antithesis. It includes no more communion with divinity, or with any reality beyond the self, than other illusions of harmony. Rousseau's concept of revery defines another psychological resource, a further way to manipulate the inner world. Society drives man to need these resources. Rousseau needs them even more than others do. His society drove him even from his island refuge. But in his extremity, he paradoxically discovers man's natural self-sufficiency again. Now only death can destroy his access to "le sentiment de l'existence."

In Book II of *The Prelude*, Wordsworth celebrates the "sentiment of Being" from a markedly different standpoint. He is not the exile driven past all ordinary consolation, but the ambitious poet, still on the first wave of confidence inspired by the memory of his past. As he summarizes this past, he draws to a climax his celebration of the gifts he received from the universe up to the age of seventeen:

> My seventeenth year was come;
> And, whether from this habit rooted now
> So deeply in my mind, or from excess
> In the great social principle of life
> Coercing all things into sympathy,
> To unorganic natures were transferred
> My own enjoyments; or the power of truth
> Coming in revelation, did converse
> With things that really are; I, at this time,
> Saw blessings spread around me like a sea.
> Thus while the days flew by, and years passed on,
> From Nature and her overflowing soul,
> I had received so much, that all my thoughts
> Were steeped in feeling; I was only then
> Contented, when with bliss ineffable
> I felt the sentiment of Being spread
> O'er all that moves and all that seemeth still;
> O'er all that, lost beyond the reach of thought
> And human knowledge, to the human eye
> Invisible, yet liveth to the heart;
> O'er all that leaps and runs, and shouts and sings,
> Or beats the gladsome air; o'er all that glides
> Beneath the wave, yea, in the wave itself,
> And mighty depth of waters. Wonder not
> If high the transport, great the joy I felt,
> Communing in this sort through earth and heaven
> With every form of creature, as it looked
> Towards the Uncreated with a countenance
> Of adoration, with an eye of love.
> One song they sang, and it was audible,
> Most audible, then, when the fleshly ear,
> O'ercome by humblest prelude of that strain,
> Forgot her functions, and slept undisturbed.
>   (II. 386-418)

Wordsworth's "sentiment of Being" resounds with the claim to supernatural significance so muted in Rousseau's account of his revery. The supernatural aura of Wordsworth's language evokes a different feeling than Rousseau's clear analytic style, and it also creates different problems of interpretation and judgment. Reading Wordsworth, one strains to discern exactly what quality of religious experience Wordsworth means by his awkwardly sublime phrasing and his bold echoes of *Paradise Lost* and Genesis. Wordsworth does not himself put his feeling of "bliss ineffable" to Rousseau's analytic question: "Quel étoit donc ce bonheur, et en quoi consistoit sa jouissance?" As I observe earlier, Wordsworth's attitude toward his memory discourages the direct scrutiny of past feeling, since for Wordsworth feelings are not themselves objects fixed in memory. If the past lives in the mind through images, there is no conclusive definition of past feeling, especially not of those most extraordinary feelings that seem to have transcended images altogether.

When Wordsworth, here and at other key points in *The Prelude*, wants to recollect feelings beyond the reach of images, he encounters the limitations of memory according to his own conception of the mind. The most blissful feelings of the past are subject to the same transformations as the painful ones. The very attributes of the mind which give images continuing life inevitably obscure the full ecstasy of those times when the fleshly eye and ear slept undisturbed. Wordsworth ventures only tentative definition of the most extreme contentment of his youth; he relies on the imagery of Milton and the Bible to convey the sublimity carried by his own images elsewhere, and he allows a certain vagueness and ambiguity of language to mark the space of what he cannot fully repossess.

Wordsworth does not define "the sentiment of Being" in the manner of Rousseau. Though he starts in an explanatory tone, Wordsworth only frustrates our desire for clearer definition. He allows alternate, even seemingly incompatible explanations to stand as equally plausible. He does not definitely trace his bliss to a natural habit of the mind, nor does he absolutely claim moments of direct supernatural revelation. Either or both explanations are possible. Instead of clarifying the origin of his most extraordinary feeling, Wordsworth turns aside from causal explanation altogether. Whatever the cause, the effect is what matters, and the effect (characteristically for Wordsworth) transcends psychological definition: "I, at this time, / Saw blessings spread around me like a sea."

Meanings are set in motion by Wordsworth's figurative language, but the range or limits of meaning remain unclear. The verb "spread" brings the blessings he saw in relation to the sentiment of Being "spread" over all things, and the image of the sea recurs in the "mighty depth of waters" echoed from the Bible further on. But this resonance of language does not define "bliss ineffable" according to the literal meaning of *define*: that is, to mark the limits of a thing, to make it distinct by fixing its boundaries in relation to other things. He celebrates a range of feelings, culminating in "bliss ineffable"; the line which separates the furthest reach in his experience from the rest is not distinctly drawn. Indefiniteness itself seems the essential character of Wordsworth's bliss. To feel the sentiment of Being is to be open (in varying degrees) to the indefinite: that is, to be open to the infinite, the formless presence of spirit spread through, over, beneath, around all things.

Wordsworth's sublime indefiniteness (or indefinite sublimity) is enough to distinguish his bliss from Rousseau's reduced and exclusive retreat. What we respond to most directly, however, is Wordsworth's indefinite *presentation* of his feeling. This difference from Rousseau is difficult to discuss, partly because Wordsworth's lack of precision has the effect of making his "sentiment of Being" less interesting than Rousseau's as an idea. The act of clarification offers Rousseau a different kind of satisfaction than the act of revery, and even though Rousseau praises the perfect sufficiency of revery, his writing shows that he remains as attracted as ever by rational analysis.

Wordsworth, in a way, is more consistent, for he tries to preserve in his language the indefiniteness that he values in his ideal experience. He refuses, therefore, to satisfy that part of our intelligence which seeks to stabilize shadows of ideas into fixed shapes in relation to each other. According to those expectations of argument, the natural habits of the mind must seem contrary to direct supernatural revelation. Yet Wordsworth will not identify his "bliss ineffable" with either alternative exclusively. As a child, he did not experience the range of his feelings in terms of contraries. Though the adult poet cannot, now, lose himself again in infinite Being, he protects his continuing belief in that spiritual reality from becoming caught in the definiteness of thought. Insofar as he succeeds, however, we cannot think very precisely about his meaning. We can only observe how he tries to give his former bliss the substantiality of a real presence, without fixing its shape either as an idea or even as a finished past event in his inner life.

"The sentiment of Being," in Wordsworth's language, does not stabilize into an altogether inward condition, "un état d'âme," in Rousseau's sense. Wordsworth manages to make his feeling seem indistinguishable from awareness of cosmic Being, the vital spirit of the whole created universe. The same words designate both his feeling and the external object of feeling, without these terms either merging altogether or separating into distinct entities. Wordsworth's peculiar use of the word "sentiment" accounts for part of the strange effect. Ordinary "sentiment" appears in Wordsworth elsewhere, usually with a moral or social adjective to imply respectable "human sentiments" like gratitude or charity.[17] For his deeper, spiritual intuitions, Wordsworth characteristically relies on the more flexible word "sense,"[18] as in "Tintern Abbey," "a sense sublime / Of something far more deeply interfused" (ll. 95-96). In Book II of *The Prelude* a more limited word is dislocated from ordinary and even from Wordsworth's own usual language, as if to mark the space of an even stranger experience than "sense" could register. By using the more definite "sentiment," Wordsworth makes the space seem full of some palpable substance, but we do not know exactly what it is. The extreme reach of his childhood experience is related to "sense," and also to moral "sentiment," but it is not quite the same as either, nor can the difference be exactly measured.

The uncertain meaning of Wordsworth's word "sentiment" belongs to the larger ambiguity about the precise role of the senses in this experience of seeing and hearing what is invisible and inaudible, or at least what becomes "most audible" beyond the fleshly ear. To feel the sentiment of Being ultimately transcends sensory experience without positively excluding it. Nor does Wordsworth specify the exact relation of the inner to the outer world in this experience. His grammar is more ambiguous than Rousseau's. "Sentiment" may, redundantly, only extend the inwardness of "felt," as if to say, "I felt the feeling." But we hear "sentiment" as though it also named an object out in the universe: "*That* is what I felt." The object of feeling seems to exist apart from the inner world; it is itself active, the subject of the verb "spread." Although Wordsworth presents no real audible or visible world in the passage, the imagery of Genesis evokes the created universe, the same natural universe so richly alive in the poet's own images elsewhere. The word "Being" thus takes on objective natural and supernatural presence. Wordsworth's "Being" includes the poet's inner life, without being located exclusively there.

What seems to be at stake in Wordsworth's ambiguity is the relationship of an ideal to other, less perfect forms of experience. In the "bliss ineffable" of youth, his Being participated fully in cosmic Being.

The boundary between feeling and objective spirit did not exist for him any more than did the sense of conflict between natural habits of the mind and supernatural revelation. The adult poet cannot altogether transcend his sense of separateness, and he can only evoke transcendence through conscious (even awkward) ambiguities of language. But the fact that he now must settle for less than "bliss ineffable" does not confine him to the contrary position of damnation or utter exile. Lesser, partial, imperfect experiences (even the somewhat strained experience of his language) confirm belief in the ideal more than they expose what is absent or lost or impossible. The poet's language shows that he still has the power to keep open the boundary between feeling and objective spirit, and this power testifies to the still potent blessing of his youth.

Wordsworth tries to place his ideal of absolute contentment in a more flexible relation to the rest of his experience than does Rousseau. All that is not Rousseau's ideal seems to oppose it. That is to say, reality for Rousseau has an adversary relationship to "le sentiment de l'existence." Indeed, all the forms of Rousseau's ideal originate in protests against reality. "Le sentiment de l'existence" is what social man does not have, or it is the antithesis of the exile's anxiety. Even Rousseau's walking trips oppose reality; they are, literally, *vacations* in which he empties his mind of society for an interlude. Wordsworth, by contrast, wants to place his "bliss ineffable" at the end point of a continuum, all the points of which are relatively valuable as they point toward the ideal. Any experience open to the "sentiment of Being" exemplifies for Wordsworth a version of his absolute happiness in youth, even though it may not reach the extreme of his contentment, then.[19]

In *The Prelude* there is no urgent measurement of what has been lost between *then* and now. Wordsworth does not allow "bliss ineffable" to represent either an altogether inaccessible past or a radical rejection of the present. Intimations of loss yield to the wonder of what does survive and what movement in the direction of the ideal the poet can now accomplish. Through memory and through the substantiation of memory by other sources of spiritual insight, like Milton or the Bible, he shows himself still open to the sentiment of Being, not as perfectly open as before, but not closed off from it either. Therefore, the "one song" of Creation heard by the boy and the poet's song of creation must not be forced into sharp opposition. His song is less than the "one song," but it also looks toward that supernatural harmony with an eye of love. His song confirms the presence of the harmony which he cannot altogether join, rather than lamenting his exclusion from it.

The self-conscious poet has lost, it is true, the unreflective openness of his youth. Then, he could freely join the timeless and more-than-human in himself to eternal Being. In contrast to Rousseau, Wordsworth does make the child epitomize the ideal, for the child is not yet bound to a distinct sense of self nor to perceptions of his place in the temporal world of things and other people. Instead of that freedom, an elaborate sense of self dominates the poet's consciousness. He is so full of himself that he makes his life the subject of an epic poem. Yet Lionel Trilling is only partially right to reduce Wordsworth's self-consciousness to a version of Rousseau's concern for personal authenticity: "the gratifying experience of the self as an entity."[20] Wordsworth accepts his growth to self-consciousness without further lament only because a more than personal sense of Being remains alive in his consciousness. Memory and imagination affirm Wordsworth's faith in the "sentiment of Being," for (we have seen in all the examples from *The Prelude*) these powers of the mind give new and enduring life to the poet's supernatural awareness.

Rousseau cherishes a narrower, secular conception of the self in his idea of "le sentiment de l'existence." His ideal of self-sufficiency in revery is consistent with his lifelong reverence for the autonomous human figure. Utter withdrawal from all action and even from perception is the logical extreme of his view that the origin and goal of experience is in the inner world of the single, human being, "l'unité numérique, l'entier absolu."

Wordsworth identifies the poetic mind with a tradition of poets and prophets who allow the human self to become worthy of reverence only because of the individual's bond to other forms of Being. It may be argued that without a clear theological structure, and without the direct possibility of "bliss ineffable," Wordsworth's cosmic Being fades into a merely rhetorical figure. His "sentiment of Being" is unquestionably more elusive to the secular reader than Rousseau's "sentiment de l'existence." Yet Wordsworth's resistance to Rousseau's isolating egotism represents one of the most urgent commitments of the English imagination in the nineteenth century. Against the modern suspicion that all experience only reverts back to the paltry entity of the human self, Wordsworth asserts his continuing belief in the vitality of the larger universe and in his power to participate in its life. However indefinite, the sentiment of Being survives in his consciousness. The poetic mind discovers versions of that sentiment amidst all the forms of experience—though "bliss ineffable" is no longer attainable, majestic minds still possess the power to join "a world of life" beyond the prison of the individual human self:

> . . . in a world of life they live,
> By sensible impressions not enthralled,
> But by their quickening impulse made more prompt
> To hold fit converse with the spiritual world,
> And with the generations of mankind
> Spread over time, past, present, and to come,
> Age after age, till Time shall be no more.
> Such minds are truly from the Deity,
> For they are Powers; and hence the highest bliss
> That flesh can know is theirs—the consciousness
> Of Whom they are, habitually infused
> Through every image and through every thought,
> And all affections by communion raised
> From earth to heaven, from human to divine.
>   (XIV. 105-118)

Part Three

English Vision and French Symbols

7

Victor Hugo and Wordsworthian Perception

In Victor Hugo's poem, "Ce qu'on entend sur la montagne," the mingled voices of man and nature become audible to the poet stationed upon a mountaintop. Truth, to the poet on the mountain, transcends the personal feeling revered by Rousseau. Sublime visions and voices come to Hugo, as to Wordsworth on the top of Snowdon. The poet's experience has the grandeur of supernatural revelation: "J'écoutai, j'entendis, et jamais voix pareille / Ne sortit d'une bouche et n'émut une oreille" (I. 726).[1] (I listened; I heard; and no such voice ever came from a mouth nor struck an ear.)

"Ce qu'on entend sur la montagne" was written in 1829, a late date in European Romanticism for a poet to proclaim new visionary power. But the poem came only at the beginning of Hugo's career as a visionary poet, and it announced what was still a new ambition for French poetry. Only since Victor Hugo, wrote Baudelaire in 1859, has poetry in France, as in England and Germany before, attained its proper stature; only since Hugo has the French poet risen to interrogate the mystery of man, nature, and divinity.[2]

Yet by 1859 the avant-garde of French poetry, most notably Baudelaire himself, had already descended from Hugo's sublimity. *Les Fleurs du Mal* appeared in 1857. The famous first poem challenges all pretensions to solitary grandeur. Mired in the common ground of shame, remorse, and disappointment, Baudelaire goads and tempts the reader to join him in a more profane brotherhood: "—Hypocrite lecteur,—mon semblable,—mon frère." (—Hypocritical reader,—my likeness,—my brother.)

In England, the Wordsworthian aspiration to sublimity had a more durable influence than any of its counterparts in the French tradition. The English poets coming after Wordsworth's great early period (1798-1805), first Shelley and Keats, then Tennyson, Arnold, and the other Victorians, labored under Wordsworth's idea of the poet's sacred gift of vision. They sought to equal Wordsworth's sublimity and they were moved, to anxiety if not to emulation, by his image of a blessed community of poets, "the noble Living and the noble Dead" (*The Prelude*, XI. 399). Only at the end of the century in England, and with the help of a new aesthetic imported from France, did the poetic values of Wordsworthian Romanticism begin to be seriously challenged. Yeats in the 1890s invoked Mallarmé to support a stand against the movement of English poetry since Wordsworth.[3] Yet even Yeats's criticism of "the old lyric afflatus" expressed nothing like the revulsion against Hugo much earlier in the century in France. In a sense, Yeats's effort to assert new religious authority for poetry continued the Wordsworthian tradition even while reacting against it.

By English standards, romantic sublimity arrived in French poetry late and left early. The French pattern may show only the feebleness of influence that could be exerted by the comparatively inferior poets writing in France in the first half of the nineteenth century. It is possible that romantic sublimity never took hold in France mainly because Hugo, the grand practitioner of the sublime, was simply not as good a poet as Wordsworth. English admirers of Wordsworth in the mid-nineteenth century suggest this judgment in the terms of their disdain for the French poet-prophet. George Eliot was bored by the "two rather stout volumes" of *Les Contemplations*, in which Hugo "discourses of 'Dieu,' 'l'univers,' 'les anges,' and 'le tombeau.' "[4] George Lewes, one of the least provincial of Victorian critics, concurred in the general English verdict. Hugo is deficient "in the cardinal qualities of Vision and Sincerity."[5] His poems are "the cant of literature, not the experience of life." In Lewes's judgment, Hugo's weakness appears particularly in the quality of his figurative language. Instead of registering "the imaginative perception of obscure relations," as figurative language ought to do, Hugo's metaphors stop at "the mere jingle of verbal suggestions."

Lewes was not advancing a new aesthetic in his criticism of Hugo.

He judged the French poet by the standards Wordsworth developed at the beginning of the century to defend his own style, thereby justifying Wordsworth's belief that great poets create the taste by which they will be valued. Wordsworth's example is implicit in Lewes's objection to Hugo, as is Coleridge's famous distinction between Fancy and Imagination: the one a source of mere verbal embellishment, the other an impassioned discovery of hidden truth.

The Victorians saw that Hugo failed to create an effective French version of Wordsworthian sublimity. Though it is tempting still to stop with the Victorian judgment that Hugo is simply inferior, modern distance from Romantic values makes it easier to see that Hugo is also significantly different from an English Romantic. The main convictions behind English Romantic vision remain alien to Hugo. Both at his best and at his worst, Hugo relies on poetic devices that are not only different but even opposed to the concept of imaginative vision in English Romanticism. It seems natural that French poetry became influential in the English turn against "the old lyric afflatus" when we realize that even Victor Hugo was following a contrary if somewhat tangled path all along.

The poem "Ce qu'on entend sur la montagne" illustrates vividly the problem posed by Hugo for the Wordsworthian. The poem takes place on a mountain—the established vantage point for the European poet as visionary by the middle of the eighteenth century. The familiarity of the literary landscape exposes the poet on a mountain to Lewes's charge—this is the "cant of literature, not the experience of life." Wordsworth, I have argued, is remarkable for transcending any simple opposition between literature and life in poetry that is entirely devoted to a new grounding of literature in experience at the same time that it is openly, deliberately literary. Although we recognize the conventions of the literary sublime when Wordsworth is on a mountaintop or mountain pass in *The Prelude*, we are also made to believe that this poet has actually been in these high places. This is a record of real experience as well as a new version of a literary convention. Wordsworth moves through vast and sometimes obscure landscapes in *The Prelude*, but we retain a remarkably sure sense of where he is and how he got there. We know how and when he crossed the Alps, visited Chartreuse, toured the Italian lakes, climbed Mount Snowdon. The first problem in "Ce qu'on entend sur la montagne" is that Hugo offers no comparable impression of real places and experience:

Avez-vous quelquefois, calme et silencieux,
Monté sur la montagne, en présence des cieux?
Etait-ce aux bords du Sund? aux côtes de Bretagne?
Aviez-vous l'océan au pied de la montagne?
Et là, penché sur l'onde et sur l'immensité,
Calme et silencieux, avez-vous écouté?
Voici ce qu'on entend:—du moins un jour qu'en rêve
Ma pensée abattit son vol sur une grève,
Et, du sommet d'un mont plongeant au gouffre amer,
Vit d'un côté la terre et de l'autre la mer.

                                        (I. 726)

(Have you sometimes, calm and still, climbed up a mountain to the presence of the skies? Was it on the banks of the Sund? on the coast of Brittany? Was the ocean at the foot of the mountain? And there, leaning over the endless rolling waves, calm and still, did you listen? This is what one hears:—at least, one day while in a dream, my mind alighted on a shore and, from the top of the mountain diving into the briny deep, I saw the earth on one side, the sea on the other.)

Hugo appears to be a constant sojourner on one mountaintop or another. It is not at all clear what mountain he has ascended on this occasion or when the event occurred. The poem does not start out from the ground at a particular place on a particular day. In a peculiar reversal of the expected movement, Hugo describes some time when his lofty thought *descended* to the scene below him. It could have been any scene where the mountains meet the sea. The questions to the reader in stanza one immediately generalize the landscape of sublime vision. The sense of an extraordinary individual experience is barely present here in comparison to Wordsworth's description of crossing the Alps or the ascent of Snowdon:

It was a close, warm, breezeless summer night,
Wan, dull, and glaring, with a dripping fog
Low-hung and thick that covered all the sky;
But, undiscouraged, we began to climb
The mountain-side. The mist soon girt us round,
And, after ordinary travellers' talk
With our conductor, pensively we sank
Each into commerce with his private thoughts:
Thus did we breast the ascent, and by myself
Was nothing either seen or heard that checked
Those musings or diverted, save that once

The shepherd's lurcher, who, among the crags,
Had to his joy unearthed a hedgehog, teased
His coiled-up prey with barkings turbulent.
This small adventure, for even such it seemed
In that wild place and at the dead of night,
Being over and forgotten, on we wound
In silence as before. With forehead bent
Earthward, as if in opposition set
Against an enemy, I panted up
With eager pace, and no less eager thoughts.
Thus might we wear a midnight hour away,
Ascending at loose distance each from each,
And I, as chanced, the foremost of the band;
When at my feet the ground appeared to brighten,
And with a step or two seemed brighter still;
Nor was time given to ask or learn the cause,
For instantly a light upon the turf
Fell like a flash, and lo! as I looked up,
The Moon hung naked in a firmament
Of azure without cloud, and at my feet
Rested a silent sea of hoary mist.

         (XIV. 11-42)

Wordsworth begins the passage with his midnight climb up the mountain. He masterfully accomplishes the movement from "small adventure" to sublime vision. The mist and fog are first elements in the real landscape at the same time as they create a portentous atmosphere, separating the travelers from each other and silencing their ordinary talk. The travelers were not seeking a vision, yet in retrospect it was the goal of a pilgrimage dimly understood: "With forehead bent / Earthward, as if in opposition set / Against an enemy." Without any forcing of the storyteller's art, Wordsworth follows the silent ascent to its completion, even while he makes the final vision come as a sudden revelation, more extraordinary than what could have been anticipated from a midnight outing.[6]

"Ce qu'on entend sur la montagne" does not show the poetic mind's voyage from the ordinary to the sublime. Hugo presents himself more as a sage than a traveler. Whereas Wordsworth records the flashes of vision that interrupt and transform the small adventures of his life, Hugo appears to dwell habitually in the sublime. What he hears and sees from his exalted station is not a private revelation. Here is the voice which *one* hears on the mountain. The poem becomes an impersonal, authoritative, even dogmatic statement, independent of the poet's individual history or sensibility. Perhaps it is that impersonality which George Eliot was registering in her disparaging term "discourses." The voices heard on the mountain are supposed to be important in themselves rather than in relation to the poet's or anyone's individual hearing of them. Hugo's poems sound like "discourses" partly because Hugo demands attention for the substance of vision rather than for the drama of visionary experience.

The five main stanzas of "Ce qu'on entend sur la montagne" present, through a long sequence of images, what one hears on the mountain. At first the noise is a single, though confused sound, "un bruit large, immense, confus." Sweet and strident tones blend mysteriously, so that it sounds like the music of a vast symphony. Eventually, two distinct voices can be discerned: one, glorious and triumphant, comes from the sea; the other, more melancholy, from the earth where men live. The poet identifies the sound of the sea as Nature's voice, rising to God in a song of praise:

> Or, comme je l'ai dit, l'océan magnifique
> Epandait une voix joyeuse et pacifique,
> Chantait comme la harpe aux temples de Sion,
> Et louait la beauté de la création.
> Sa clameur, qu'emportaient la brise et la rafale,
> Incessamment vers Dieu montait plus triomphale,
> Et chacun de ses flots que Dieu seul peut dompter,
> Quand l'autre avait fini, se levait pour chanter.
> Comme ce grand lion dont Daniel fut l'hôte,
> L'océan par moments abaissait sa voix haute;
> Et moi je croyais voir, vers le couchant en feu,
> Sous sa crinière d'or passer la main de Dieu.
>
> (I. 727)

(Now, as I said, the magnificent ocean poured forth its joyous and peaceful voice; it sang like the harp in the temples of Zion, and praised the beauty of Creation. Its clamor, swept away by breeze and squall, ceaselessly rose to God, ever more triumphant; and each of its waves, which only God can tame, rose up one after another to sing. Like the great lion with whom Daniel dwelt, the ocean at times softened its roar; and I thought I saw in the flaming sunset, the hand of God run through its golden mane.)

After the climactic vision of God's hand in the sunset, the poem descends to a rather tedious rendering of earth's voice:

Cependant, à côté de l'auguste fanfare,
L'autre voix, comme un cri de coursier qui s'effare,
Comme le gond rouillé d'une porte d'enfer,
Comme l'archet d'airain sur la lyre de fer,
Grinçait; et pleurs, et cris, l'injure, l'anathème,
Refus du viatique et refus du baptême,
Et malédiction, et blasphème, et clameur,
Dans le flot tournoyant de l'humaine rumeur
Passaient, comme le soir on voit dans les vallées
De noirs oiseaux de nuit qui s'en vont par volées.
Qu'était-ce que ce bruit dont mille échos vibraient?
Hélas! c'était la terre et l'homme qui pleuraient.

(I.727)

(Meanwhile, beside this majestic fanfare, creaked the other voice, like the cry of a frightened steed, like the rusty hinge of an infernal gate, like the brazen bow on the iron lyre; sobs, cries, insults, anathema, the last sacrament spurned and baptism spurned; and curses, blasphemy, noise whirled around in this human din, as at night one sees in the valleys, passing flights of dark nocturnal birds. What was this noise with a thousand echoes? Alas! it was the earth and man weeping.)

The weakness of the stanza describing earth's voice may come from our difficulty in connecting Hugo's figurative language for this part of the event to any perceptible sights or sounds. The imagery loses its connection to audible sound; we do not believe that the poet on the mountain actually heard the human sounds named: "et pleurs, et cris, l'injure, l'anathème, / Refus du viatique et refus du baptême." The image of dark nocturnal birds in the valley is the most effective in the stanza, but it does not seem to register any visible or audible reality in this scene; moreover, it is unclear why the human din, as distinct from nature's music, should be rendered in imagery taken from nature.

The general import of Hugo's confusing figurative language is, of course, obvious enough. In contrast to the majestic harmony of the sea, human sound is grating and ominous. But Hugo's similes render in terms of sound only a formulated (and rather conventional) idea of human misery, not a perception of any particular sound heard on any occasion. The poet possesses a repertory of sensory images which give diverse concrete form to the idea of human discord. The images gain their expressiveness from literary allusion; the rusty hinge, for example, recalls both Milton's gate of Hell in *Paradise Lost* (II. 880-881) and

Milton's source in Virgil's description of the underground in the *Aeneid* (VI. 573-574). Hugo echoes images from earlier literature to express in concrete terms a general and abstract conception of the human condition. All he has done here with the traditional image of sound is to transfer its reference from Hell to earth. The human world becomes a Hell, but not because of any sound heard by the poet on this or any particular occasion.

In Wordsworth's poetry, literary and mythic undertones extend without replacing images of perception:

> . . . and I would stand,
> If the night blackened with a coming storm,
> Beneath some rock, listening to notes that are
> The ghostly language of the ancient earth,
> Or make their dim abode in distant winds.
>
> (II. 306-310)

The wonder of childhood in *The Prelude* is that, then, the poet actually saw and heard the universe in ways that he will, only later, meet again in literature and myth. When Wordsworth says "the earth / And common face of Nature spake to me / Rememberable things" (I. 586-587), he depends upon his images of real sound, like the sound of thunder before a storm, to revitalize the conventional literary image of Nature's voice.

Even in poems of general statement, where Wordsworth does not record any personal experience, the grounding of his metaphor in perception is crucial to its often surprising effect. The sonnet, "Thought of a Briton on the Subjugation of Switzerland," for example, seems at first more like a discourse by Hugo, in that Wordsworth states an idea (a "thought") through images of sound. The poem appeals to England to preserve itself as the remaining stronghold of liberty now that Switzerland has been subjugated. Wordsworth gives concrete form to the analogy between Switzerland and England through the image of Nature's different voices, but the political idea at first seems abstract and separable from the metaphor:

> Two voices are there; one is of the sea,
> One of the mountains; each a mighty Voice:
> In both from age to age thou didst rejoice,
> They were thy chosen music, Liberty!
>
> (ll. 1-4)

Wordsworth's seemingly straightforward political lament, however, takes a strange turn by the end through the suggestiveness of his
sensory images. The bereft figure of Liberty is more pitiable than the
subjugated lands, for the imagery of sound endows the nature of those
places with indomitable force, regardless of their political destiny:

> There came a Tyrant, and with holy glee
> Thou fought'st against him; but hast vainly striven:
> Thou from thy Alpine holds at length art driven,
> Where not a torrent murmurs heard by thee.
> Of one deep bliss thine ear hath been bereft:
> Then cleave, O cleave to that which still is left;
> For, high-souled Maid, what sorrow would it be
> That Mountain floods should thunder as before,
> And Ocean bellow from his rocky shore,
> And neither awful Voice be heard by thee!
>
> (ll. 5-14)

Although the poet laments the fate of Switzerland and fears for the
future of England, his sensory images in a way limit the power of any
Tyrant to subjugate Nature's power. Moreover, the poet's own destiny also seems strangely detached from that of Liberty, the "high-
souled Maid." Whether or not Liberty is bereft, the poet hears the
music of Nature with his own ears; he does not depend upon Liberty
for the bliss of hearing Mountain floods thunder and Ocean bellow.
The word "bliss" in the poem refers to the experience of hearing Nature's mighty voices. Wordsworth's images of perception indirectly
assert the poet's continuing and independent responsiveness to the living force of Nature. The images suggest that the poet's "bliss" survives, separable from political liberty. Beneath the political lament,
the images somewhat paradoxically express the poet's private freedom
from politics altogether. He ends by seeming as invulnerable to political catastrophe as the voices of sea and mountain, for his ear cleaves
to that music and his own voice can re-create it in the language of the
poem.

The absence of any comparable grounding in perception keeps
Hugo's notion of earth's voice a more limited rhetorical figure than
Wordsworthian images of sound. In comparison to Wordsworth,
even Hugo's description of the sea does not really owe its significance
to an act of hearing. Hugo's comparison of the sea to a wild beast may
seem analogous to Wordsworth's bellowing Ocean, but Hugo's image

of the lion in Daniel's den seems too specific to derive from sensory suggestion. There is no sensory reason to hear *Daniel's* lion in the pauses of ocean waves. Wordsworth compares the sound of water to thunder or to the bellows of a strange god or beast; in *The Prelude*, he recalls that as a child he heard wolves in the sound of the howling wind. But to connect the pauses between sounds with a particular Biblical beast, as Hugo does, shows a different activity of mind. Hugo uses the image of Daniel and the lion to exemplify the idea of savage force subject only to God's will. The poet sees this idea embodied in the pauses of the sea, but the idea itself seems clear and fully formulated independent of sensory perception.[7]

In Hugo's poetry, the landscape characteristically embodies ideas and corresponds to other embodiments of ideas in literature and legend. The figurative comparisons are quite specific and they have public, traditional resonance; their spiritual meanings are clear to the educated reader. Hugo makes the world spiritually significant by connecting earthly things to spiritual images already present in the culture before and apart from his experience. There seems no limit to the number and variety of images available to the poet. His repertory of images can sustain him not just through five stanzas, but through hundreds, even thousands of lines of poetry.[8]

Baudelaire responded to the impression of plentitude in Hugo's figurative language when he praised him for opening the reservoirs of analogy for French poetry. Hugo has a vast store of similitudes, Baudelaire remarked admiringly (1086). He does not distinguish Hugo's analogies between the human, the natural, and the supernatural from other forms of figurative language. The perspective of English Romantic poetry, however, exposes the severely limited structure of Hugo's comparisons. The vision granted to Wordsworth on the top of Snowdon depends upon quite different figures of speech:

> A hundred hills their dusky backs upheaved
> All over this still ocean; and beyond,
> Far, far beyond, the solid vapours stretched,
> In headlands, tongues, and promontory shapes,
> Into the main Atlantic, that appeared
> To dwindle, and give up his majesty,
> Usurped upon far as the sight could reach.
> Not so the ethereal vault; encroachment none
> Was there, nor loss; only the inferior stars
> Had disappeared, or shed a fainter light

In the clear presence of the full-orbed Moon,
Who, from her sovereign elevation, gazed
Upon the billowy ocean, as it lay
All meek and silent, save that through a rift—
Not distant from the shore whereon we stood,
A fixed, abysmal, gloomy, breathing-place—
Mounted the roar of waters, torrents, streams
Innumerable, roaring with one voice!
Heard over earth and sea, and, in that hour,
For so it seemed, felt by the starry heavens.
(XIV. 43-62)

Wordsworth first strives to re-create the impression of a vision that "fell like a flash," extraordinary and totally absorbing in its visual impressiveness. The long, complex sentences, with their unfolding subordinate clauses, create an impression of intricacy that is registered in detail and also apprehended all at once. Wordsworth describes the spectacle without naming its spiritual meaning, except that his metaphoric language itself animates and thus spiritualizes the landscape. The sea of mist "rested," the hills "upheaved" their backs like primordial monsters. Most strikingly, the scene revealed complex and mysterious relationships at work, as between living and feeling beings. The relation of the moon to the sea and to the ocean of mist is felt to be a relationship of powers, variously usurped upon or supreme. Metaphors of power dominate the language: "majesty," "usurped upon," "encroachment," "sovereign elevation." It is not obvious what spiritual significance such metaphors have, nor does the poet hurry to circumscribe the symbolic implications of the description. We are first encouraged to be impressed, as he had been, by the extraordinary, mysterious vitality of this spectacle. The impression of vitality is the first revelation; we cannot be sure what else it all may mean.

Like Hugo, Wordsworth intimates spiritual meanings through figurative language that is recognizably literary (and specifically Biblical and Miltonic). But Wordsworth's metaphors do not make precise correspondences between the misty night landscape and any specific spiritual events known from religious or literary tradition. The description of the scene may bring to mind Milton's version of the Creation, for example, but Wordsworth's allusiveness works more loosely than Hugo's, with more open suggestiveness. More precise interpretation comes only later, as the poet's speculation after the vision has partially dissolved.

In Book XIV of *The Prelude*, it is the interpretive passage (63-129) following the vision that disappoints many readers. The meaning of the Snowdon emblem is relatively clear: the poet's vision of order and power in the landscape has revealed to him the living spirit of Nature. Upon reflection, the vision further seems to represent symbolically the order and power of the ideal human mind, that is, the poetic mind. By showing at the same time the living power of both Nature and the poetic mind, the vision (as Wordsworth interprets it) is supposed to disclose the bond between Nature and the mind and the relationship of both to divinity. Presumably, the very act of vision (and the act of making the emblem out of vision) confirms all these truths, for Wordsworth within the poem is demonstrating the mutual exertion of power between parts of the majestic mind while he is explaining it.

The problem posed by the Snowdon emblem concerns not so much its meaning as its uncertain persuasiveness after the marvelous and mysterious vision. David Ferry argues that Wordsworth's vision in Book XIV is more ambiguous than the interpretation he puts on it: "But the abstract explanation of the image is more orderly than the image itself, and makes an insufficient account of the mists and of the abyss of roaring waters."[9] Ferry sees Wordsworth's vision instead as an emblem of the poet's deep uncertainty about the value of the poetic imagination: "It is power against power—the power of the clarifying moon, which not only discovers but even creates the order of natural things, over against the power of the abyss, that nature whose name is not order and harmony but chaos and mystery."

Without fully engaging in the far-reaching implications of Ferry's view, I am interested to consider how much is said about the difference between Wordsworth and Hugo by the very character of the problem posed by Wordsworth's vision and emblem. The problem in Wordsworth arises precisely because his language of vision seems to promise unpredictable spiritual meanings in the world of "sensible impressions." One dissents from Wordsworth's interpretation by pursuing further the suggestiveness of his figurative language. The spiritual meanings shadowed forth in Nature are not firmly established beforehand in Wordsworth's language. His own explanation may be disappointing, not only because it is too simply optimistic, but also because Wordsworth seems to retreat from the excited sense of discovery which his own language initiates. We are led to expect a revelation, but the emblem seems too simply contrived to restate the conception of the poetic mind already established in earlier books of *The Prelude*.

If Hugo's interpretations of his visions are not comparably disappointing, that is because Hugo's language of vision creates no Wordsworthian expectations. Hugo never suggests that physical forms shadow forth mysterious meanings to be shaped through imaginative perception, for acts of perception do not govern Hugo's figurative language. The imagery is dominated by formal similes which keep the objects in the poem separate and clear; each simile expresses a distinct spiritual meaning. The significance of the landscape is firmly controlled all along by the established associations of the similes: the harp of Zion, the lion of Daniel, the rusty gate of Hell. Wordsworth's metaphors show how the mind discovers and builds relationships among the objects of perception. Hugo's method, by contrast, recalls the "fixities and definites" in Coleridge's idea of Fancy. Two opposing sets of images illustrate a single contrast between harmony and discord, nature and man, sea and earth, divine power and human confusion. The harp of Zion merely opposes the lyre of iron. No relationship unfolds between the images of music and those of beasts. Hugo creates the effect of a catalogue of examples, each one further preserving its fixed, distinct identity by occupying a whole line or stanza. Instead of Wordsworth's movement toward the discovery of relationship, an impression of clearer separation emerges from the form and statement in Hugo. What was first heard as a confusing single sound is finally analyzed into two distinct and contrasting voices.

Hugo's design, however, creates its own problems. At the end, Hugo too wishes to assert a bond between Nature and man, but his imagery intimates no basis for reconciliation, nor any relationship other than antithesis. His similes identify, with much less ambiguity than in Wordsworth, only a contrast between the human and the natural, not the possibility of any bond between them.

In the meditation at the end of the poem, Hugo acknowledges his helplessness to explain the bond between Nature and man which he nevertheless asserts. The stanza shows Hugo in an unfortunately recurrent posture—announcing his discovery of confusion in grandiose platitudes:

> Alors je méditai; car mon esprit fidèle,
> Hélas! n'avait jamais déployé plus grande aile;
> Dans mon ombre jamais n'avait lui tant de jour;
> Et je rêvai longtemps, contemplant tour à tour,
> Après l'abîme obscur que me cachait la lame,

L'autre abîme sans fond qui s'ouvrait dans mon âme.
Et je me demandai pourquoi l'on est ici,
Quel peut être après tout le but de tout ceci,
Que fait l'âme, lequel vaut mieux d'être ou de vivre,
Et pourquoi le Seigneur, qui seul lit à son livre,
Mêle éternellement dans un fatal hymen
Le chant de la nature au cri du genre humain?

(I. 728)

(Then I paused in meditation; for my faithful spirit, alas, had never spread its wings so wide. Never through my shadow had so much light glimmered; and I dreamed for a long time, contemplating in turn, first the dark abyss concealed by the waves, then the other bottomless abyss opening in my soul. And I wondered why we are here; what, after all, is the goal of all this; what is the purpose of the soul; which is better: to be or to live; and why does the Lord, who alone reads in His Book, eternally combine in a fatal marriage, the song of nature with the cry of mankind?)

Hugo now interprets the music as "un fatal hymen," but this ambiguous image of union is itself contained within a series of bewildered questions. Even in the last line, the two voices remain separate across the caesura. The marriage between Nature and man seems formal and, in a sense, merely doctrinal, for the mystery of God's design remains impenetrable. The earlier figurative comparisons do not yield a unifying insight and Hugo puts them aside. The rusty gate of Hell, the lion, the horse, the harp, the lyre all disappear as the poet broods upon the inscrutable mystery of God.

From the point of view of English Romantic theory, Hugo's failure to attain a fuller vision of the marriage between man and Nature might be attributed to the weakness of his imagination—weakness implicit in the limited uses of metaphor earlier in the poem. Hugo's epigraph to "Ce qu'on entend sur la montagne" intimates, however, a more traditional Christian explanation for the limitations of poetic vision (though no theology can explain the flatness of the final stanza). The epigraph alludes to St. Paul: "O altitudo." In the Bible, the passage continues: "O the depth of the riches and wisdom and knowledge of God! How unsearchable are his judgments and how inscrutable his ways! For who has known the mind of the Lord, or who has been his counselor?" (Rom. 11: 33-34). Spiritual truth is ultimately hidden in the mind of the Lord, beyond human reach. Nature, the Creation of God, shows forth His power. The human mind may apprehend the divine significance of the Creation, but Nature, like the Bible it so often calls to mind, only confirms His inscrutability rather than revealing His secret.

Wordsworth is reluctant to acknowledge that any spiritual truth is inherently inaccessible to the poet. The creative power of the human mind is a faculty of spiritual insight, capable of discovering the bonds between man and Nature, and between the earthly and the divine. It is because of these bonds that natural forms can symbolize the nature of the mind at the same time as they shadow forth the divine order of the universe outside the mind. The poetic mind recognizes that natural images have a double reference; they are both mirror and lens, for while reflecting the creative power within the mind, they also open to view the riches and wisdom of God.

Book XIV and other parts of *The Prelude* illustrate, as do passages in Coleridge's poetry and prose in different ways, that the English Romantic faith in the spiritual power of the poetic mind is subject to ambiguity, qualification, wavering. Yet for all the uncertainty or false assurance we may feel at times in both Wordsworth and Coleridge, their confidence in the value of art cannot be divorced from their commitment to a relationship between the poetic mind and divinity. The relationship is discovered and then discovered again through the poet's repeated acts of imaginative perception. The idea of imaginative perception sanctifies the poetic vocation; it directs the poet to revere his experiences in nature, and it defines even the special virtue of metaphoric language. The very possibility of writing poetry becomes inseparable from faith in this religious as well as aesthetic principle. It is no wonder that Wordsworth draws back from the darker implications of the Snowdon vision, or that the Victorians saw the possible loss of Wordsworth's faith as a crisis for poetry itself.

Victor Hugo displays no comparable anxiety in "Ce qu'on entend sur la montagne." Retaining the orthodox distinction between the mind of man and the mind of God, Hugo's discourse seems oddly humble despite its rhetorical grandiosity. Hugo on the mountain rediscovers spiritual bewilderment as the irremediable human condition. Although the poet suffers from the same limitations of insight as other men, his confidence in the high mission of poetry seems unshakeable. Hugo does not stake his authority on the claim to holy insight. The poet's vision only summons other men back to faith in the inscrutable wisdom of God.

8

Victor Hugo: From Spectacle to Symbol

Hugo's frequently declamatory tone may mislead us to expect a boldness not really asserted by either his poetry or criticism. In comparison to the English Romantics, Hugo proposes only a modest conception of the poet's spiritual power. In the Preface to the volume, *Les Voix intérieures* (1837), Hugo's image of the poet as "echo" implies even more humility than he seems to realize:

> La Porcia de Shakespeare parle quelque part de cette *musique que tout homme a en soi.*—Malheur, dit-elle, à qui ne l'entend pas!— Cette musique, la nature aussi l'a en elle. Si le livre qu'on va lire est quelque chose, il est l'écho, bien confus et bien affaibli sans doute, mais fidèle, l'auteur le croit, de ce chant qui répond en nous au chant que nous entendons hors de nous. (I. 919)

> (Shakespeare's Portia speaks somewhere of that *music which every man has in himself.* Woe, she says, to the man who does not hear it! This music, nature too possesses. If the book you are about to read is anything at all, it is the echo, no doubt confused and weakened, but faithful, the author believes, to that song which answers within us to the song which we hear outside of ourselves.)

It is hard to know from Hugo's language in what sense poetry is to echo nature's voice, or whether there is an important distinction in his mind between echoing nature and echoing human response to nature. But the very image of an echo differs fundamentally from the central image of the poet's music in English Romanticism, the Aeolian harp.

The touch of the breeze moves the Aeolian harp to music. The harp does not merely echo the breeze which may, indeed, be inaudible until received by the instrument and transformed to music. Poetic genius is a special fitness to receive the motions of life in the natural universe and out of them to generate music or a new order of meaning. The making of an echo is less mysterious. It does not invite the same reverent or speculative attention. In comparison to the Aeolian harp, an echo is objective, impersonal. It reproduces a sound that has a distinct, prior existence of its own.

According to Hugo in the Preface to *Les Voix intérieures*, the poet performs at once as an echo of the voices of man, of nature, and of "les événements," the public world of circumstance:

> Si l'homme a sa voix, si la nature a la sienne, les événements ont aussi la leur. L'auteur a toujours pensé que la mission du poète était de fondre dans un même groupe de chants cette triple parole qui renferme un triple enseignement, car la première s'adresse plus particulièrement au coeur, la seconde à l'âme, la troisième à l'esprit. *Tres radios*. (I. 919)

> (If man has his voice, and nature has hers, then events have theirs too. The author has always thought that the poet's mission was to cast into a single group of songs this triple voice which yields a triple lesson: the first speaks most particularly to the heart, the second to the soul, the third to the mind. *Tres radios*.)

Although Hugo distinguishes different voices and different human faculties, his rhetorical flourishes gloss over the crucial relationships: between man and nature, between heart and soul and intellect. Hugo's tone of public proclamation does not encourage us to speculate about the basic nature of the poetic process. As in "Ce qu'on entend sur la montagne," Hugo calls attention to the importance of the sounds echoed by the poet rather than to the process of their becoming poetic speech. He summons the reader to heed the diverse voices of the universe audible in his poems. We are not invited to contemplate the mysterious workings of the poet's instrument, nor do we think of him as the single maker of the song he sings. The position of the poet as echo is more grandiose, yet more self-effacing at the same time.

The relatively successful poem, "Spectacle rassurant," shows the poet perform as echo of a more delicate music than in "Ce qu'on entend sur la montagne." The very range of tones in Hugo's poetry is worth remarking, for the poet as echo hardly possesses a distinctive voice of his own:

> Tout est lumière, tout est joie.
> L'araignée au pied diligent
> Attache aux tulipes de soie
> Ses rondes dentelles d'argent.
>
> La frissonnante libellule
> Mire les globes de ses yeux
> Dans l'étang splendide où pullule
> Tout un monde mystérieux!
>
> La rose semble, rajeunie,
> S'accoupler au bouton vermeil;
> L'oiseau chante plein d'harmonie
> Dans les rameaux pleins de soleil.
>
> Sa voix bénit le Dieu de l'âme
> Qui, toujours visible au coeur pur,
> Fait l'aube, paupière de flamme,
> Pour le ciel, prunelle d'azur!
>
> Sous les bois, où tout bruit s'émousse,
> Le faon craintif joue en rêvant;
> Dans les verts écrins de la mousse
> Luit le scarabée, or vivant.
>
> La lune au jour est tiède et pâle
> Comme un joyeux convalescent;
> Tendre, elle ouvre ses yeux d'opale
> D'où la douceur du ciel descend!
>
> La giroflée avec l'abeille
> Folâtre en baisant le vieux mur;
> Le chaud sillon gaîment s'éveille,
> Remué par le germe obscur.
>
> Tout vit, et se pose avec grâce,
> Le rayon sur le seuil ouvert,
> L'ombre qui fuit sur l'eau qui passe,
> Le ciel bleu sur le coteau vert!

La plaine brille, heureuse et pure;
Le bois jase; l'herbe fleurit . . . —
Homme! ne crains rien! la nature
Sait le grand secret, et sourit.

(I. 1061-1062)

(All is light, all is joy. The busy-footed spider hangs his rings of sil-
ver lace on the silky tulips. The shivering dragonfly mirrors the
globes of his eyes in the splendid pool, swarming with a whole
mysterious world. The rose, in her new youth, seems to mate with
the scarlet bud; the bird sings, full of harmony, in the boughs full of
sun. His voice blesses the God of the soul who, always visible to the
pure in heart, makes the dawn, that fiery lid, for the sky, that clear
blue eye. In the woods, where all noises soften, the timid fawn plays
and dreams; in the green casing of the moss shines the beetle, living
gold. The moon at dawn is warm and pale, like a joyful convales-
cent; tenderly she opens her eyes of opal, pouring down the sweetness of the sky! The gillyflower and the bee frolic together, kissing
the old wall. The warm furrow merrily awakens, stirred by the hidden seed. Everything is alive, and alights with grace: the ray of sun
on the open threshold, the fleeting shadow on the running stream,
the blue sky on the green hillside! The plain shines, happy and pure;
the woods twitter, the grass blossoms . . . —Man! have no fear!
Nature knows the great secret, and smiles.)

The graceful varied rhythms and sound patterns of "Spectacle rassurant" make audible the delicate awakening of spring, while the
imagery of the poem records the visual spectacle. As in "Ce qu'on
entend sur la montagne," there is little sense of specific occasion in the
poem, but the absence of personal drama seems appropriate here,
effectively placing the poet as spectator of a scene that is complete in
itself and separate from him. Hugo holds only a transparent lens to the
scene, the visual counterpart of an echo. He may enlarge the tiny creatures of nature—the spider, the dragonfly, the beetle—or he may
focus on the large masses of shape and color, "le ciel bleu sur le coteau
vert." But the lively serenity of the scene is made to seem autonomous;
it owes nothing, apparently, to the modifying power of the poet's eye.
Hugo's tone is matter-of-fact, even when he attributes emotions to the
landscape: "Tout est lumière, tout est joie," "La plaine brille, heureuse
et pure; / Le bois jase; l'herbe fleurit." The simple declarative renders
the feelings of nature as unmistakable as color or light.

Hugo's attentiveness to spring in "Spectacle rassurant" seems to suspend or discipline the poet's inner life, in accord more with the aim of

an Imagist description than a Wordsworthian meditation. Daffodils become a spectacle or "show" in "I Wandered Lonely as a Cloud" because of the poet's response to them, even more so since the poem presents the memory of an experience rather than the direct perception of a scene. Similarly, in the simple lyric, "Lines Written in Early Spring," Wordsworth interposes his experience on a particular remembered occasion between the reader and the scene. He does not echo spring; he is the instrument that composes the scene into "a thousand blended notes":

> I heard a thousand blended notes
> While in a grove I sate reclined,
> In that sweet mood when pleasant thoughts
> Bring sad thoughts to the mind.
>
> (ll. 1-4)

Wordsworth's originality (and his perversity) in a poem such as "Lines Written in Early Spring" comes from his refusal to accept, merely as a matter of course, the pleasure generally and conventionally associated with nature. To find "pleasure" in a scene of playful birds and budding trees does not indicate an extraordinary personal response. Wordsworth's simplicity of diction, rhythm, and stanza in part acknowledges the normality of the scene and of his feeling. Yet the poem also has a more assertive undertone. Wordsworth insists that we make more of his experience of this ordinary event. He presents his perception as though it were remarkable, even preposterous:

> The budding twigs spread out their fan,
> To catch the breezy air;
> And I must think, do all I can,
> That there was pleasure there.
>
> (ll. 17-20)

This scene, Wordsworth tells us, composed itself in his mind in terms of metaphors: the budding twigs, to his perception, were like a fan, spread purposefully to catch the breeze and also graciously, as if to refresh the birds and even the speaker himself. His metaphoric perception was so complete that he cannot help but believe a sentient power was present in the motion. Pleasure was in the scene, a feeling akin to human emotion, though significantly purer than the feelings of the happy-sad human observer.

Wordsworth objected to the personifications of eighteenth-century descriptive poetry partly because, as a rhetorical convention, personification in itself expressed no special passion, while he regarded with religious reverence his moments of seeing life and feeling in natural forms.[1] Metaphors which animate natural objects must dramatize the responsiveness of the mind to the hidden life of the universe. In "Lines Written in Early Spring," imaginative perception generates religious emotion. Wordsworth protests that his feeling of belief is involuntary, unarguable, for it inheres in the very activity of his perception—in the laws which govern his mode of seeing, hearing, and remembering. The early lyric already illustrates the laws of Imagination invoked in the "Preface of 1815": "Imagination . . . has no reference to images that are merely a faithful copy, existing in the mind, of absent external objects; but is a word of higher import, denoting operations of the mind upon those objects, and processes of creation or of composition governed by certain fixed laws."[2]

The style of "Spectacle rassurant" is not mechanical, yet neither is it "imaginative," in Wordsworth's sense. Hugo makes the blessedness of spring objective rather than the inward persuasion of the observer. The tone is closer to a Blake song, like "The Ecchoing Green," than to Wordsworth:

> The Sun does arise,
> And make happy the skies;
> The merry bells ring
> To welcome the Spring;
> The skylark and thrush,
> The birds of the bush,
> Sing louder around
> To the bells' chearful sound,
> While our sports shall be seen
> On the Ecchoing Green.
>
> (ll. 1-10)

Like "Spectacle rassurant," Blake's song simply declares the presence of feeling in the landscape. But in "The Ecchoing Green," Blake compares the earth to an echo, not the poet. The landscape echoes the jubilance of the children who sing the song. It is the gift of innocence, in Blake's view, to extend human happiness to all objects in the universe. The declarative assurance of the poem expresses the certitude of innocence. To the children the happiness of nature is literal.

Hugo's matter-of-fact tone is more puzzling, for the landscape of "Spectacle rassurant" does not seem to echo any person's inner state. At the end of the poem, a reassuring lesson for men is announced: "Homme! ne crains rien! la nature / Sait le grand secret, et sourit." The ending turns the poem public and didactic—having recorded the state of nature, the poet draws the lesson for the congregation of readers. There is no sense that this poet, this human observer, has shared in Nature's secret, nor is his lack of participation made to seem noteworthy. The poem ends on a note of achievement rather than disappointment, even though from the perspective of English Romanticism, little of what a poet might be expected to want from a springtime scene has been achieved.

Hugo's apparent indifference to his individual inner life in "Spectacle rassurant" sets him apart from English poets in the Romantic period and also later. He does not question his exclusion from Nature's secret, nor does he measure his lack of feeling against the richer inward experience of other poets, as Hardy, for example, does so suggestively in "The Darkling Thrush."

> I leant upon a coppice gate
>   When Frost was spectre-gray,
> And Winter's dregs made desolate
>   The weakening eye of day.
> The tangled bine-stems scored the sky
>   Like strings of broken lyres,
> And all mankind that haunted nigh
>   Had sought their household fires.
>
> The land's sharp features seemed to be
>   The Century's corpse outleant;
> His crypt the cloudy canopy,
>   The wind his death-lament.
> The ancient pulse of germ and birth
>   Was shrunken hard and dry,
> And every spirit upon earth
>   Seemed fervourless as I.
>
> At once a voice arose among
>   The bleak twigs overhead
> In a full-hearted evensong
>   Of joy illimited;
> An aged thrush, frail, gaunt, and small,
>   In blast-beruffled plume,
> Had chosen thus to fling his soul
>   Upon the growing gloom.

> So little cause for carollings
>   Of such ecstatic sound
> Was written on terrestrial things
>   Afar or nigh around,
> That I could think there trembled through
>   His happy good-night air
> Some blessed Hope, whereof he knew
>   And I was unaware.

The English poet, standing at the demise of the nineteenth century, takes his bearings in relation to the poetry of the century gone by. His concern is with the limits of his perception—what he sees and hears and what he can or cannot make of it. Lingering past dusk in the shrunken winter scene, Hardy perceives the decay of the Romantic landscape. The lyre is broken and only a death-lament can be heard in the wind. For this poet, "terrestrial things" mainly confirm the hard and dry reality of his own desolation. The English poet, however, even when surrounded by a scene as "fervourless" as his own spirit, is still attuned to any remaining sign of mysterious vitality. And the sound of joy still does come to him suddenly in the song of the thrush, even though this bird has almost human pathos and bravery rather than the mysterious blessedness of the Romantic bird. Hearing the aged thrush, the poet does not easily nor altogether disbelieve that a secret does still tremble through Nature's voice.

Whereas Hugo, in "Spectacle rassurant," is content to report that Nature has and knows a secret, "The Darkling Thrush" expresses Hardy's rather different concern with his individual responsiveness to reassuring natural signs. The fact that the bird sings matters to Hardy, but it matters most in relation to what he thinks, feels, believes in response to hearing that song. The subtlety of Hardy's last two stanzas is in their understatement of response. The poet can still hear birdsong as "ecstatic sound"; he can still regard that sound as spiritually significant, but his own voice does not burst forth in joy. For a moment, in stanza three, a new tone begins, "At once a voice arose among. . . ." But the lyricism quickly descends to the more sober narrative tone, "An aged thrush, frail, gaunt, and small." In the last stanza, the poet's voice sounds more puzzled than thrilled. The act of perception for Hardy no longer has the persuasiveness asserted by Wordsworth, "And I must think, do all I can / That there was pleasure there." Instead, a bare possibility of faith comes out of the incongruity between the poet's different perceptions. There is so little visible cause for happiness in the scene, and yet the bird sounds so happy—out of this incongruity, the poet "could think" there is some secret cause for the bird's ecstatic sound.

"The Darkling Thrush" records both an achievement and a disappointment, to be measured in relation to all those famous other English poems where cuckoos, thrushes, nightingales, and skylarks aroused poets to rich experiences of feeling and belief. Hardy reconsiders the possibility of moving from perception to faith. To discern blessed hope in the song of a bird involves a sequence of mental acts—a sequence that he can still perform, but only tentatively and with new uncertainty about its significance. In "The Darkling Thrush," Hardy (like Stevens, Frost, and many other twentieth-century poets in English) is as interested in reevaluating this psychological sequence as he is in any more personal or more general subject.

The bird in "Spectacle rassurant" stays apart from the famous birds in English poetry since Wordsworth, for Hugo's bird articulates a blessing independent of the poet's response or lack of response:

> L'oiseau chante plein d'harmonie
> Dans les rameaux pleins de soleil.
>
> Sa voix bénit le Dieu de l'âme
> Qui, toujours visible au coeur pur,
> Fait l'aube, paupière de flamme,
> Pour le ciel, prunelle d'azur!

(The bird sings, full of harmony, in the boughs full of sun. His voice blesses the God of the soul who, always visible to the pure in heart, makes the dawn, that fiery lid, for the sky, that clear blue eye.)

Hugo simply echoes the clear blessing to be heard in the bird's song, without questioning the extent of his response or the psychological origin of his sense of blessing. The bird's song does not seem to arouse his memory, as in Wordsworth's "To the Cuckoo"; he does not imagine himself joining the bird in song or flight, like Keats in "Ode to a Nightingale." He expresses no yearning, or hope, or illusion of being with a bird or like a bird. Nor does he show a more characteristically modern questioning of the fictive character of his poetic bird. Its blessing seems clear beyond question, apart from the poet's mental experience on this or another occasion.

The bird in "Spectacle rassurant" declares the presence and power of God to be manifest in the dawn and in the sky. But how does the poet (or the bird) come to compare the sky to the pupil of an eye? and what exactly does it mean for the natural sky to be the opening through which divine light enters the world? God, says the bird, is always visible to the pure heart. Some mode of cognition other than natural perception is implied—intuition or faith, perhaps only doctrinal teaching. The bird's song has the tone of a creed to be learned by heart. The cryptic brevity of the images recalls the peculiar combination of reticence and presumption in "Ce qu'on entend sur la montagne." Hugo simply lists the spiritual meanings of nature; he names the true and permanent spiritual identity of things, without claiming his experience of perception as the authority for what he announces.

Metaphors that start in perception tend to characterize the appearances of things at some particular time. Daffodils do not always appear to dance, nor do branches always move like fans. Wordsworth may take inward possession of a spectacle and thus seem to release it from time, but his metaphors originate in his mind's encounter with the changing world of appearances, just as the whole imaginative experience begins in a particular place at a particular time. Thus, Wordsworth's metaphors and similes characteristically refer to actions; in rhetorical terms, the metaphor centers on verbs and verbal forms of speech. Even similes which start by comparing substantives go on to disclose the action of things as the point of comparison: "I wandered lonely as a cloud / That floats on high . . . ," "She shall be sportive as the fawn / That wild with glee across the lawn / Or up the mountain springs." In the "Preface of 1815," Wordsworth's examples of imaginative language are all metaphors in the verbs of sentences: three metaphoric uses of "hang" (from Virgil, Shakespeare, and Milton); from Wordsworth's own poetry, the nightingale's voice "buried" among trees, and the leechgatherer: "Motionless as a cloud the old man stood," like "a sea-beast crawled forth, which on a shelf / Of rock or sand reposeth." Images of stillness are still perceptions of a thing's action—what it does rather than what it is. The imagination, in Wordsworth's view, perceives the hidden meaning of motions, or discovers action, volition, spirit even in the appearance of total stillness.

Hugo's figurative language makes natural things represent timeless spiritual truths more conclusively. Instead of Wordsworth's verbs, Hugo's metaphors are often substantives in apposition to a noun; they confer new, more exalted names on natural things. To call the sky the pupil of an eye, for example, implies no particular encounter of the mind with an object. Hugo does not brood over the glimpses of eternity shadowed forth in his response to temporal appearances. The symbolic meaning of natural things is as securely attached to them as their color or shape or name. The spiritualizing metaphors are no more contingent on acts of perception than is a royal title.[3]

Hugo's brief poem, "Unité," from Les Contemplations, shows how the kind of symbolic identification implicit in Hugo's individual metaphors can govern the structure of a whole poem:

> Par-dessus l'horizon aux collines brunies,
> Le soleil, cette fleur des splendeurs infinies,
> Se penchait sur la terre à l'heure du couchant;
> Une humble marguerite, éclose au bord d'un champ,
> Sur un mur gris, croulant parmi l'avoine folle,
> Blanche, épanouissait sa candide auréole;
> Et la petite fleur, par-dessus le vieux mur,
> Regardait fixement, dans l'éternel azur,
> Le grand astre épanchant sa lumière immortelle.
> —Et moi, j'ai des rayons aussi! —lui disait-elle.
>
>   (II. 526)

(Above the tawny hills on the horizon, the sun, that flower of all infinite splendor, was looking down on earth at the end of day. A humble daisy, blooming at the edge of a field, on top of a gray wall crumbling among wild oats, was spreading her pure white halo. And the little flower above the old wall was gazing in the eternal blue toward the great star pouring forth its immortal light: "I too have beams," she said.)

"Unité" appears in the first section of Les Contemplations, entitled "Aurore." The two volumes of Les Contemplations form an autobiographical record of the poet's development from 1830 to 1855. Symbolic interpretation of nature belongs, by the design of the volume, to the period of the poet's early maturity. But "Unité" is not itself an autobiographical poem. There is no individual voice in the poem, nor any record of feelings or experience. The poet is unindividualized except for his power to register the symbols offered by nature. At the end, he only echoes the flower's assertion of its own symbolic status.

The poem ends rather flatly; the interesting part comes earlier. After the neutral description of the first line, "Unité" opens into a tribute to the sun, "Le soleil, cette fleur des splendeurs infinies." The metaphor stands in apposition to the noun. The sun is given the new title of flower, and the title is simply declared. At first, the metaphor here may not seem to spiritualize the object, since the sun already has more traditional spiritual dignity than a flower. But it is symptomatic of Hugo's metaphoric practice that the flower in line two is less an object in nature than a figure of speech, part of a rhetorical formula of praise that does, after all, exalt the sun. The sun is the flower of creation, the finest part of the universe, the most splendid of splendors. Although Hugo hints some visual analogy between sun and flower as he pictures the sun bending over the hills at dusk, the metaphor announces the sun's permanent value rather than its impressiveness at a particular time. The suggestion of flowerlike grace in the movement of the sun at twilight is not elaborated. Instead, Hugo turns to identify the flower, the main object of his attention.

The humble white daisy illuminates the dreary wall as the sun gives radiance to the brown earth. Two actions are compared, but there is no development of movement in the metaphor. The daisy does not act notably like the sun; it unfolds its petals in the way that flowers do. Curiously Hugo does not take advantage of the natural fact that daisies close their petals at night, a fact registered in the very name of the English flower, "days-eye." Hugo's daisy is fully open at twilight. Moreover, the placement of words in the lines (their displacement even from ordinary usage) diverts attention from the verbs to the nouns and adjectives, especially to the isolated adjective, "Blanche." The metaphor depends on the color and form of the petals, their halo of white, not on the impression made by this flower's behavior at a particular time.

Hugo reinforces the permanent spiritual meaning of the flower by taking advantage of the symbols fixed in language, partly from etymology. "Candide" come from the Latin *candidus* and designates both the color white and its traditional figurative meaning. The white daisy represents humble but radiant purity, as the very name of the flower in French, "marguerite," signifies purity and preciousness, through its derivation from the Latin, *margarita* or pearl. The association with the name of an early Christian saint, the virgin and martyr, Marguerite, and also the Biblical allusion to "the pearl" in Matthew (13:45-46) are more pertinent to the resonance of the symbol than any naturalistic fact.

Like the halo of a saint, the white circle of petals on the flower represents symbolically the purity of the object and its relationship to the light of God. Like other emblems of divinity—the pearl, a halo, the sun itself—the flower embodies divine light in material form. The analogy between flower and sun discloses the unity of nature from high to low and also the repetition of divine symbols: in nature, history, the Bible, and even in the forms of language.

Natural things in Wordsworth's poetry never acquire such clear and permanent symbolic identity. Chance encounters in the world of time—hearing the song of a solitary reaper, coming upon a leechgatherer or an old blind beggar—yield only glimpses of symbolic meaning. Terrestrial things do not articulate their own symbolic meanings, especially since Wordsworth's imagination tends to discover spirituality in the least articulate things. The poet's mind creates the symbol in our presence; sometimes he even unmakes it again before the end of the poem. In "To a Butterfly," for instance, Wordsworth broods upon the symbolic implications of a butterfly he has been watching, only to turn away in the second stanza of the poem from the symbol he has begun to create:

> I've watched you now a full half-hour,
> Self-poised upon that yellow flower;
> And, little Butterfly! indeed
> I know not if you sleep or feed.
> How motionless!—not frozen seas
> More motionless! and then
> What joy awaits you, when the breeze
> Hath found you out among the trees,
> And calls you forth again!
>
> This plot of orchard-ground is ours;
> My trees they are, my Sister's flowers;
> Here rest your wings when they are weary;
> Here lodge as in a sanctuary!
> Come often to us, fear no wrong;
> Sit near us on the bough!
> We'll talk of sunshine and of song,
> And summer days, when we were young;
> Sweet childish days, that were as long
> As twenty days are now.

The poet has been watching the butterfly for a "full half-hour" without being able to discern exactly what it is doing. Out of his very uncertainty, hints of symbolic meaning begin to arise. The butterfly seems to exemplify the "self-poise" of objects in nature, a serene self-absorption remarkable and strange to the self-conscious and restless observer. The poet holds the mystery of the creature in awe. His mind works upon what he sees, moving from simple exclamation—"How motionless!"—to the surprising metaphor of "frozen seas." The stillness of the small creature brings to the poet's mind an image of the vast, impenetrable forces of nature. As his mind continues its movement, imagining the joy that awaits the butterfly at the call of the breeze, the significance of the creature becomes more complex. By the end of the stanza, the butterfly may be tentatively understood as an emblem of Nature's mystery and remoteness. It also exemplifies the strange harmony of natural life, where the will of the breeze and the joy of the creature are the same, where sleeping and feeding are indistinguishable, where playful gaiety may be preceded by deathlike stillness.

Wordsworth only intimates the larger meaning of the butterfly in the terms of his response. But there is also a melancholy, even slightly impatient undertone to his meditation. The butterfly is indifferent to the speaker's attention and, perhaps for that very reason, seems to embody a poise forever denied to man. Before the subtle hint of envy or longing on the speaker's part becomes explicit, however, he turns abruptly away from the symbolic implications of the spectacle. In the second stanza, the speaker becomes suddenly assertive, patronizing, eager to hold the butterfly back from its impending flight by inviting it to share an intimacy inconceivable in the terms of the earlier symbol. The butterfly changes its meaning to the speaker or, rather, he reduces it to a particular, fragile creature come to rest on his property. The natural world of trees, flowers, earth now appears subject to human ownership. The butterfly may be safe there because of the speaker's gentleness. At the very end, he begins to entertain a new image of the butterfly as a possible companion for nostalgic musing. The essential strangeness of the butterfly is put out of mind as if the creature could be imagined to have the same inner experience as the man and his sister.[4]

In Wordsworth's poetry, the unstable symbolic meaning of natural objects is often both a strength and a problem for the poem. The process of making and sometimes undoing or withdrawing from a symbol gives dramatic movement and complexity to the poem, but we are often unsure how much the poet is in control of these effects. The sense of ironic reversal in the second stanza of "To a Butterfly" may be more vivid to the reader than to the poet; in Wordsworth there is rarely the clear distinction between speaker and poet upon which this kind of irony depends. Even so, we can feel sure that Wordsworth does mean to show how the symbolic meaning of a butterfly is contingent upon the observer. The things of nature assert no fixed meaning apart from one's power to see with the eye of imagination. Hugo's metaphors, in contrast, grant permanent validity to the symbolic terms, in the way that the bread and wine of the Eucharist have permanent symbolic meaning apart from any individual act of Communion. Recognition of the divinity symbolically present in nature does not, for Hugo, in itself signify communion. Hugo's figurative style gives natural symbols a dogmatic, almost ecclesiastical authority rather than the force of inward persuasion.

It is therefore appropriate that in one of Hugo's most explicit statements of faith, Nature appears to enact a version of the Catholic Mass. In "Relligio,"[5] the poet answers the question, "quelle est ta bible?" (what is your Bible?) by pointing to the sky:

> La lune à l'horizon montait, hostie énorme;
> Tout avait le frisson, le pin, le cèdre et l'orme,
>   Le loup, et l'aigle, et l'alcyon;
> Lui montrant l'astre d'or sur la terre obscurcie,
> Je lui dis:—Courbe-toi. Dieu lui-même officie,
>   Et voici l'élévation.
>
> (II. 778)

(On the horizon the moon was rising, enormous wafer; everything was shivering, the pine, the cedar, and the elm, the wolf, the eagle, and the halcyon; pointing to the golden star on the darkened earth, I said: "Kneel down. God himself is officiating, and this is the elevation of the Host.")

The poet boldly leaves the Church to worship in the temple of Nature. But the service there is still a form of the Mass. The moon, in a rather grotesque metaphor, symbolically represents an enormous wafer of Communion. Hugo is initiated into all the details of the natural Mass but even here he does not seem moved to take Communion, nor does he intimate how one may actually partake of the divinity embodied in natural forms.

In the absence of the poet's direct experience of communion, Hugo's poetry of nature tends toward one or another form of creed or sermon. In "Relligio," the poet preaches to a companion. In other poems, the reader, or Man generally, is lectured. Hugo characteristically establishes an initiated commentator in the poem who instructs an ignorant, perhaps skeptical, sometimes even recalcitrant audience. When Hugo uses the fiction of talking birds or flowers, he divides his voice into both commentator and audience, but with a clear distinction between the voices sustained. One voice, often the main voice in the poem, affirms the divinity symbolically present in nature. The purpose is reassurance, but the tone is often reproachful, as if the other figure were holding stubbornly to gloom. Occasionally, the resistance becomes active, and the poem approaches the form and tone of debate. The voices of nature tediously insist upon their reassuring secrets but, despite a show of patient attention, the human figure within the poem seems as unmoved as the reader.

Hugo's poetry of nature sometimes seems on the verge of acknowledging its own dullness. In "Je lisais . . . ," for example, the human voice within the poem unambiguously announces the hollowness of nature's sermon, yet Hugo nevertheless allows a black martin to preach his unpersuasive doctrine at length: "Tout est plein de jour, même la nuit; / Et tout ce qui travaille, éclaire, aime ou détruit, / A des rayons" (II. 584). (Everything is full of light, even the night; and everything that works, gives light, loves, or destroys, has beams.)

The poet shows himself dutifully attentive to the bird's pieties, but he is like an unpromising novice in an alien religious order. He never swerves from his own conviction that the essential facts of human life are sinfulness and death:

> Je répondis:—Hélas! tu te trompes, oiseau.
> Ma chair, faite de cendre, à chaque instant succombe;
> Mon âme ne sera blanche que dans la tombe;
> Car l'homme, quoiqu'il fasse, est aveugle ou méchant.—
> Et je continuai la lecture du champ.
> (II. 585)

(I answered: "—Alas! bird, you are wrong. My flesh, made of ashes, yields at every instant; my soul will not be white until the grave. For man, whatever he does, is blind or wicked.—" And I went on reading the book of the field.)

The debate seems pointless, for the man states his conviction decisively. His generalizations and paradoxes have the same authoritative tone as the bird's. There is no movement toward conversion intimated in the poem, nor even any real debate, for the bird and the man have really nothing to say to each other. Continuing reverence for the Book of Nature in the face of the man's own contrary certainty seems merely perfunctory. Nature's lesson in the poem is as pedantic and doctrinaire as a Sunday School lesson, but with even less relevance than orthodox Christian doctrine to the man's simply stated consciousness of his destiny: "Mon âme ne sera blanche que dans la tombe."

Hugo's pitting of Nature's dogma against human feeling differs from the ambivalence of feeling often expressed by Wordsworth. Different attitudes toward death, for example, do not oppose each other in doctrinal debate in Wordsworth's poetry, where the grounding of the poem in perception avoids both the didacticism and the artificiality of Hugo's talking birds and flowers. Wordsworth shows human feeling open to Nature's influence—literally, a flowing in of experience. Indeed, the experience of perception in Wordsworth's poetry is what finally distinguishes the living from the dead. The dead neither see nor hear. The living do, and this essential fact of life generates ambivalent feelings: fear, joy, sorrow, awe, reconciliation. In Wordsworth's elegiac poetry, from the Lucy sequence to the sonnet, "Surprised by Joy," the poet's perception of the still living earth variously complicates his grief for a dead person and his attitude toward his own mortality. Imaginative perception comes to seem intrinsic to mourning and also to whatever reconciliation to death may follow.

There is no counterpart to Wordsworthian elegy in the poetry of Victor Hugo. Never "surprised by joy" in a landscape, Hugo has no basis for Wordsworth's rich and ambiguous interplay of feeling and perception. Hugo seems cut off from the main sources of richness in the Wordsworthian mode by his unyielding conviction that the deepest human feelings are untouched by natural appearances. Yet by preserving the separateness of human consciousness, Hugo also avoids certain constraints of the Wordsworthian tradition. He seems freer than the English poet to turn away, simply and decisively, from spectacles which have nothing to do with him. In some of Hugo's most interesting poems after 1843 (beginning with the elegies for his daughter), Hugo abandons the effort to be either the priest or the obedient parishioner in Nature's temple. The unpersuasiveness of Nature's blessing, implicit in the style of the earlier poetry, becomes more explicit. The poet's sense of his separate consciousness either becomes the poetic subject or else frees the poet to consider other subjects. Sorrow, mourning, consciousness of sin, longing for another person or for death—these distinctively human feelings are made to overshadow all that the nonhuman world may show or signify. In the poem, "La clarté du dehors . . . ," for example, to disregard nature comes to seem like fortitude and integrity, a refusal to be distracted from the distinctively human experience of spiritual hope or despair:

> Moi, je laisse voler les senteurs et les baumes,
> Je laisse chuchoter les fleurs, ces doux fantômes,
>   Et l'aube dire: Vous vivrez!
> Je regarde en moi-même, et, seul, oubliant l'heure,
> L'oeil plein des visions de l'ombre intérieure,
>   Je songe aux morts, ces délivrés!
>
> (II. 604)

(As for me, I let the balmy scents waft through the air; I let the flowers—those sweet ghosts—whisper, and let the dawn say: "You shall live!" I look into myself, and, alone, oblivious of time, my eye full of visions of the inner shadows, I think of the dead, the liberated!)

In Hugo's late poems, the word "vision," instead of referring to the poet's knowledge of nature's hidden spirituality, comes to mean the vivid consciousness of inner states of mind and feeling: "L'oeil plein des visions de l'ombre intérieure." This idea of "vision" returns Hugo to the record of "des états d'âme," in Rousseau's sense, but with a difference, for Hugo regards the inner world itself as if it were a spectacle. He need not rely on the direct statement of feeling, as Rousseau did, for all the reservoirs of image and metaphor which he opened for the description of nature are also available for the symbolic landscape of the inner life. Through the traditional religious associations of the imagery, Hugo's symbols of feeling can seem like "visions" of objective spiritual truth, but the poet's visionary power does not sustain itself on the "quickening impulse" of "sensible impressions," in the Wordsworthian way. His inward eye does not dwell on even the memory of nature's spectacle, for his sense of spiritual reassurance or despair has its own rhythm, separate from nature and untouched by its apparent life.

The nonperceptual character of Hugo's figurative language acquires new value in poems that emphasize the separate and inward origin of human spirituality. When Hugo was ostensibly studying the Bible of Nature, the uncertain grounding of his imagery in perception was confusing. But the same kind of imagery strengthens the impressions of the poet's deliberate turning away from the visible light: "La clarté du dehors ne distrait pas mon âme" (II. 604). (Outer brightness does not distract my soul.) The surreal landscape of the mind is bright or dark irrespective of Nature's appearance:

> On croit être à cette heure où la terre éveillée
> Entend le bruit que fait l'ouverture du jour,
> Le premier pas du vent, du travail, de l'amour,
> De l'homme, et le verrou de la porte sonore,
> Et le hennissement du blanc cheval aurore.
> ("Eclaircie," II. 759)

(It feels like the hour when the awakened earth hears the sound of opening day: the first step of the wind, of labor, of love, of man, and the lock of the sonorous door, and the neighing of the white horse dawn.)

A state of spiritual illumination feels like dawn, but no natural dawn brings joy, as Wordsworth's sunrise does in Book IV of *The Prelude*. Hugo's nonperceptual imagery enforces the idea that Grace does not, cannot, originate in perception. His image of the white horse dawn positively flouts naturalistic fact. Dawn does not sound at all like the neighing of a white horse. This dawn exists in the mind, not in nature; it is a symbol of spiritual illumination in a private mythology with traditional supernatural associations—here, to Apollo and also to the white horse in the Book of Revelation.

"Le Pont," the poem that opens Hugo's last, visionary book of *Les Contemplations*, altogether separates spiritual darkness and illumination from the common light of day:

> J'avais devant les yeux les ténèbres. L'abîme
> Qui n'a pas de rivage et qui n'a pas de cime
> Etait là, morne, immense; et rien n'y remuait.
> Je me sentais perdu dans l'infini muet.
> Au fond, à travers l'ombre, impénétrable voile,
> On apercevait Dieu comme une sombre étoile.
> Je m'écriai:—Mon âme, ô mon âme! il faudrait,
> Pour traverser ce gouffre où nul bord n'apparaît,
> Et pour qu'en cette nuit jusqu'à ton Dieu tu marches,
> Bâtir un pont géant sur des millions d'arches.
> Qui le pourra jamais? Personne! ô deuil! effroi!
> Pleure!—Un fantôme blanc se dressa devant moi
> Pendant que je jetais sur l'ombre un oeil d'alarme,
> Et ce fantôme avait la forme d'une larme;

C'était un front de vierge avec des mains d'enfant;
Il ressemblait au lys que la blancheur défend;
Ses mains en se joignant faisaient de la lumière.
Il me montra l'abîme où va toute poussière,
Si profond, que jamais un écho n'y répond,
Et me dit:—Si tu veux, je bâtirai le pont.
Vers ce pâle inconnu je levai ma paupière.
—Quel est ton nom? lui dis-je. Il me dit:—La prière.

(II. 721)

(Dark shadows were before my eyes. The abyss which has no shore and no summit was there, dismal, immense; and nothing was stirring in it. I felt lost in the voiceless infinite. In the depths, through the impenetrable shade, God was discernible, like a somber star. I cried out: "My soul, o my soul! To cross over this chasm which seems boundless, and to walk up to your God in this night, you would have to build a bridge on a million arches. Who could ever do it? No one! O grief! O terror! Weep!" A pale ghost rose before me as I glanced in fear into the darkness, and this ghost had the form of a tear, the forehead of a virgin, and the hands of a child. It looked like the lily whose whiteness is its defense. Its hands drawn together emanated light. It showed me the abyss into which all dust goes, so deep that it never sends back any echo, and it said: "If you wish, I shall build the bridge." I raised my eyes toward this pale stranger. "What is your name?" I asked. It told me: "Prayer.")

The abyss in "Le Pont" is a symbolic landscape that reappears, more memorably, in the poetry of Baudelaire. We shall see that Baudelaire's landscape of despair is more interesting than Hugo's; it is more complex and elusive in its significance. Yet Baudelaire's originality, as well as his continuity with other French poetry in the nineteenth century, stands out more clearly when we realize that his symbolic landscape of the mind is also fully visible in poems by Victor Hugo.

Spiritual darkness is all the eye can see in "Le Pont." We are not tempted to mistake the scene for an actual place in nature—its shape, or rather its shapelessness—is as evidently symbolic as the image of Chaos in *Paradise Lost* (which Hugo probably had in mind for his own image):[6]

> . . . a dark
> Illimitable Ocean, without bound,
> Without dimension; where length, breadth and highth
> And time and place are lost.

(II. 891-894)

Milton paradoxically uses the essence of physical definition—the very idea of "dimension"—to designate a place apart from any place, "The womb of Nature, and perhaps her grave." In Book X of *Paradise Lost*, Sin and Death build a bridge across this abyss for easier passage between Hell and Earth. As Anne Ferry has argued, the allegorical character of Milton's language in this part of the poem separates Sin, Death, and the bridge across Chaos from other characters and places in Milton's myth.[7] Eden, or even the region where Satan and his troops reign, are "real" places in Milton's story, though their physical character also has metaphoric significance. The bridge across Chaos, in contrast, seems to have only symbolic existence. It is an emblem of the moral and spiritual condition created by Satan, born of his mind like his offspring, Sin and Death. Hugo's abyss in "Le Pont" is also a projected image. The landscape of the mind becomes visible, as in a dream or hallucination. The poet recognizes the abyss; he is not encountering it for the first time. Whether a recurrent vision of his own has returned or whether he recognizes the universal and traditional landscape of spiritual despair—*that* abyss, the one without boundary, was there.

No suggestion appears in "Le Pont" that the abyss may be illuminated by the light of nature: "On apercevait Dieu comme une sombre étoile." The dark star is not an emblem of divinity discovered in nature. The verb "apercevoir" defines an awakening of consciousness, different from natural perception. A peculiarly unnatural star figuratively expresses the poet's awareness that God is present, though infinitely remote, as alien and unwelcoming as a dark star. Natural stars in themselves play no role in the spiritual drama.

In *Paradise Lost* the bridge to boundless darkness was built for all men by Sin and Death at the time of the Fall. By imagining a bridge to God built by Prayer, Hugo tries to revise Milton's story, eliminating the figure of Christ. Natural perception cannot bridge the abyss separating man from the divine; but neither is Christ necessary. Hugo seems to argue that man has within him the power to create the exit from despair by envisioning it, just as he creates the abyss through inner vision. Prayer appears first in the form of a tear, as if to signify the power of human suffering by itself to generate its own release. The poet cries, or commands himself to cry; immediately the white phantom in the form of a tear appears.

The weakness of Hugo's argument, however, becomes apparent in his own failure to make the vision of spiritual hope strong enough to stand against the vision of despair earlier in the poem. The first six lines are the vivid part of the poem. Hugo's figure of Prayer never becomes more than a phantom patched out of Christian remnants: the face of a virgin, the hands of a child, the whiteness of a lily. The attributes of Prayer are doctrinaire, yet without living connection to the doctrine they evoke. Nor can we translate the Christian fragments into symbols of purely personal feeling, for their meaning is rooted in a definite theology. In the first part of "Le Pont," a symbolic landscape with traditional religious overtones effectively represents feelings of despair and fear. Prayer also seems to represent a state of feeling, but the poetic form for that emotion never becomes more than an awkward contrivance. The language is dull in comparison to the beginning of the poem, and the speaker remains peculiarly dissociated from his own vision.

Hugo introduces traditional religious symbols to carry spiritual promises into the void, almost as if he were anticipating T. S. Eliot: "These fragments I have shored against my ruins." But Eliot's fragments are incomparably richer than Hugo's brief and lifeless lily, child, and tear, and Eliot also expects less of them. Hugo's Prayer is supposed to build a powerful structure, "Bâtir un pont géant sur des millions des arches," yet the poem neither affirms a theology nor creates the impression of an emotion which could support the effort. As in his earlier poems of natural theology, the reassurance seems arbitrary and contrived. An optimistic voice speaks with confidence but with no accountable source of authority. The phantom Prayer in "Le Pont" is therefore no more persuasive than the pedantic black martin in "Je lisais. . . ." Hugo wants to show the human spirit capable of generating its own vision of salvation. But the reassurances in Hugo's poetry of vision can seem as remote from inward conviction as the sermons of birds and flowers.

Baudelaire, in "De Profundis clamavi" (among other poems), avoids Hugo's weakness by directly confronting the mind's incapacity to transcend its own vision of despair. As if to expose Hugo's ineffectual resolution in "Le Pont," Baudelaire actually begins his poem in prayer, but no promise of redemption ensues. The inwardness of vision in Baudelaire's poetry tends to mean that the poet is constrained to hear only his own voice and he has nothing new to tell himself. Thus, instead of Hugo's vague spiritual optimism, Baudelaire challenges the very idea of redemption through poetic vision. The challenge is profound in implication, for if the act of vision is not redemptive, the poet has no special spiritual authority and poetry must relinquish the presumption to spiritual guidance.

> J'implore ta pitié, Toi, l'unique que j'aime,
> Du fond du gouffre obscur où mon coeur est tombé.
> C'est un univers morne à l'horizon plombé,
> Où nagent dans la nuit l'horreur et le blasphème;
>
> Un soleil sans chaleur plane au-dessus six mois,
> Et les six autres mois la nuit couvre la terre;
> C'est un pays plus nu que la terre polaire;
> —Ni bêtes, ni ruisseaux, ni verdure, ni bois!
>
> Or il n'est pas d'horreur au monde qui surpasse
> La froide cruauté de ce soleil de glace
> Et cette immense nuit semblable au vieux Chaos;
>
> Je jalouse le sort des plus vils animaux
> Qui peuvent se plonger dans un sommeil stupide,
> Tant l'écheveau du temps lentement se dévide!

(I implore your pity from the depths of the dark abyss where my heart is fallen, Thou, the only one I love. It is a bleak world, with a low leaden sky, where horror and blasphemy swim in the night. A sun without warmth hovers for six months, and the other six months night covers the earth; it is a land more barren than the polar wastes—no beasts, nor brooks, nor grass, nor woods! There surely is no horror in the world greater than the cold cruelty of this icy sun and this vast night, like old Chaos. I envy the fate of the lowest animals who can sink into dumb sleep, so slowly does the skein of time unwind!)

Echoes of Hugo's vocabulary—"gouffre obscur," "un univers morne," "immense nuit"—identify the same abyss evoked in "Le Pont."[8] The image of Chaos, suggested by Hugo's description, is explicit in "De Profundis clamavi." The dissociation of this landscape from nature is explicit too, in the paradoxically frozen sun and in the dark, cold barrenness of the scene, empty of all natural life.

In "De Profundis clamavi," however, Baudelaire uses the traditional overtones of his imagery to quite different effect than Hugo. Whereas Hugo wants to generalize the character of his despair so that his redeeming vision will also have public authority, Baudelaire manipulates the impression of familiarity to suggest the common tedium of his condition. His sense of the abyss may represent the universal plight of the fallen spirit, but Baudelaire's speaker seems more concerned with how his commonness shades into cliché. He seems to regard even his own despair as a cliché, if only because he has known it so long. There is a peculiar flatness to the poetic voice, as if, to him, even horror had become mundane: "Or il n'est pas d'horreur au monde qui surpasse / La froide cruauté de ce soleil de glace." He seems too much the connoisseur of horror to be aroused by talking about it.

In its most straightforward form, in the form most often attempted by Hugo, the symbolic representation of feeling works by objectification. Instead of stating feeling directly ("I feel horror, dread, hopelessness"), the poet shows us a world of objects. The symbolic objects represent feeling; we infer from the poet's descriptive language what feelings govern his experience. Symbolic vision thus releases the poet from the banality of a direct vocabulary of emotion. A limitless reservoir of things—from nature, from other literature, from the Bible—becomes available to express the inner life, to give it variety and significance.

Baudelaire, however, makes the relationship of feeling to symbolic vision less straightforward, even paradoxical. In his language, feelings often become so objectified that they no longer even seem to belong to the poetic voice. The sense of dissociation between feeling and vision that is confusing at the end of "Le Pont" becomes a device for irony in "De Profundis clamavi." The vision of the abyss represents horror, but the feeling of horror no longer dominates the poet's tone, as it does in Hugo's direct exclamation, "ô deuil! effroi!" In "De Profundis clamavi," horror becomes an object, out there, in the symbolic landscape: "Où nagent dans la nuit l'horreur et le blasphème." Baudelaire treats the name of his feeling as though it were a thing, separate from him, and, in a sense, it is separate, for the voice in the poem seems devoid of horror. The poet sounds more bored than afraid; or, if afraid, then only of his own tedium.

Baudelaire thus uses symbolic vision to distance his voice from the monotony of his emotions. The symbol of feeling becomes, at least in part, ironic, for it registers the absence rather than the presence of lively feeling in the poet. Baudelaire plays the monotonous rhythm of his voice against the extremity of his symbols. Whereas Rousseau used the rhythms of his prose to suggest more intensity, more immediacy of emotion than his words of feeling could contain, Baudelaire turns his more varied metaphoric language to the reverse effect of exposing how dull even his extremity of feeling is. He dramatizes the peculiar horror of coming to feel less not more than the content of his language states.

Yet the Baudelaire poem still records "un état d'âme." The drama in "De Profundis clamavi" is totally inward; as in Rousseau, the important relationship is between the poet's feeling (or lack of feeling) and his language, rather than between the mind and any external reality. That the poet is confined to his exclusively inner world is, indeed, the essence of his monotonous plight, for despite the initial form of prayer, the poem intimates no possibility that any presence from outside the mind could penetrate this abyss. Nor can his mind alone create even the illusion of other forms. From Baudelaire's point of view, Hugo is naïve to grant suffering the power to generate a phantom visitor to the abyss. Baudelaire insists instead upon the sterile repetitiveness of spiritual despair. As in many other poems by Baudelaire, the tedium rather than the intensity of the inner life becomes Baudelaire's main theme in "De Profundis clamavi"—indirectly through the style of the entire poem, and then, explicitly, in the lament of the final stanza:

> Je jalouse le sort des plus vils animaux
> Qui peuvent se plonger dans un sommeil stupide,
> Tant l'écheveau du temps lentement se dévide!

(I envy the fate of the lowest animals who can sink into dumb sleep, so slowly does the skein of time unwind!)

No Wordsworthian perception of nature's mysterious "self-poise" complicates Baudelaire's envy of beasts. His image of dumb sleep represents only his desire to escape consciousness of monotony. He can imagine no release other than bestial oblivion, for by the end of the poem, even the act of envisioning the abyss seems part of the monotony of being there. The skein of time continues its slow unwinding, whether or not the poet busies himself with futile descriptions of his plight.

Instead of moving toward some moral or religious resolution, in the manner of Hugo, Baudelaire turns the act of symbolic vision self-consciously against itself. The "état d'âme" in the poem seems utterly hopeless, yet there is an odd tone of triumph at the end. Though the image of the skein offers no promise of escape, the image itself is new in the poem and it has a satisfying decisiveness. The unexpected grammatical turn of the last sentence suggests a play of mind at odds with the yearning for oblivion. As the formal design of the sonnet comes neatly to completion, one is drawn to separate the satisfaction of the poetic form from the hopelessness of statement within the poem. Regardless of what Baudelaire says about endless monotony, the poem itself does finally manage to interrupt, if not actually halt, the dull unraveling of time.

In "De Profundis clamavi," the sonnet itself is the one object to appear in the abyss. This object is not a bridge to salvation. Yet Baudelaire's design gives the aesthetic gesture a symbolic importance it does not have for Victor Hugo. The completed form of the poem in itself becomes a symbol of human freedom and inventiveness. Though the poet envisions no escape from the abyss, in the end he unexpectedly does succeed in forming his inner emptiness into a definite shape. He contrives the decisive ending by himself, with no aid from external impressions. No new experience has changed or even touched his mind. His consciousness is not penetrated even by any outside measure of time. Yet though he remains as deep in the abyss as before, the gesture of the poem also represents the unpredictable and subtle power of the poet's spirit to rescue itself from oblivion by the very way he expresses his yearning for it. Through a surprising turn of image and phrase, the poet shapes his formless despair into the strict form of the sonnet. He asserts control, if not mastery, over his inner void by containing it in the clear forms of his art.

9

The Lovely Behavior of Things
Hopkins and Baudelaire

When the sole satisfaction of poetic form replaces belief in even the possibility of other satisfactions, all kinds of figurative language come to seem equally attractive—but also uniformly sterile. Although Baudelaire creates his poetic designs with images, the things that make up his imagery seem to have no value in themselves. They have no life of their own; they represent no possibilities of experience in the world. Nature offers one among other sources of metaphor, but natural images hold no special promise. They do not even create the presence in the poem of an order of life separate from consciousness. Like Hugo, Baudelaire often deforms the natural image, as if to insist upon the mind's separation from nature as an actual influence. In the abyss of the mind, stars can be dark, dawn can neigh like a horse; the sun can be cold, night can last six months. The denaturalized image represents an inner state at the same time as it obliterates the presence of nature as a real spectacle, a living force offering gifts or demanding response. In this kind of image, nature does not press on the mind, guiding the poet's mood, nor does the outside world resist human moods by the force of its own asserted life.

In many poems by Baudelaire, the only reality that imposes itself on the mind is time. And even time, to Baudelaire, lacks the palpable objective form common to English nineteenth-century poetry in images of changing natural appearances: seasons, sunrises, the blossoming or decay of flowers. Baudelaire's experience of time is more abstract and hardly separable from an inner state. His skeins and clocks intrude without warning or disappear altogether. The rhythm of time is variable, as entirely dependent on consciousness as all the other images in the poetry.

Nineteenth-century English poetry offers few counterparts to the French dissociation of consciousness from the forms of outer things. In "The Darkling Thrush," Hardy's bird still has the power to obtrude itself on human awareness, though the significance of the perception is uncertain. In a sense, the winter desolation in the poem projects and represents the poet's own spiritual deadness, yet that cold dusk also has a strong, natural presence of its own in Hardy's language, in contrast to the purely symbolic abyss of Hugo and Baudelaire.

Gerard Manley Hopkins, in individual images and parts of poems, seems at times to go further than other Victorians to withdraw the mind from the influence of external appearances. Like Hugo and Baudelaire, Hopkins asserts the thoroughly inward sources of spiritual life or death through paradoxical manipulations of light and darkness: "I wake and feel the fell of dark, not day." In "No Worst, There Is None," the Romantic landscape of the sublime becomes purely figurative, symbolic of totally inward spiritual conditions: "O the mind, mind has mountains; cliffs of fall / Frightful, sheer, no-man-fathomed. Hold them cheap / May who ne'er hung there." But these paradoxes and conceits, important as they are to Hopkins' reputation as a "modern" poet, rarely dominate an entire poem. Hopkins is especially interesting in comparison to Baudelaire because Hopkins so remarkably combines earlier and post-Romantic devices of style with the basic forms of English Romantic perception. Compared to other Victorians, Hopkins does react more decisively against Wordsworthian perception, both by his Catholicism and by his affiliation with seventeenth-century religious poetry. Yet Hopkins is most remarkable when he succeeds in renewing the English Romantic idea of imaginative perception at the same time as he probes its limitations. The beautiful poem, "Hurrahing in Harvest," illustrates this achievement:

> Summer ends now; now, barbarous in beauty, the stooks rise
> Around; up above, what wind-walks! what lovely
> behavior
> Of silk-sack clouds! has wilder, willful-wavier
> Meal-drift moulded ever and melted across skies?

I walk, I lift up, I lift up heart, eyes,
Down all that glory in the heavens to glean our Saviour;
And, eyes, heart, what looks, what lips yet gave you a
Rapturous love's greeting of realer, of rounder replies?

And the azurous hung hills are his world-wielding shoulder
Majestic—as a stallion stalwart, very-violet-sweet!—
These things, these things were here and but the beholder
Wanting; which two when they once meet,
The heart rears wings bold and bolder
And hurls for him, O half hurls earth for him off under his
    feet.[1]

Hopkins begins with the excitement characteristic of the English poet in the nineteenth century: "Summer ends now; now, barbarous in beauty." A marvelous event is happening, in time, in nature. The poet watches; he exclaims, describes, responds. It is true that this poet-observer is more openly an inventor of language than Wordsworth; his sound effects and surprising metaphors are frankly meant to dazzle. But in stanzas one and two of "Hurrahing in Harvest" poetic inventiveness remains obedient to the act of natural perception. The images of silk-sack clouds and meal-drift, the soaring effects of the sound and rhythm register the impression made by wind, cloud, and sheaves of corn, a visual reality apart from the poet's figurative contrivances. The sense of "love's greeting" is a response to the "lovely behaviour" of the landscape on this day.

When Hopkins uses the image of lips, he evokes a more definite sense of spiritual greeting than the feelings of blessing in Wordsworth's poetry. Yet Hopkins does not follow Hugo to envision the soul invisibly, directly kissed by Spirit, as in "Eclaircie": "une âme obscure, épanouie en tout, / Avance doucement sa bouche vers nos lèvres" (a hidden soul, in full bloom, gently brings her mouth near our lips). Hopkins only compares his feeling to the greeting of lips, human lips presumably, as if to exclaim that no human greeting gives more substantial love than what he feels on this occasion. To Hopkins, it is important that "love's greeting" through nature is real and round, with sensory weight and presence to the eye as well as to the heart. True to the Wordsworthian idea of the poet, Hopkins both perceives and creates the glory of a reality which exists in nature apart from him, "these things were here and but the beholder / Wanting." The landscape now greets him with love because he sees it imaginatively, with "heart, eyes," "eyes, heart."

Wordsworthian imagination, however, cannot altogether account for the rapture of "Hurrahing in Harvest." The imagination alone cannot create belief in "our Saviour," nor does it allow the heart boldly to hurl earth away. Though at the end "half hurls" qualifies the boldness slightly, there is an ecstasy in the imagery and sound of Hopkins' last stanza beyond the reach of Wordsworth's meditative joy.

Hopkins' poem defies natural limits, including the ambiguous and generous limits of natural feeling marked by Wordsworth. Even the title, "Hurrahing in Harvest," flouts natural expectation for, as Hopkins acknowledges, harvest signals the end of summer as well as its fulfillment. Yet Hopkins intimates none of the natural sorrow associated with all endings, however rich and beautiful they may be.

Wordsworth leads only part of the way to Hopkins' joy. The sadness of autumn does not altogether disappear, for example, from Wordsworth's celebration in "The Solitary Reaper." Wordsworth does hear a melancholy undertone in the reaper's song and the poem ends not in rapture but with a measured acknowledgement of time gone by: "The music in my heart I bore / Long after it was heard no more." Wordsworth's subtlety in the poem is in the balance between the melancholy beauty of natural time—music that fills the valley and then is heard no more—and the poet's simultaneous feeling of more enduring harmony. The reaper participates in this harmony by her age-old ritual, and the poet indirectly enters it by his imaginative response to her. He carries her song out of its limited place in time, yet the undertone of melancholy remains, even in the enduring music of his own poem.

Hopkins hurls past Wordsworth's measured celebration to the fuller rapture open to the Christian beholder of harvest. An unexplained act of religious faith lifts Hopkins from Wordsworth's valley to the definite image of a Saviour in the heavens. In the last stanza of "Hurrahing in Harvest," Hopkins displays the clarity and freedom of the imagination empowered by Christian faith. Beautiful forms, reminiscent of pagan deities, appear in the images of "the world-wielding shoulder" and "stallion stalwart." Wordsworth yearned to see again the pagan gods, granting them clarity and excitement difficult to equal by his own more ambiguous perceptions of nature. Hopkins answers Wordsworth's lament in "The World is Too Much With Us" by making the

Christian seem the true inheritor of pagan myth. Some version of Proteus rising in the sea is made to seem, paradoxically, less alien to Hopkins' Christian than to Wordsworth's naturalistic imagination.

Hopkins clarifies the cloudy affirmations of earlier nineteenth-century English poetry by returning the imagination to a firmer grounding in Christian faith. But Hopkins' flight of language and spirit transcends the natural without at all denying the reality or beauty of nature's "lovely behaviour." The poem does not belittle the beautiful natural world. The stooks, the silk-sack clouds, and then, finally, the azurous hung hills, remain *here, now* in the poem. Whatever else the poet's spirit beholds, these things are beautiful in themselves, full of sweetness, color, warmth, and motion.

I have been arguing that neither Hugo nor Baudelaire grant nature the power to make any comparable impression on a beholder. In Hugo's poetry, the very character of the figurative language withholds vitality from nature even when that effect jars with the poet's ostensible piety. In the late visionary poems, Hugo's flights and descents of spirit lead him away from natural appearances rather than toward the complex adjustment of perception and faith seen in Hopkins. Baudelaire goes much further than Hugo to admit, even insist upon the essential deadness behind appearances. The sterility of the object— especially the object most graceful and lively on the surface—is often what the Baudelaire poem is finally about, sometimes in playfulness, more often with an undertone of bitter and vindictive disappointment:

> Avec ses vêtements ondoyants et nacrés,
> Même quand elle marche on croirait qu'elle danse,
> Comme ces longs serpents que les jongleurs sacrés
> Au bout de leurs bâtons agitent en cadence.
>
> Comme le sable morne et l'azur des déserts,
> Insensibles tous deux à l'humaine souffrance,
> Comme les longs réseaux de la houle des mers,
> Elle se développe avec indifférence.
>
> Ses yeux polis sont faits de minéraux charmants,
> Et dans cette nature étrange et symbolique
> Où l'ange inviolé se mêle au sphinx antique,
>
> Où tout n'est qu'or, acier, lumière et diamants,
> Resplendit à jamais, comme un astre inutile,
> La froide majesté de la femme stérile.

(In her flowing and iridescent clothes, she appears to dance even as she walks, like those long snakes which holy jugglers wave rhythmically at the end of their batons. Like the bleak sand and the bright desert sky, both insensitive to human suffering; like the endless network of the rolling waves, she slowly unfolds, remote, indifferent. Her polished eyes are made of enchanting stones; and in this strange and symbolic nature, where undefiled angel and ancient sphinx combine, where all is pure gold, steel, light, and diamonds, there forever shines, like a useless star, the cold majesty of the sterile woman.)

In a tone of casual appreciation, this sonnet begins in praise of a woman's lively appearance. The poem is not the symbolic projection of an inner state, like "De Profundis clamavi," nor is it ostensibly a poem about the relation of the mind to nature. We may place it more easily in a sonnet tradition of lovers' complaints—praise and lament for the mysterious beauty of an inaccessible woman. As in other love sonnets, however, the figurative language in the poem generalizes the theme. To Baudelaire's mind, this woman resembles nature in its most mysterious and majestic forms. In a sense, Baudelaire is not talking about his feelings for a woman at all. The poem uses the figure of a lively woman to probe the relationship of the mind to all beautiful appearances and to assert the value of art as a form of insight and possession.

In the sonnet tradition, the poet-lover, often under a guise of nonchalance, threatens the unreceptive woman with her dependence on his power to preserve beauty through art. Baudelaire, in this sonnet (as in the more famous poem "La Charogne"), continues this traditional theme, but with a difference, for this poet seems intent upon showing his power to destroy rather than to preserve the woman. The sonnet does, in effect, destroy her. The poet first exposes the essential emptiness behind her surface beauty; then he seems to discard her altogether as a real living presence within the poem. In the last stanza, the ambiguous word "resplendit" does not refer mainly to the glitter of the woman's presence, as one expects, but to the brilliance of the symbol which displaces her. By the end, the particular woman disappears into the symbol which the poet announces with a mixture of bitterness and satisfaction. Her nature has come to represent the essence of sterility in human form and, more generally, the majestic emptiness of all superficially beautiful appearances.

Baudelaire intimates the final symbolic statement of the poem even in his casual opening description, for he announces right away the possible deceptiveness of this woman's appearance. Her glittering clothing makes her look as if she were dancing even when she is not. The general observer, "on," naïvely believes his eyes, but Baudelaire presents himself as more knowing, not bound to appearances for his knowledge of reality.

Baudelaire's language claims a different authority over the reader than does Wordsworthian imaginative perception. Baudelaire seems to articulate what is objectively and always true about this woman, rather than the implications of his response to her on any particular occasion. While Wordsworth invites us to witness, if not accompany, the movement of his mind from appearance to meaning, Baudelaire more abruptly reports that he knows what cannot be seen. He does not show the progress of his mind toward knowledge. He therefore discourages the sense of shared experience between poet and reader that is one effect of metaphors rooted in perception. Wordsworth summons us to "Behold" the solitary reaper. Hopkins, in "The Starlight Night," exclaims, "Look at the stars! Look, look up at the skies!" The English poet invites us to see appearances anew; his metaphoric language teaches new ways of seeing. Even in poems of private meditation, images of perception draw the reader to follow the mind's movement from appearance to meaning: "I've watched you now a full half-hour / Self-poised upon that yellow flower." Wordsworth suggests that the appearance of the butterfly has meaning, however uncertain his grasp of it. His mind seeks that meaning by brooding over what his eye sees. When Wordsworth compares the butterfly to "frozen seas," the surprising metaphor is still rooted in the impression of motionlessness. Though the strange leap between images suggests some special power, if not idiosyncrasy, to the poet's activity of mind, we feel that he nevertheless relies on processes of observation and thought also available to us.

I do not want to exaggerate the impression of secret authority in the opening lines of Baudelaire's sonnet, for the tone is light, casual, admiring. More obscure and sinister undertones, however, quickly appear in the comparison of the woman's movement to "ces longs serpents que les jongleurs sacrés / Au bout de leur bâtons agitent en cadence." Jugglers and their batons are playful and gay, but there is also some further connotation of trickery, some secret magic or sleight-of-hand. Even more important is the sudden obscurity of the simile. Baudelaire speaks as if we all know about snakes at the end of jugglers' batons, presumably in some esoteric ritual. Since we probably do not know, the actual effect of the comparison is to increase the poet's air of special authority. The poet here seems to possess mysterious, esoteric stores of analogy. Instead of participating in his act of imaginative discovery, we wait, with a vaguely ominous expectation, for him to disclose his meaning as he will.

Like Hugo, Baudelaire creates the effect of a catalogue of comparisons. The woman's movements are as subtle as the apparent dance of snakes, as elusive as the shifting of sands, as the network of ocean currents, but like all these mysterious motions, hers too are only deceptive appearances of life. They are "insensibles" in more than one way. Their deadness is callous to human need, and also hidden, inaccessible to the senses, as in Hugo's use of "insensible" in "La Pente de la rêverie": "Une pente insensible / Va du monde réel à la sphère invisible" (I. 770). (An imperceptible slope goes from the real world to the invisible sphere.) One cannot see, but the poet knows, that all these motions are motiveless, mysteriously self-generated and self-referring. The last line of stanza two completes the sequence of comparisons by explaining the hidden truth of the woman and of a kind of motion: "Elle se développe avec indifférence."

Baudelaire's idea of nature's indifference is not unlike Wordsworth's sense of "self-poise" in "To a Butterfly," but instead of Wordsworth's never completed approach to the meaning of his perceptions, Baudelaire lightly yet decisively announces the point of his analogies. There is no illusion of following the poet's mind toward the discovery of meaning. Baudelaire's effects seem more coolly premeditated. The shifts of tone—playful, solemn, then light again—the surprising juxtaposition of images, the delay of the main clause of the sentence, the controlled pace of explanation—Baudelaire uses all these poetic devices to render the poem what I would call an act of disclosure rather than of discovery. We rely on the poet's authority; we are made dependent on his disclosure of meanings not to be apprehended through any common act of perception.

Paradoxically, Baudelaire possesses the hidden meaning of a beauty whose essence is its very resistance to possession. Superficially, the woman seems elusive because of her constant motion. But the poet has penetrated to a more profound inaccessibility. The woman cannot be possessed because her apparent vitality covers only coldness, deadness, sterility. There is sexual revenge in penetrating the woman's surface and announcing that what one has possessed is sterile and useless. The poet exposes and, in a sense, even destroys the woman's apparent vitality through his poetic act. The last line of the poem is motionless, without a verb; the only verb in the last stanza is "resplendit," announcing the permanent, motionless illumination of the symbol revealed.

The poet is the destroyer of appearances and the creator of symbols. The woman, like the precious jewels and other forms of nature in the poem, asserts no energy; she creates nothing. It is only the poet who makes something out of barrenness and he can choose whether to be playful, reverent, or derisive toward the object he has made. Yet the poet's power may finally seem as strangely useless and sterile as the woman's beauty. The poet accomplishes no progress toward any real act of possession within the poem, as sonnets of courtship often do. Further interchange between the self and an object, human or natural, is impossible if, in penetrating the lovely behavior of appearances, one reaches only essential sterility.

Insofar as Baudelaire shows the poetic mind penetrating to the hidden truth of the object, one may say that he at last introduces into French poetry a concept of the imagination as insight, a faculty of knowledge, the destroyer rather than the creator of illusion. But if what the imagination discloses is only the mysterious emptiness of the outer world, one is not as far from Rousseau as may first appear. The deepest insight attained by the poetic mind in Baudelaire's sonnet only confirms the poet's utter isolation. His imagination has no power to create fuller union with the world outside his mind. Instead, he exposes the essential impossibility of union, or even of lesser forms of relationship.

Unlike Rousseau, the poet does not openly confess disappointment. He takes his revenge on insensible beauty through a posture of indifference, a show of cool satisfaction with his perfect symbol. By the end, the poem resembles the woman—self-contained and self-referring. The difference between the poet and the woman, however, is that his coldness seems the surface rather than the deepest secret of his nature. His posture seems artificial—not inherent, not useless, but purposeful, even though the purpose refers only back to the self. Given the impossibility of union with the beauty he admires, the poet defiantly withdraws from experience to the self-contained satisfaction of his imagination. The relationship between desire and imagination becomes more covert than it was for Rousseau, since Baudelaire does not indulge his sensibility by withdrawing to more responsive, imaginary objects. The symbol created by his imagination does not satisfy desire any more than nature does. Yet though the self-sufficiency of the poem differs from Rousseau's retreat to fantasy, it is still a response to the disappointments of experience. The coldness of the Baudelaire poem is a discipline of disappointment. It asserts control over the inevitable isolation of the mind by transforming the consciousness of emptiness into the beautiful and self-sufficient forms of art.

When George Henry Lewes criticized Hugo for writing "the cant of literature" rather than "the experience of life," he did not foresee that French poetry (and then, modern poetry, more generally) would go much further than Hugo to challenge the poetry of "experience," in the Wordsworthian sense. In both "De Profundis clamavi" and the sonnet, "Avec ses vêtements ondoyants . . .," an impression of experience is created by Baudelaire, but then challenged, teased, emptied of significance within the poem. Though the unique value of the poem as a verbal gesture against the tedium or sterility of experience becomes more explicit and programmatic with Mallarmé, Baudelaire already displays this attitude through the design of his poems and the character of his figurative language.

The poetry of Hopkins, as well as innumerable examples from other post-Romantic English poets, suggests the persistence in England through the nineteenth century of faith in the potential if not actual value of experience rooted in perception: "these things were here and but the beholder/Wanting." The English poet continues to question the quality of his beholding for his joy or disappointment in things. If he experiences the world imaginatively, he will know that he lives in "a world of life." Nevertheless, by the end of the century, Wordsworthian imaginative perception no longer represents sacred truth. Yeats, for example, turns to French ideas about poetry because the French seem free of the worn-out English reverence for perception. In "The Autumn of the Body," Yeats asserts that the Wordsworthian mode is based on a mistaken faith in the vitality of things. The poet, Yeats argues, must no longer woo the world through what he sees and hears, for the beauty of the sensory world is only an illusion. Yeats will go on to complicate and modify this attitude, but in 1898 he cites Mallarmé for an ideal of poetic language free of false reverence for appearances that are, in themselves, only air and dust and moisture:

> It was only with the modern poets, with Goethe and Wordsworth and Browning, that poetry gave up the right to consider all things in the world as a dictionary of types and symbols and began to call itself a critic of life and an interpreter of things as they are. . . . Man has wooed and won the world, and has fallen weary, and not, I think, for a time, but with a weariness that will not end until the last autumn, when the stars shall be blown away like withered leaves. He grew weary when he said, "These things that I touch and see and hear are alone real," for he saw them without illusion at last, and found them but air and dust and moisture. . . . Mr. Symons has written lately on Mallarmé's method, and has quoted him as saying that we should "abolish the pretension, aesthetically an error, despite its dominion over almost all the masterpieces, to enclose within the subtle paper other than—for example—the horror of the forest or the silent thunder in the leaves, not the intense dense wood of the trees," and as desiring to substitute for "the old lyric afflatus or the enthusiastic personal direction of the phrase" words "that take light from mutual reflection, like an actual trail of fire over precious stones."[2]

Part Four

Ideas of the Symbol in Coleridge and Baudelaire

10
Beauty and Taste

The French influence on the turn away from Romanticism in English is impossible to formulate simply. Poet-critics like Yeats and T. S. Eliot mix homage to French mentors with diverse other loyalties, including only half-acknowledged loyalty to English Romanticism itself. The actual debt to the French is hard to calculate in each instance, for, as in all such matters of literary influence, foreign names often appear as glamorous but only superficial decoration in writings more intricately and deeply rooted in the writer's own national tradition.

Baudelaire's importance is especially difficult to measure. His poetry and criticism are generally acknowledged to be the first French writing in the nineteenth century to affect the course of English poetry; before Baudelaire, French poetry was the lame stepchild of Romanticism. By the end of the century, the French had become the avant-garde of modernism. Baudelaire's pivotal position in this transformation seems unquestionable. Yet to judge the specific character of his originality (and then, the somewhat separate issue of the force exerted by his example) involves some of the knottiest problems in modern literary history. There is not only Baudelaire's confusing relationship to English Romanticism through his interest in Poe, but also the diffusion of Baudelaire's influence through a variety of later writers in both French and English.

Most simply stated, Baudelaire seems to lead in two almost contrary directions. Yeats's early essays show the first path: from Baudelaire to the later French Symbolists and to the spiritualized cult of Art
at the end of the nineteenth century. Yeats's essay, "The Autumn of
the Body," praises French Symbolism for repudiating "outward
things" and the picturesque and declamatory style in which the
idolatry of things reaches its weary limit. In "The Symbolism of
Poetry," Yeats announces that now the imagination is about to resume
its legitimate spiritual function by purifying itself of both things and
opinions about things:

> I see, indeed, in the arts of every country those faint lights and faint
> colours and faint outlines and faint energies which many call "the
> decadence," and which I, because I believe that the arts lie dreaming
> of things to come, prefer to call the autumn of the body. . . . The
> arts are, I believe, about to take upon their shoulders the burdens
> that have fallen from the shoulders of priests, and to lead us back
> upon our journey by filling our thoughts with the essences of things,
> and not with things.[1]

T. S. Eliot in 1930, however, reinterpreted the importance of
Baudelaire and later French poetry in terms quite contrary to Yeats's
prophecy. Attending directly to Baudelaire's own writing, rather than
to the cult of Art elaborated by the later Symbolists more appealing to
Yeats, Eliot remarked the new vividness of *things* in French poetry
following Baudelaire. Eliot argued that Baudelaire was "the first
counter-romantic in poetry" because he created a modern poetic
language out of the common, even sordid things of his contemporary
world. Although Eliot shared Yeats's dislike for the picturesque and
the declamatory, he saw Baudelaire restoring the intensity of temporal
things for the uses of poetry, rather than allowing them to fade away:
"It is not merely in the use of imagery of common life, not merely in
the use of imagery of the sordid life of a great metropolis, but in the
elevation of such imagery to the *first intensity*—presenting it as it is,
and yet making it represent something much more than itself—that
Baudelaire has created a mode of release and expression for other
men."[2]

It seems paradoxical that the French example both discredits things
in poetry and also charges them with new intensity. Both attitudes
toward things do, however, appear in Baudelaire's own poetry and

criticism. The apparent contradiction looks sharper perhaps in retrospect because later writers (both French and English) split apart what were more closely related attitudes for Baudelaire. One way to understand Baudelaire's (somewhat loose) consistency is to recognize that, in one way or another, he avoids the English Romantic ambiguity about temporal things. In their different ways, Yeats and Eliot were both right to see in French poetry following Baudelaire alternatives to what they disliked in the English Romantics. Since Baudelaire does not try to root spirituality in natural perception, he does not revere outward things or expect revelations from them. Nor does he brood over things in the ruminations that Eliot regarded as so tiresome in most English poetry since the seventeenth century

Yet to criticize English nineteenth-century poetry in the name of either "the imagination" (like Yeats) or "the imagery of common life" (like Eliot) may seem only to cover filial ingratitude with French airs. We can still hear Coleridge in Yeats's language for the symbol: "to give a body to something that moves beyond the senses," and also in Eliot's definition of the modern poet's action on the imagery of common life: "presenting it as it is, and yet making it represent something much more than itself." In turning the Romantics' own critical vocabulary against them, Yeats and Eliot undoubtedly belittled their own literary parentage, as prophets of liberation tend to do. Yet their use of this vocabulary through the filter of French poetry and criticism also suggests real departures from English Romantic attitudes. Starting with Baudelaire, the French transformed the key terms of English Romantic theory—"imagination," "symbol," "beauty," "form"—if only by releasing this critical vocabulary from the shadow of Wordsworth and Coleridge. My study of Rousseau and Victor Hugo tries to show that the main critical terms of English Romanticism gathered no comparable burden of meaning in the first half of the nineteenth century to the French. When the terms of English criticism began to appear in mid-century France, they expressed from the start the interests and values of writers indifferent to the English Romantic legacy, if not altogether ignorant of it.

I shall attend in detail here to an early point in this intricate story. The contrast between the critical writing of Coleridge and Baudelaire elucidates the baffling way in which French criticism became Romantic (in the English sense) and counter-romantic simultaneously. Baudelaire comes closer than any earlier French critic in the nineteenth century to the English interest in the processes of poetic creation. Yet he undermines the English interpretation of those processes even while he introduces the subject into French criticism for the first time.

Baudelaire knew English aesthetic theory mainly from Poe,[3] a peculiar source since Poe himself challenged Wordsworth and Coleridge at the same time as he appropriated fragments of their critical vocabulary. Baudelaire went even further than Poe to change the significance of the key terms of English Romantic theory. Without arguing against Coleridge (without even mentioning his name),[4] Baudelaire absorbed Coleridgean terms like "imagination," "symbol," "beauty," and turned them to his own uses.

The turnabout from Coleridge to Baudelaire appears as soon as any of the key terms are pressed for specific meaning. "Beauty," perhaps the most elusive, offers a good starting point because it most quickly reveals separate controversies of taste and the seasoning of philosophy with prejudice of different sorts. At the risk of too schematic a formulation of theoretical positions, I will first examine the concept of Beauty to show differences in the general biases of Coleridge and Baudelaire as critics. Before attending directly to their ideas of the symbol, it is necessary to understand how they each handle the vocabulary of criticism, with whom they are arguing, and why.

Coleridge on Beauty in the "Principles of Genial Criticism" shows right away English bias against French taste at the beginning of the nineteenth century:

> Should an Englishman gazing on a mass of cloud rich with the rays of the rising sun exclaim, even without distinction of, or reference to its form, or its relation to other objects, how beautiful! I should have no quarrel with him. First, because by the law of association there is in all visual beholdings at least an indistinct subsumption of form and relation: and, secondly, because even in the coincidence between the sight and the object there is an approximation to the reduction of the many into one. But who, that heard a Frenchman call the flavor of a leg of mutton a beautiful taste, would not immediately recognize him for a Frenchman, even though there should be neither grimace or characteristic nasal twang?[5]

As a "genial critic," Coleridge is not above a rather nasty chauvinism. Coleridge's "geniality" refers more to creative genius than to sociable good humor, and the French, according to Coleridge, cannot understand the nature of creative genius. Coleridge habitually excludes the French from serious aesthetic philosophy. He tends to picture them at dinner tables where the flow of food and conversation diverts the mind from serious thought. Although Coleridge also likes to be conversational—he is genial in that sense too—he nevertheless aspires to keep aesthetic conversation formal, that is, technical and philosophical.

To the philosophic mind according to Coleridge, "the Beautiful, contemplated in its essentials, that is, in *kind* and not in *degree*, is that in which the *many*, still seen as many, becomes one."[6] The flavor of mutton, or even of some more delectable edible, cannot be called beautiful because the senses of taste and smell are not "susceptible of distinction of parts." Unlike the eye and ear, the palate therefore allows no "multeity in unity," to use Coleridge's deliberately difficult phrase. Mutton, according to Coleridge, does not even attain the first category of the Agreeable: "that which is congruous with the primary constitution of our senses." Coleridge asserts that the color green, for example, is naturally agreeable to the eye. But only the second, lesser definition of the Agreeable can account for the appeal of mutton: "those things which have by force of habit (thence called a second nature) been made to agree with us."

Baudelaire has little interest in Coleridge's kind of technical distinction between the senses. In the "Salon de 1846," for example, he nonchalantly praises the use of color by the painter Decamps by comparing its effect to that of pungent food:

Les mets les plus appétissants, les drôleries cuisinées avec le plus de réflexion, les produits culinaires le plus âprement assaisonnés avaient moins de ragoût et de montant, exhalaient moins de volupté sauvage pour le nez et le palais d'un gourmand, que les tableaux de M. Decamps pour un amateur de peinture. ("De Quelques coloristes," 637)

(The most appetizing dishes, the most thoughtfully prepared tidbits, the most piquantly seasoned products of the kitchen, had less relish and tang, and exhaled less fierce ecstacy upon the nose and the palate of the epicure than M. Decamps' pictures possessed for the lover of painting.)

Baudelaire is famous for suggesting correspondences between different sensory experiences and between tastes, smells, colors, and aesthetic and spiritual feelings. In "La Chevelure," the exotic fragrance of the woman's hair is a single "parfum," yet also a "fôret aromatique," rich with subtly distinguishable aromas. No sunrise offers the lover as rich an experience of "multeity in unity" as he discovers in the perfume of his mistress' hair.

Although Baudelaire himself characteristically disdains the crude confusions of contemporary French taste, his argument does not follow Coleridgean distinctions:

> Nous avons, tous tant que nous sommes, même les moins *chauvins*, su défendre la France à table d'hôte, sur des rivages lointains; mais ici, chez nous, en famille, sachons dire la vérité: la France n'est pas poëte; elle éprouve même, pour tout dire, une horreur congénitale de la poésie. Parmi les écrivains qui se servent du vers, ceux qu'elle préférera toujours sont les plus prosaïques. Je crois vraiment,— pardonnez-moi, vrais amants de la Muse!—que j'ai manqué de courage au commencement de cette étude, en disant que, pour la France, le Beau n'était facilement digestible que relevé par le condiment politique. C'était le contraire qu'il fallait dire: quelque politique que soit le condiment, le Beau amène l'indigestion, ou plutôt l'estomac français le refuse immédiatement. ("Théophile Gautier," 1041-1042)

> (All of us, even the least chauvinistic, have been capable of defending France at dinner parties in distant lands; but here, at home, among ourselves, let us tell the truth: the French are not poetic; indeed they have an innate horror of poetry. Of the writers who use verse, they will always prefer the most prosaic. I really believe— forgive me, true lovers of the Muse!—that I lacked courage at the beginning of this essay when I said that for the French, the Beautiful is easily digestible only when seasoned with politics. I should have said the opposite: no matter how political the seasoning may be, the Beautiful brings on indigestion, or more precisely, the French stomach rejects it instantly.)

Perhaps the now familiar snobbery of the hungry artist joins Baudelaire's metaphor of indigestion to Coleridge's contemptible mutton. Lovers of Beauty since the beginning of the nineteenth century disdain bourgeois gluttony. Yet Baudelaire, even when he attacks the French appetite, still does not pursue a Coleridgean idea of taste.

Baudelaire's categories are larger and looser than Coleridge's hierarchy of the Beautiful and the Agreeable. Baudelaire's argument attacks the antiaestheticism which is one of the main legacies of Rousseau: the French worship "le Vrai" instead of "le Beau"; they disdain imagination in favor of supposed knowledge about the world; they cannot digest originality because they are surfeited with slogans of social and political justice. Beauty may be distinguished from politics more easily than from the Agreeable, and without a philosophic disquisition in the manner of Coleridge. Baudelaire aims at a large public target in terms sharp enough to touch the general reader, "le philistin ennemi," in his everyday prejudices.

Coleridge, even when he writes in the Bristol press (where the "Principles of Genial Criticism" were first published), conducts a technical debate with other aestheticians, like Francis Jeffrey and Archibald Alison, the author of *Essays on the Nature and Principles of Taste* in two volumes (1790). The importance of Beauty is accepted by all participants in the English debate. The problem is how to define Beauty, and how to account for it psychologically.

Modern controversy about the coherence and also the originality of Coleridge's position in this debate often tends to overshadow the main purpose of his interest in it.[7] For my subject, however, Coleridge's reasons for caring to disagree with the English associationist aestheticians are perhaps more interesting than the actual value of his definitions and distinctions. By attending to the motive of Coleridge's technical argument, we can better appreciate the significance of Baudelaire's indifference to this entire aspect of English eighteenth-century thought.

The technical argument about Beauty in eighteenth-century English philosophy, like comparable arguments about other subjects, was a way of opening traditional values and inherited prejudices to what was thought to be scientific scrutiny. Empirical psychology has the effect (if not the intention) of challenging traditional elites and supposedly objective hierarchies of value. In relation to art, empirical psychology challenges an absolute standard of taste by making the definition of Beauty contingent upon individual experience. Beauty does not arise from any inherent quality in things, nor does it refer to any universal principle of composition. Starting from Locke's analysis of mental experience, Alison and Jeffrey define Beauty to be the feeling aroused in the individual through associations recalled to the mind by certain objects.[8] The cutting edge of the empirical argument appears behind the seemingly bland truism that the connection between objects and feelings varies according to experience. Once that ground is granted, the philosophic basis for any universal aesthetic principles becomes difficult to sustain. Like Jeffrey, one is led to acknowledge that all tastes are equally just and true, insofar as each individual speaks only of his own emotions.

Although Lockian aestheticians retreat in various ways from total relativism, the logic of the associationist argument undermines an objective hierarchy of taste along with a hierarchy of the senses.[9] Only by reference to nonaesthetic values do some forms of Beauty deserve more respect than others. The end of art being to promote innocent pleasure, for example, some forms of Beauty are worthier than others for this moral end. Even the moral discrimination between feelings, however, is flexible, a matter of degree or merely of social agreement. Jeffrey accepts this relativism, politely chiding aesthetic snobbery by a show of reasonable tolerance: "It is a strange aberration indeed of vanity that makes us despise persons for being happy—for having sources of enjoyment in which we cannot share:—and yet this is the true source of the ridicule, which is so generally poured upon individuals who seek only to enjoy their peculiar tastes unmolested."[10]

Coleridge is in an awkward position because he *does* despise what he regards as bad taste, and yet he also wants to maintain the insights of empirical psychology which seem to erode the philosophic ground for such arrogance. Coleridge has to argue with the associationists partly because the Lockian analysis of the mind has so much intellectual authority for him. He will not follow the example of, say, Samuel Johnson who preserves the moral and intellectual authority of literary judgment apart from a scientific scrutiny of mental structure. Coleridge sees his own importance to come precisely from his effort to make aesthetic judgment more rigorously philosophic, that is, rooted in the study of mental structure and development which was the most far-reaching endeavor of philosophy in eighteenth-century England. Coleridge is not content to justify his aesthetic values apart from principles of psychology. He accepts the intellectual claims of empirical psychology. But he also wants to force a psychological approach to aesthetic theory into the service of universal values.

Coleridge's critical theory thus tries to reconcile the idea of objective and universal aesthetic principles with the recognition that aesthetic as well as other kinds of experience take place in the mind of the beholder. Aided by his reading in post-Kantian German philosophy,[11] Coleridge insists upon the mind's capacity for intuitive responses, not dependent upon acquired experience. In Coleridge's psychology, the human mind innately has the capacity to respond to the harmony that is actually in certain objects, for example, in a wheel.[12] To go further, the mind desires this experience. An individual may, of course, be in fact unresponsive to Beauty. Coleridge can imagine an

Iroquois Sachem who finds in Paris nothing so beautiful as the cook-shops. Intuitive taste may be dormant or corrupted. "Great depression of spirits" may render even the cultivated mind insensible. But the universal and permanent meaning of Beauty transcends these accidents and peculiarities of experience. Since the human mind itself is a complex and harmonious structure, it is organized to find pleasure in all other analogous forms of composition, and this discovery is the essence of aesthetic experience: "The Beautiful arises from the perceived harmony of an object, whether sight or sound, with the inborn and constitutive rules of the judgement and imagination: and it is always intuitive. As light to the eye, even such is beauty to the mind, which cannot but have complacency in whatever is perceived as preconfigured to its living faculties."[13]

The associationist aestheticians discourage philosophic arrogance partly by building the meaning of philosophic terms out of general usage, with the implication that ordinary language represents common human experience. Since "all men" call sounds and even smells beautiful, argues Alison, there seems no reason to outlaw this general reality of experience. The difficult and peculiar terminology of Coleridge's criticism may be understood as part of his effort to free aesthetic philosophy from the limited rule of general experience. Coleridge insists that his philosophic language is not idiosyncratic, yet it is not derived from common speech either. The impersonal technicality of Coleridge's prose makes it clear that this is neither a private voice we are hearing nor is it the voice of general experience. The philosophic meaning of terms like Beauty and Taste refer to ideas that are really ideals, and therefore not manifest in everyday talk. Taste refers to the universal laws of the mind—thus Coleridge retains the impartiality of psychology. But Taste also designates an ideal, for few if any men actually follow the order inherent in the structure of the mind. The laws of the mind interesting to Coleridge are potential, not compulsory. Psychology, in this Coleridgean sense, turns away from the description of actual and general experience, and becomes instead a way of reestablishing universal ideals on an impartial intellectual foundation.

The spirit of proselytism, to use Jeffrey's pejorative term, is thus given new strength in Coleridge's psychological approach to aesthetic judgment. His way of enclosing the idea of Beauty in the framework of psychology reinforces the didactic authority of art. Since artists come closest to the ideal of Taste, they are most fully human, that is, they most fully realize what the structure of the mind allows and intends. The laws of art are even less arguable than other laws, for history shows the arbitrary, the accidental, and the transient in human society, while the structure of the mind is permanent and universal.

Wordsworth, we have seen, shares Coleridge's desire to make psychology yield new general authority for the special character of the artist's experience. The didacticism of English Romantic poetry relies on the psychological argument that the poetic mind differs from other minds only by being *more* what other minds are potentially and ought to become: "what we have loved, / Others will love, and we will teach them how" (*The Prelude*, XIV. 446-447). Wordsworth's ambiguous language of feeling, however, does not satisfy Coleridge's standard of the intellectual rigor required for aesthetic philosophy. There is an irritable defensiveness in Coleridge's technical prose. He insists that he has to punish the natural tendencies of the language in order to articulate truth. Grace of style in philosophy even comes to seem a dangerous seduction. Intellectual rigor demands distinctions, not simply contrasts but subtle differentiations. Symbol differs from Allegory, Reason from Understanding, Imagination from Fancy, the Beautiful from the Agreeable. "Taste," Coleridge protests, is a sloppy metaphor which confuses two separate Greek words, one meaning "sensation" and the other, "love for the beautiful." Whereas Wordsworth relies on the flexibility of "sense," "sentiment," "sensation," to draw the reader through the whole range and, especially, to the outmost limit of his experience, Coleridge instead disintegrates ordinary words and chastises the careless reader. To confuse a taste for turtle with an aesthetic experience reveals a basic incapacity for aesthetic discussion: "If a man, upon questioning his own experience, can detect no difference in *kind* between the enjoyment derived from the eating of turtle, and that from the perception of a new truth; if in *his* feelings a taste *for* Milton is essentially the same as the taste *of* mutton, he may still be a sensible and a valuable member of society; but it would be desecration to argue with him on the Fine Arts."[14]

However marked the differences between Coleridge and Wordsworth as aestheticians, a much greater distance separates both of them from Baudelaire. The two English poet-critics both try to give their aesthetic values permanent and impartial philosophic authority. They try, in other words, to be aestheticians in a tradition which makes the study of mental processes the surest starting-point of knowledge and judgment. Baudelaire has no comparable philosophic pretentions. For him, all aesthetic systems bear the taint of the French Academy where an arrogantly provincial neoclassicism masquerades as aesthetic philosophy. Baudelaire's critical essays are more occasional than Coleridge's; he reviews exhibitions of painting or praises particular new painters and writers, usually as a gadfly to established taste. These essays do not aspire to be "genial criticism," in Coleridge's sense of establishing the psychological origins of aesthetic creation and response. Although Baudelaire articulates poetic principles, he deliberately keeps the critic's art impressionistic, using what he calls his naïve personal response to goad the intellectual pretensions of others: "Je me suis orgueilleusement résigné à la modestie: je me suis contenté de sentir; je suis revenu chercher un asile dans l'impeccable naïveté" (691). (I proudly resigned myself to modesty; I became content to feel; I returned to seek refuge in impeccable naïveté.)

Baudelaire's sophisticated naïveté differs from Coleridge's intellectual righteousness partly as a matter of tone—it is the difference between the aggressively precise obscurity in Coleridge's manner and Baudelaire's pose of casual blasphemy. But Baudelaire's indifference to systematic aesthetic theory also separates him from both Coleridge and Wordsworth in more substantial ways. Whether Baudelaire is kneeling before the goddess Beauty or whether he more sharply defines the particular character of beauty in contemporary objects, he shows little zeal for justifying his responses through a psychological study of mental structure and development. Baudelaire neither defends nor attacks associationist theories of the mind. Sometimes he sounds like a Lockian; at other times he seems to differ. Mainly he does not labor to coordinate his principles with that kind of intellectual structure.

In the essay on Gautier, for example, Baudelaire chides the public for confusing science and politics with art. He seems to be making philosophic distinctions when he differentiates "le Beau" from "le Vrai" and "le Bien." But following Poe, Baudelaire really abandons the philosophic definition of Beauty for a posture of devotion to what is essentially undefinable, "un sphinx incompris." Indeed, by separating Beauty from Truth, Baudelaire in effect repudiates the necessity and even the possibility of Coleridge's kind of philosophic effort. Beauty cannot be contained in categories devised by the intellect. Beauty is a mysterious goddess, not to be explained but only evoked by lofty expressions of devotion: "cet immortel instinct du Beau," "une Beauté supérieure," "la Beauté pure," "le *Beau* est l'unique ambition, le but exclusif du Goût."

Baudelaire's vocabulary in the essay on Gautier comes from the French Parnasse (including Gautier himself) reinforced by Poe. It is Poe who gives Baudelaire fragments of Coleridgean terminology but already turned around by Poe's own rejection of Coleridge's philosophic pretensions. Poe begins his essay, "The Poetic Principle," by announcing, "I have no design to be either thorough or profound."[15] With his dictum against mixing "the obstinate oils and waters of Poetry and Truth," Poe abandons Coleridge's complex structure of the mind. According to Poe, Coleridge ruins the attraction of art, as well as his own prose style, by caring so much for the intellect. Poe's critical language carries an aura of psychological definition but without any of Coleridge's straining after precision: "An immortal instinct, deep within the spirit of man, is thus, plainly, a sense of the Beautiful. This it is which administers to his delight in the manifold forms, and sounds, and odors, and sentiments, amid which he exists."

Poe's tone of vague exaltation brushes away the principle of multeity in unity along with the hierarchy of the senses and all Coleridge's other technical distinctions.[16] Instead, Poe loosely separates "spirit" from intellect and thus changes Coleridge's idea of intuition to an explicitly anti-intellectual "instinct" of the spirit. Nothing remains of Coleridge's psychology but a diffuse feeling of aspiration, mysteriously born in the spirit and associated with many kinds of things and feelings. Poe lists them all together, without rank or distinction. The artist feels the true poetic effect "in the surf that complains to the shore, in the fresh breath of the woods, in the scent of the violet, in the voluptuous perfume of the hyacinth . . . in all noble thoughts, in all unworldly motives, in all holy impulses, in all chivalrous, generous, and self-sacrificing deeds. He feels it in the beauty of woman, in the grace of her step . . . "[17]

Baudelaire's ideal Beauty in the essay on Gautier is almost as flexible in substance as Poe's "supernal Beauty." Because both Poe and Baudelaire release Taste from the philistine rule of intellect, they do not even attempt Coleridge's kind of philosophic definition. Coleridge's Taste *is* intellectual. The perception of Beauty is both intuitive and intellectual, for Coleridge's model of the mind considers intuition itself a mode of intellect. All forms of intellect have truth as their object, and this is also true of aesthetic intuition. For Coleridge, therefore, the value of Beauty does depend on its truth. The principle of multeity in unity claims to register the true harmony in the composition of certain objects and the true structure of the mind and the true relation between object and the mind in aesthetic experience.

The denigration of intellect which Baudelaire echoes from Poe repudiates the main purpose of Coleridge's aesthetic philosophy. The cult of Art derived from Baudelaire and Poe detaches spirituality from the intellect much more radically than Coleridge and even Wordsworth were willing to do. The true poetic effect for Baudelaire and for Poe arouses vague spiritual longings rather than the complacency of the mind in compositions congruent with the mind's own internal structure. In the cult of Art, rigor comes in the disciplined devotion of the artist to whatever form of Beauty his spiritual longings conjure. The exact psychological processes of the aesthetic act remain mysterious, and the character of the object matters less than the artist's posture of devotion.

Coleridge values psychology because he believes that he can use it to ground the spiritual significance of art in the permanent structure of the mind. Coleridge hopes to make the psychology of aesthetic creation and response confirm the permanent and objective validity of spiritual values. But the always precarious faith of the English Romantics that science and spirituality could be reconciled proved less enduring than they had hoped. Some admirers of Coleridge, most notably I. A. Richards, tried to preserve Coleridge's scientific approach to aesthetic theory while allowing his religious commitments to fade.[18] Poe and Baudelaire (followed by the later French Symbolists and early Yeats) turned the other way by detaching the spirituality of art from Coleridge's philosophic structure. The artist, according to Poe and Baudelaire, feels spiritual yearning; the pursuit of Beauty through art is the concrete form of the artist's spirituality. This belief is not to be argued through a systematic study of the mind. It is felt by the artists themselves and evoked for others through the aura of spiritual longing which becomes the dominant tone of late nineteenth-century aestheticism.

Baudelaire's disdain for the devotees of "le Vrai" is a social posture as well as an aesthetic and religious position. In Baudelaire's criticism, the worship of Beauty is frankly, even defiantly, aristocratic. Whereas the English Romantics sought to reconcile a vision of the artist's superiority with an enlightened view of social harmony, Baudelaire is openly a snob. He does not participate in the uneasy effort of Wordsworth and Coleridge to make the artist a figure of inspiration to other men. Instead, he savors the feeling of aristocratic separateness, even while lamenting the modern artist's social isolation. Baudelaire does not shrink from social arrogance, nor does he labor to rationalize it through a structure of general psychology. He celebrates Poe as the pure aristocrat destroyed by vulgar American democracy. Gautier for him embodies the artist as priest, aristocrat, glorious fanatic, the unrecognized hero of a society in which science and democracy have destroyed all other forms of distinction.

The posture of social defiance in Baudelaire's criticism may seem too facile, but in my opinion, his aristocratic bravado saves him from the rather vapid loftiness into which the cult of Art otherwise tends to deteriorate. Baudelaire improved Poe and achieved a more various influence than Poe, partly because he sharpened the worship of Beauty into a weapon for social satire, criticism, and lament. Baudelaire's wit and intellectual clarity appear most effectively in his criticism when he uses the cult of Beauty as an instrument to flail the complacent degradation of his society.

Baudelaire reargues the relation between art and society to a French audience that expects criticism to attend directly to social values. The separation of art from truth and virtue was a theme already full of social resonance in French criticism before Baudelaire. I have earlier suggested how Rousseau's obsession with the relationship between artifice and social injustice kept him apart from the English interest in the psychology of the poetic process.[19] The untruthfulness of art was more a social than an epistemological problem for Rousseau, or at least it was the social elaboration of his argument that survived to dominate French critical debate through the Romantic period. Under the influence of Poe, Baudelaire introduces into French criticism a new concern for poetic principles. But in a sense, Poe has the appeal of seeming to bring a kind of aesthetic philosophy new to France, while his message actually reinforces the disregard for epistemology and the psychology of perception so striking in French criticism earlier.

Baudelaire uses the cult of Beauty to challenge Rousseau's values while still continuing the social emphasis of Rousseau's thought. Despising the reign of style in eighteenth-century France, Rousseau asserted that art both causes and comes from social corruption. In post-revolutionary France, however, Baudelaire sees the Rousseauist slogans masking only spiritual emptiness and the middle-class scramble for money and power. With the help of Poe's poetic principles, Baudelaire thus turns Rousseau's formula around. In a society deadened by false professions of truth and virtue, the artist alone preserves the life of the spirit. He is not thoroughly redeemed because he too suffers from the pervasive spiritual decay of his culture. But insofar as he can be purified, he is so by his priestlike devotion to Art. Now that a degraded society waves Rousseau's banner of truth and virtue, the superior spirit must seek refuge in the discipline of Art.

Baudelaire's devotion to Beauty (like Rousseau's contrary devotion to "la vérité") comes most alive through the social outrage that seems characteristic of important French criticism since Rousseau, regardless of its abstract allegiances. Baudelaire ridicules the public, toys with democratic prejudices and pretensions. He is witty, blasphemous, condescending. Most important, he concentrates his critical attention on the objects which represent for him contemporary spiritual deadness. Paradoxically, Baudelaire in his social arrogance, engages his imagination with contemporary things more specifically than the English Romantics ever do, for all their affirmation of social good will. It is this social specificity that links Baudelaire's cult of Beauty to the imagery of contemporary life. Since Baudelaire does not single out certain things as "pre-configured" to the structure of the mind, there is no reason, according to his concept of Beauty, to limit aesthetic pleasure to the forms envisioned by Coleridge. The artist, in Baudelaire's view, may show his devotion to Beauty by the quality of his attention even to the most sordid things. Baudelaire enlarges the range of things which can generate "the true poetic effect" even beyond what Poe implied. Though Poe loosens the Coleridgean definition of a beautiful form, he tends to regard conventionally pretty things as the most suggestive, especially when tinged with sadness—the smell of flowers, a beautiful woman's death. Baudelaire goes further than Poe to show how the artistic spirit may be aroused by all kinds of things, even by ugly things. The artist's love of Beauty may manifest itself through irony and criticism as well as through delight and longing. The artist may transform patently ugly things into formal beauty, or he may show his spirituality by his protest against the absence of spirit in the things of his world.

The connection in Baudelaire's prose between the worship of Beauty and social criticism appears in his earliest essays, before he read Poe.[20] In the "Salon de 1846," for example, Baudelaire explains how to make an artistic image out of the black suit and coat of contemporary Parisian fashion. Arguing against the draping of modern heroes in classical garb, Baudelaire directs the modern artist to pursue his love of beauty by apprehending the symbolic significance of contemporary things:

> Et cependant, n'a-t-il pas sa beauté et son charme indigène, cet habit tant victimé? N'est-il pas l'habit nécessaire de notre époque, souffrante et portant jusque sur ses épaules noires et maigres le symbole d'un deuil perpétuel? Remarquez bien que l'habit noir et la redingote ont non-seulement leur beauté politique, qui est l'expression de l'égalité universelle, mais encore leur beauté poétique, qui est l'expression de l'âme publique;—une immense défilade de croque-morts, croque-morts politiques, croque-morts amoureux, croque-morts bourgeois. Nous célébrons tous quelque enterrement. ("De l'Héroïsme de la vie moderne," 678)

> (But all the same, has not this much-abused garb its own beauty and its native charm? Is it not the necessary garb of our suffering age, which wears the symbol of a perpetual mourning even upon its thin black shoulders? Note, too, that the dress-coat and the frock-coat not only possess their political beauty, which is an expression of universal equality, but also their poetic beauty, which is an expression of the public soul—an immense cortège of undertaker's mutes [mutes in love, political mutes, bourgeois mutes]. We are each of us celebrating some funeral.)

Baudelaire deftly shows by his own example how to make a modern symbol. Superficially, the modern uniform of black suit and coat embodies the political ideal of equality. The artist, however, penetrates this surface by his ironic disdain for contemporary political ideals. The artist's spiritual yearning allows him to see the hollowness of modern equality, so that contemporary fashion for him becomes an ironic symbol. The black uniform embodies the equality in desolation of modern man, "le symbole d'un deuil perpétuel."

Baudelaire's image of modern society as an immense funeral parade draws together in a single stroke political, religious, and personal versions of grief and disillusionment, rather like Eliot's spectral crowd over London Bridge in *The Waste Land*. The artist makes a common thing represent something more than itself by perceiving it as the outward form of a spiritual condition. Baudelaire recognizes the spiritual poverty of his culture in the material forms of contemporary fashion. At the same time, by virtue of his artistic spirit, he transforms the mundane and the material into "la beauté poétique." Sordid contemporary things become beautiful when they are made to embody spiritual reality—even though the reality revealed is, in fact, the death-struggle of spirit in contemporary life: "Ces plis grimaçant, et jouant comme les serpents autour d'une chair mortifiée, n'ont-ils pas leur grâce mystérieuse?" ("De l'Héroïsme . . . ," 678). (Those grinning creases which play like serpents around mortified flesh—have they not their own mysterious grace?) Baudelaire's modern Parisian has no redeeming Grace, but Baudelaire does grant him grace of a sort. Perhaps the artist shows mainly his own grace by re-creating the contemporary figure as a new Laocoon, damned but also ennobled by the cut and fold of his coat.

Although Baudelaire worships a mysterious goddess Beauty, he serves this goddess through his half-ironic, half-celebratory attentiveness to contemporary things. All good art attends to the forms of beauty characteristic of its own culture, Baudelaire argues. That is why aesthetic systems cannot account for the art of diverse countries and times. In an essay occasioned by the "Exposition universelle" of 1855, the only general principle that Baudelaire acknowledges binds the definition of Beauty to historical conditions:

Le Beau est toujours bizarre. Je ne veux pas dire qu'il soit volontairement, froidement bizarre, car dans ce cas il serait un monstre sorti des rails de la vie. Je dis qu'il contient toujours un peu de bizarrerie, de bizarrerie naïve, non voulue, inconsciente, et que c'est cette bizarrerie qui le fait être particulièrement le Beau. C'est son immatriculation, sa caractéristique. . . . Or, comment cette bizarrerie, nécessaire, incompressible, variée à l'infini, dépendante des milieux, des climats, des moeurs, de la race, de la religion et du tempérament de l'artiste, pourra-t-elle jamais être gouvernée, amendée, redressée, par les règles utopiques, conçues dans un petit temple scientifique quelconque de la planète, sans danger de mort pour l'art lui-même? ("Exposition universelle de 1855," 691)

(*The Beautiful is always strange.* I do not mean that it is coldly, deliberately strange, for in that case it would be a monstrosity that had jumped the rails of life. I mean that it always contains a touch of strangeness, of simple, unpremeditated and unconscious strangeness, and that it is this touch of strangeness that gives it its particular quality as Beauty. It is its endorsement, so to speak—its mathematical characteristic. . . . Now how could this necessary, irreducible and infinitely varied strangeness, depending upon the environment, the climate, the manners, the race, the religion and the temperament of the artist—how could it ever be controlled, amended, and corrected by Utopian rules conceived in some little scientific temple or other on this planet, without mortal danger to art itself?)

There is calculated blasphemy against the neoclassic aesthetician in Baudelaire's praise of "bizarrerie." Baudelaire enjoys the mischief of a word which connotes oddity, perversity, exoticism—all the qualities that the neoclassic aesthetician abhors. Yet Baudelaire also, and more seriously, expands the term "bizarre" to connote a larger and, specifically, a historical conception of individuality. Beauty is that which is individual and characteristic in a single work of art, in a single artist, or in the art of a particular culture.

Baudelaire's interest in the "bizarrerie" of culture sets him apart in yet another way from the main English concern for the structure of the mind. Empirical psychology presents a model of individual mental development, but the Lockians do not study the history of culture. Although Baudelaire's historical conception of beauty is quite compatible with Lockian psychology (since it makes beauty depend on the variable circumstances of experience), Baudelaire goes far beyond the cautious relativism of the English associationists when he makes "bizarrerie" the one common attribute of beauty. Moreover, Baudelaire does not draw upon empirical psychology for his argument. His idea of cultural particularity continues within the framework of French Romanticism, and he draws primarily on French sources, like Stendhal's *Histoire de la peinture en Italie* (1817).[21]

Baudelaire's historical perspective antedates his reading of Poe and continues through the essays and poems of the 1850s. Like Rousseau, he is not interested so much in the actual history of the past, as in using the idea of history to undermine ostensibly absolute standards of judgment. Rousseau, we have seen, shocks us with his personal "bizarrerie" in the *Confessions*, yet he also rationalizes his peculiarity through the history of his development. Instead of judging Rousseau's character by fixed moral or psychological principles, we are to enter sympathetically into the unique play of circumstance and temperament in his history.[22] Though Baudelaire is interested in art more than in sensibility, he similarly uses the idea of history to protest against fixed principles of judgment. What is needed is "une théorie rationnelle et historique du beau, en opposition avec la théorie du beau unique et absolu" ("Le Beau, la mode et le bonheur," 883) (a rational and historical theory of beauty, in opposition to the theory of unique and absolute Beauty). Baudelaire, like other French Romantic critics, is attracted to a historical theory of beauty mainly because it releases contemporary French art to be modern. Standards that pretend to be universal can be shown to reflect the particular cultures of other times and places.

Baudelaire's commitment to contemporary forms of beauty coexists, more or less compatibly, with his devotion to the goddess Beauty. At times, particularly in the essays directed to creating a modern subject for painting, Baudelaire sacrifices the high-toned worship of Art in order to clear space for the individuality of the modern artist:

> Avant de rechercher quel peut être le côté épique de la vie moderne, et de prouver par des exemples que notre époque n'est pas moins féconde que les anciennes en motifs sublimes, on peut affirmer que puisque tous les siècles et tous les peuples ont eu leur beauté, nous avons inévitablement la nôtre. Cela est dans l'ordre.
>
> Toutes les beautés contiennent, comme tous les phénomènes possibles, quelque chose d'éternel et quelque chose de transitoire,— d'absolu et du particulier. La beauté absolue et éternelle n'existe pas, ou plutôt elle n'est qu'une abstraction écrémée à la surface générale des beautés diverses. L'élément particulier de chaque beauté vient des passions, et comme nous avons nos passions particulières, nous avons notre beauté. ("De l'Héroïsme . . . ," 677)

> (Before trying to distinguish the epic side of modern life, and before bringing examples to prove that our age is no less fertile in sublime themes than past ages, we may assert that since all centuries and all peoples have had their own form of beauty, so inevitably we have ours. That is in the order of things.
>
> All forms of beauty, like all possible phenomena, contain an element of the eternal and an element of the transitory—of the absolute and of the particular. Absolute and eternal beauty does not exist, or rather it is only an abstraction creamed from the general surface of different beauties. The particular element in each manifestation comes from the emotions; and just as we have our own particular emotions, so we have our own beauty.)

In "De l'Héroïsme de la vie moderne," Baudelaire acknowledges the "eternal" component of beauty only to dismiss it as an insignificant abstraction. As when reading Rousseau, one is struck here by the paradoxical French tendency to intensify the abstractness of words like "la Beauté" (or "l'amour") while believing in the abstractions less than the English Romantics do. Baudelaire likes to use the grand abstraction, "la Beauté," in his criticism. Yet the vital character of beauty for him derives from passions and human passion changes, subject to the conditions of culture.

T. S. Eliot found Baudelaire's modernity liberating, but also alien and even disappointing. Indeed, contrary to Baudelaire's own principles, Eliot finally withholds ultimate praise for Baudelaire's poetry because it is, in Eliot's view, an achievement limited by modern culture.[23] In this respect, Eliot does not relinquish the ahistorical bias of English criticism shared by critics as different in other ways as Samuel Johnson, the associationists, and Coleridge. For although Coleridge, like Eliot, praises the individuality of different artists, he seeks always to judge the excellence of art by standards that transcend the contingencies of culture.

By comparison to Baudelaire, Coleridge's praise of particular poets always leans toward the permanent and universal values revealed through individual forms of art. Nature's inexhaustible variety commends the artist to pursue his own nature freely, but the stamp of individuality is not what Coleridge values most. Like the artist, the genial critic seeks to register variety while joining the many into one. The axiom "multeity in unity" defines the beauty of true aesthetic philosophy as well as the beauty of other objects in art and life. It is the balance between the particular and the universal which Coleridge seeks, or rather the revelation of universal principles through forms that have their power because they most freely obey the unchanging laws of nature and the mind. Shakespeare, therefore, can be praised by Coleridge as though he were contemporary to Wordsworth—the terms of praise are the same as those used by the philosopher to define Beauty and the permanent structure of the mind capable of apprehending it. Coleridge sees Milton's character more palpably shaped by the spirit of his age, but the excellence of *Paradise Lost* also points to permanent spiritual, aesthetic, and intellectual values:

> In his mind itself there were purity and piety absolute; an imagination to which neither the past nor the present were interesting, except as far as they called forth and enlivened the great ideal, in which and for which he lived; a keen love of truth, which, after many weary pursuits, found a harbour in a sublime listening to the still voice in his own spirit, and as keen a love of his country, which,

after a disappointment still more depressive, expanded and soared into a love of man as a probationer of immortality.[24]

History does not change the meaning of Beauty for Coleridge any more than it changes the meaning of "purity," "piety," and "truth." The power of aesthetic principles to accommodate writers as different as Wordsworth and Shakespeare and Milton confirms the philosophic value of the principles as well as the permanent worth of the writers.

Historical distinctions matter little to Coleridge for the further reason that aesthetic principles affirm permanent religious truth. Coleridge's idea of "multeity in unity" starts and ends in the religious idea of the eternal relationship of things to spirit. The highest degree of multeity in unity is the revelation of One Spirit in the many forms of matter: "The Mystics meant the same, when they define beauty as the subjection of matter to spirit so as to be transformed into a symbol, in and through which the spirit reveals itself; and declare *that* the *most* beautiful, where the most obstacles to a full manifestation have been most perfectly overcome."[25] Coleridge's idea of Beauty and the idea of the symbol come together to transcend the blasphemies of contemporary passion. We shall have to return to consider the constraints this attitude implies for the material of poetry and for the appropriate attitudes to take toward that material. For the moment, I simply want to remark that for Coleridge the desire to rise from matter to spirit, from the many to the One, is the human passion most pertinent to aesthetic experience, and that passion is made to seem permanent, as free from historical contingency as the turning of a plant to the light.

11
Symbolic Light

Pater's essay on Coleridge shows the chafing of a later English generation against the philosophic pretensions of English Romanticism. Pater named Coleridge's chief offense to be "an excess of seriousness." Coleridge's writing lacks "the excitement of the literary sense," according to Pater, for "there is a certain shade of unconcern . . . which may be thought to mark complete culture in the handling of abstract questions."[1] Pater preferred Wordsworth's looser suggestiveness to Coleridge's ungenial philosophy, yet there is hardly a shade of unconcern in Wordsworth's manner of abstract discussion either. For Wordsworth as well as for Coleridge, philosophic levity was a social vice, signifying culture only in the worst sense. With the notable exception of Byron, the English Romantics specifically disliked the urbanity which Pater admired (and which he learned to admire partly under the new influence of the French).

We can see the difference that a shade of unconcern makes to the idea of the symbol in the contrast between Baudelaire and Coleridge. To understand that the difference is more than social manner, we need to look directly at Coleridge's most serious claims for the symbol. The best example in the criticism comes from "Appendix B" of *The Statesman's Manual*. Coleridge creates and explains two symbols—a flowery meadow in sunlight and the growth of a plant. Further, he puts before us the progress of his own mind in creating the symbols, so that the movement of mind in the passage becomes, in a sense, another symbol. Like Wordsworth, Coleridge in "Appendix B" simultaneously performs and explains the workings of the poetic mind. He shows by his own example what it means to subject matter to spirit and how the mind may progress to the symbol where "the most obstacles to a full manifestation have been most perfectly overcome."

Coleridge begins in a digression, a pause for repose in the thickets of religious philosophy: "If you have accompanied me thus far, thoughtful reader, let it not weary you if I digress for a few moments to another book, likewise a revelation of God—the great book of his servant Nature."[2]

Like Wordsworth, Coleridge proposes to explain the revelation of divinity through nature, though his gentle reflectiveness prepares for a somewhat different experience of revelation than Wordsworth's midnight vision on a mountaintop. As in the poem, "Frost at Midnight," Coleridge quietly allows his "abstruser musings" to be interrupted by the calm of the outer world. He starts with a familiar scene, noticed in the midst of his philosophic labors, almost as if by chance:

> I have at this moment before me, in the flowery meadow, on which my eye is now reposing, one of its most soothing chapters, in which there is no lamenting word, no one character of guilt or anguish. For never can I look and meditate on the vegetable creation without a feeling similar to that with which we gaze at a beautiful infant that has fed itself asleep at its mother's bosom, and smiles in its strange dream of obscure yet happy sensations.

Coleridge's commonplace scene does have Wordsworthian counterparts, for example in the landscape of "Lines Written in Early Spring," but Coleridge stays more apart from the scene than Wordsworth, resting his eye on it as through a window. His first image of "happy smiles" claims no extraordinary imaginative response to nature. Coleridge does not want to make the revelation of spiritual truth in nature too dependent on extraordinary occasions or special gifts of imagination. The spiritual drama he goes on to present belongs to all gentle and pious minds, and it is available in all the commonplace occasions of life. The conventionally pretty scene evokes agreeable associations of birth and warmth. The associations are natural, or at least so habitual as to seem like a second nature (to use Coleridge's own language for the Agreeable in the "Principles of Genial Criticism").

Upon further introspection, the agreeable feeling is seen to blend melancholy and pleasure, as often for Wordsworth too. Coleridge, however, offers a more elaborate statement of the complex feeling:

The same tender and genial pleasure takes possession of me, and this pleasure is checked and drawn inward by the like aching melancholy, by the same whispered remonstrance, and made restless by a similar impulse of aspiration. It seems as if the soul said to itself: From this state hast thou fallen! Such shouldst thou still become, thyself all permeable to a holier power! thyself at once hidden and glorified by its own transparency, as the accidental and dividuous in this quiet and harmonious object is subjected to the life and light of nature; to that life and light of nature, I say, which shines in every plant and flower, even as the transmitted power, love and wisdom of God over all fills, and shines through, nature! But what the plant is by an act not its own and unconsciously—that must thou make thyself to become—must by prayer and by a watchful and unresisting spirit, join at least with the preventive and assisting grace to make thyself, in that light of conscience which inflameth not, and with that knowledge which puffeth not up!

Coleridge's soul addresses itself a full discourse of religious philosophy. Drawn inward, the pleasure of the scene meets a complex spiritual life: ideas and feelings, remonstrances and aspirations. The philosophic phrasing is more densely charged than Wordsworth's. Coleridge brings to the scene his habitual language of meditation, a peculiar blend of Scripture and intricate philosophic distinction: "accidental and dividuous," "transmitted power," "preventive and assisting grace," "knowledge which puffeth not up."

Coleridge reproaches the fallen state of his spirit brought to consciousness by the meadow. The scene represents an ideal openness to light. The human spirit is both pleased and rebuked to see the holy light of the sun compose the "accidental and dividuous" in nature into harmonious unity, for the mind recognizes its own "impulse of aspiration" in this beauty. Like the meadow, the parts of the mind ought also to be joined by openness to the love and wisdom of God. Part of the spirit aspires to this openness, but the mind recognizes its own failures in the very act of contemplating the ideal.

Coleridge's landscape arouses the mind to contemplate its own ideal condition, but the analogy articulates distinctions as well as correspondences between nature and the human spirit. Nature embodies ideal spirituality, but unconsciously. Part of responding to the meadow is to realize that human spirituality depends on the fullest development of consciousness, particularly in the form of conscience. Therefore, although the light of nature is itself an actual form of divine presence, human openness to the divine differs intelligibly from the openness of a meadow to sunlight.

Coleridge's metaphor of light distinguishes human spirituality from sensory faculties and appearances. The "light of conscience" responds to the visible scene, but its full power is moral and intellectual. The light of conscience, for Coleridge, shines inward, on human experience.[3] Conscience is the inner counterpart of the sun, responsive to its power, but mainly directed to organize the shadows, the particulars, "the accidental and dividuous" within the moral and intellectual life of man.

If Coleridge were to stop here, perhaps his analogy would assert no deeper bond between nature and the human spirit than we have seen in a French poet like Victor Hugo. Though Coleridge does describe a particular occasion, and though his meadow has more sensory presence than, say, Hugo's white horse dawn, one may feel that Coleridge marks the distinction between the human and the natural too sharply to evoke the Wordsworthian sense of a deep bond. For Wordsworth, the poet's power of spiritual love reveals itself through the act of imaginative vision. When Wordsworth recalls a sunrise that he saw on the way home from a party in youth, he feels again that his life is guided by vows made for him by nature. To see the beauty of the sunrise, either actually or in memory, reassures the spirit, for one feels that the imagination participates in the divine power of the sun as together they illuminate the visible scene. Wordsworth's imagination bestows magnificence on the sunrise together with and in the same way as the sun itself. Coleridge may seem more like Hugo in contriving to interpret a natural scene so that it exemplifies a traditional idea of spirituality in itself without connection to nature. The burden of Coleridge's correspondence between nature and spirit falls on the metaphor of light, and there seems no reason other than religious and literary tradition to call conscience a light. The "light of conscience" is a figure of speech, perhaps only an arbitrary verbal convention.

Characteristically, however, Coleridge only pauses for breath where we think he has come to conclusion. The figurative reading of nature in "Appendix B" progresses by gradual and definite stages from the "happy smiles" of the commonplace scene, to the more elaborate analogy between literal and figurative light, and finally, to the climactic and altogether inward beholding of a "symbol established in the truth of things."

> But further . . . I seem to myself to behold in the quiet objects, on which I am gazing, more than an arbitrary illustration, more than a mere *simile*, the work of my own fancy. I feel an awe, as if there were before my eyes the same power as that of the reason—the same power in a lower dignity, and therefore a symbol established in the truth of things. I feel it alike, whether I contemplate a single tree or flower, or meditate on vegetation throughout the world, as one of the great organs of the life of nature. LO!—with the rising sun it commences its outward life . . .

As if the deepening of contemplation revealed the unnoticed shallowness of what came before, Coleridge himself acknowledges the limitations of the sun on the meadow as a symbol. Even while he continues to take pleasure in what may now seem the work of Fancy, the new symbol of the plant arouses a different awe:

> LO!—with the rising sun it commences its outward life and enters into open communion with all the elements, at once assimilating them to itself and to each other. At the same moment it strikes its roots and unfolds its leaves, absorbs and respires, steams forth its cooling vapors and finer fragrance, and breathes a repairing spirit, at once the food and tone of the atmosphere, into the atmosphere that feeds it. Lo!—at the touch of light how it returns an air akin to light, and yet with the same pulse effectuates its own secret growth, still contracting to fix what expanding it had refined. Lo!—how upholding the ceaseless plastic motion of the parts in the profoundest rest of the whole it becomes the visible *organismus* of the entire silent or elementary life of nature and, therefore, in incorporating the one extreme becomes the symbol of the other; the natural symbol of that higher life of reason, in which the whole series (known to us in our present state of being) is perfected, in which, therefore, all the subordinate gradations recur, and are re-ordained *in more abundant honor.*

There is no counterpart in nineteenth-century French literature to Coleridge's symbol of the plant. Through the symbol Coleridge beholds the law of organic growth as a marvelous spectacle for the mind. The language swarms with activity—complex, intricate, miraculous exchanges of power and nourishment. The awe of Wordsworthian

vision enters Coleridge's tone when he goes beyond sensory appearances to behold the invisible processes of nature's relation to the light
and the mind's relation to the law of growth in nature.[4]

Coleridge registers the secret and intricate harmony of natural
growth. What we admire with our eye is beautiful, but it is only the
outward and final development of an invisible miracle. The flower is
the material result of the creation; in thought, the activity that comes
before the flower appears even more wonderful. The plant, any plant,
has the active power to use the energy of light for its own growth at
the same time as the very process of growth nourishes the air in return.

When Coleridge beholds in the growth of the plant "the natural
symbol" of human reason, the essence of the symbol is the power of
natural things to receive light and to return "an air akin to light." Reason is Coleridge's name here for the human capacity to receive divine
light, "the ground and source of all the rest," like the plant's capacity
to receive the light of the sun. In a Note earlier in "Appendix B," Coleridge had tried to define Reason directly, without the aid of a symbol,
but the abstract definition is barely intelligible: "and this we can no
otherwise define than as the capability with which God has endowed
man of beholding, or being conscious of, the divine light. But this very
capability is itself that light, not as the divine light, but as the life or
indwelling of the living Word, which is our light; that is, a life whereby
we are capable of the light, and by which the light is present to us."[5]

It is difficult to keep hold of the different meanings of light in the
abstract definition; the repetitions seem finally more incantatory than
illuminating. The Biblical rhythm and phrasing dignifies the abstractions but without making them more intelligible. Only through the
symbol of the plant does Coleridge's idea of Reason take on a form
that the mind can grasp, as if to confirm Coleridge's belief that an idea
in the highest sense cannot be conveyed but by a symbol.[6]

We understand what it means for the plant to be capable of absorbing the light by a mysterious inherent power related to the source of all
energy in the universe. We can also understand how this capability is
the ground upon which all other processes of growth depend. We cannot, of course, verify Coleridge's analogy between the plant and the
mind, nor can we prove the divine source of life, in nature or in man.
Yet the symbol does make palpable the idea of a fundamental capability for life and the way that principle joins man to nature and both to

the source of life in the universe. Our minds assimilate the symbol to our intuitive knowledge of our own consciousness. We can contemplate how the mind is like a plant, transforming what it absorbs by a capability for growth distinct from any element of experience. Coleridge's symbol reveals a natural law of process at the heart of life, every organism breathing in what the universe offers, sending forth its own life-giving spirit, all the while that it is also absorbed thoroughly in its own natural and particular growth into roots and leaves and flowers.

Coleridge contemplates his symbol with awe, the high excitement of having discovered more than an arbitrary illustration. The laws of growth are actually true for the plant, scientifically true, and the mind is not merely like a plant in a fanciful way. Indeed, the power to discover philosophic truth in nature, and the power to incorporate philosophic truth in symbols is the very process of absorbing, respiring, and growing into form which the symbol of the plant represents. The truth of the symbol seems confirmed by the very process of mind performed by Coleridge in the making of the symbol.

The act of consciousness involved in the creation of symbol raises the mind above the forms of nature. For Coleridge more clearly than for Wordsworth, the natural symbol belongs to a *lower* degree in a hierarchy crowned and completed by man. But, in a sense, Coleridge's idea of the natural symbol also challenges man's false sense of superiority, for nature embodies more perfect obedience to divine law than man generally attains. The symbol from dumb nature represents the ideal of human aspiration. The mind recognizes in nature the laws which can and should but generally do not guide the life of consciousness. As we have already seen in relation to Beauty, the laws interesting to Coleridge represent the ideal rather than the actual rule of human experience. Reason *ought* to be "the ground and source of all the rest," but the proper order of the mind may be corrupted, disorganized by false allegiances. The plant, like the meadow, represents the ideal of permeability to the light. Although the plant's unconscious fidelity to natural and divine law has less dignity than ideal human spirituality, it also rebukes the actual fallen spirit. Coleridge's symbolic reading of nature is therefore both exalting and sad, for the human spirit recognizes in the symbol how openness to divine light should be but is not as habitual for man as growth is to the plant:

O!—if as the plant to the orient beam, we would but open out our minds to that holier light, which "being compared with light is found before it, more beautiful than the sun, and above all the order of stars" (Wisdom of Solomon, vii.29)—ungenial, alien, and adverse to our very nature would appear the boastful wisdom which, beginning in France, gradually tampered with the taste and literature of all the most civilized nations of Christendom, seducing the understanding from its natural allegiance, and therewith from all its own lawful claims, titles, and privileges.

Baudelaire's idea of the symbol proposes a much less solemn conception of the mind's natural allegiance. In "Notes nouvelles sur Edgar Poe," Baudelaire shows how to make symbols of spirit from nature in a way that seems only to extend the boastful and seductive wisdom which Coleridge blames on the French. The judgment of Poe as a decadent writer is the subject, and it involves Baudelaire in characteristically acerbic reflections upon the relation of art to society, to nature, and to philosophic pedantry:

Le mot *littérature de décadence* implique qu'il y a une échelle de littératures, une vagissante, une puérile, une adolescente, etc. Ce terme, veux-je dire, suppose quelque chose de fatal et de providentiel, comme un décret inéluctable; et il est tout à fait injuste de nous reprocher d'accomplir la loi mystérieuse. Tout ce que je puis comprendre dans la parole académique, c'est qu'il est honteux d'obéir à cette loi avec plaisir, et que nous somme coupables de nous réjouir dans notre destinée. —Ce soleil qui, il y a quelques heures, écrasait toutes choses de sa lumière droite et blanche, va bientôt inonder l'horizon occidental de couleurs variées. Dans les jeux de ce soleil agonisant, certains esprits poétiques trouveront des délices nouvelles; ils y découvriront des colonnades éblouissantes, des cascades de métal fondu, des paradis de feu, une splendeur triste, la volupté du regret, toutes les magies du rêve, toutes les souvenirs de l'opium. Et le coucher du soleil leur apparaîtra en effet comme la merveilleuse allégorie d'une âme chargée de vie, qui descend derrière l'horizon avec une magnifique provision de pensées et de rêves.
    Mais ce à quoi les professeurs jurés n'ont pas pensé, c'est que dans le mouvement de la vie, telle complication, telle combinaison peut se présenter, tout à fait inattendue pour leur sagesse d'écoliers. Et alors leur langue insuffisante se trouve en défaut, comme dans le cas—phénomène qui se multipliera peut-être avec des variantes—où une nation commence par la décadence et débute par où les autres finissent.[7]

(The phrase *decadent literature* implies that there is a scale of literatures, an infantile, a childish, an adolescent, etc. This term, in other words, assumes something fatal and providential, like an ineluctable decree; and it is altogether unfair to reproach us for fulfilling the mysterious law. All that I can understand in this academic phrase is that it is shameful to obey this law with pleasure and that we are guilty to rejoice in our destiny.—This sun, which a few hours ago crushed everything with its direct white light, is soon going to flood the western horizon with variegated colors. In the play of light of the dying sun certain poetic spirits will find new delights; they will discover there dazzling colonnades, cascades of molten metal, paradises of fire, a sad splendor, the pleasure of regret, all the magic of dreams, all the memories of opium. And indeed the sunset will appear to them like the marvelous allegory of a soul charged with life which descends behind the horizon with a magnificent store of thoughts and dreams.

But what the narrow-minded professors have not realized is that, in the movement of life, some complication, some combination may appear, quite unforeseen by their schoolboy wisdom. And then their inadequate language fails, as in the case—a phenomenon which perhaps will increase with variants—where a nation begins with decadence and thus starts where others end.)

The phrase "littérature de décadence," Baudelaire explains, imposes upon human affairs an order drawn from the natural process of birth, growth, and decay. Baudelaire plays with the natural metaphor, particularly to undermine its ordinary moral and social connotations. He dismisses the idea that natural law embodies an ideal for human aspiration or grounds for reproach. If decay is the law of history as well as nature, why blame the decadent for accomplishing the natural destiny of culture? Or is the decadent reprehensible only for enjoying what the metaphor asserts to be inevitable?

With characteristic nonchalance, Baudelaire scoffs at the schoolboy wisdom of the academic mind. One might argue that his dismissive gesture does not really engage itself against serious theories of natural law, like either Rousseau's in the second *Discours* or Coleridge's in the idea of the natural symbol. Baudelaire does not conduct a serious philosophical argument in "Notes nouvelles sur Edgar Poe," nor does he acknowledge that the idea of free will within a providential view of history is a classic paradox in Western thought. Baudelaire does not review earlier ways of thinking about this paradox. His tone is casual, dependent upon quick changes in the ground of argument to disarm a more pedantic opposition. He needles the doctrinaire naturalist from two directions at the same time. If culture is altogether determined by

natural law, how can decadent literature be subject to moral judgment? Anyway, culture does not always follow the same laws as nature. There are spiritual accidents, unpredictable complications which
distinguish the movement of human life in society and in individuals
too. Thus Poe, a "decadent" at the dawn of a new culture in America.

Baudelaire mischievously turns the idea of decadence against a
morality based on the analogy between the human and the natural.
The poetic mind does recognize itself in nature but not in a straightforward moralistic way. The artist's pleasure in sunset positively flouts
the order of nature. As if indifferent to the normal and natural pleasure of morning or springtime, crushed by "la lumière droite et
blanche," the poetic spirit awakens to delight as the day declines. The
rich shading of color in sunset offers more and more unusual "motive
for metaphor," in Wallace Stevens' phrase. The poetic spirit pleases
itself by discovering symbols in nature, but it does not bow to the natural order as if nature possessed inherent moral and spiritual meaning.

Baudelaire's image of the sunset plays with natural appearances in a
way alien to both Wordsworth and Coleridge. Coleridge began with
the look of a meadow in sunlight but moved quickly to the organizing
light of the scene, and then to the invisible laws of growth in the plant.
For Wordsworth, the magnificence of sunrise comes also from the
impression of order, the mountains drenched in empyrean light above
and yet still in relation to the common ground. Even a sunset—"the
deep radiance of the setting sun"—illuminates the place of man in the
order of nature as it glorifies the form of the shepherd in Book VIII of
The Prelude. Wordsworth and Coleridge respond to revelations of
natural and spiritual order in the spectacles of sunlight, and they show
how the mind itself belongs to this order by its very power to see what
is revealed.

Baudelaire has no allegiance to the English Romantic idea of natural
order. The things of nature for Baudelaire do not possess the power of
Coleridge's plant to embody the laws that govern both nature and the
mind. Baudelaire makes the sunset a sheerly visual spectacle with no
inherent meaning aside from what "certains esprits poétiques" may put
there. The distinction between what is objectively there in the object
and what the poetic mind creates becomes sharper than in English
Romanticism. Indeed, it is the glory of the poetic imagination to create
rich delight out of what is essentially an indifferent object. The poetic
spirit discovers in the sunset the most fantastical shapes: "des colon-

nades éblouissantes, des cascades de métal fondu, des paradis de feu."
The feelings elicited by the spectacle are equally fabulous: "une splendeur triste, la volupté du regret, toutes les magies du rêve, tous les
souvenirs de l'opium."

Baudelaire implies no inherent correspondence between the natural
process of the sun setting and the poet's exotic feelings. It is true that
the flood of color at the end of day has natural, or at least habitual,
associations. Just as spring connotes birth and warmth, sunsets evoke
a mood of luxurious nostalgia and easeful death. The visual event of
sunset seems to invite acquiescence in decline; like autumn, such gorgeous decay may seem richer than the clear intensity which came
before. But the "correspondence" is only the Lockian connection
between an appearance and certain habits of feeling, not between an
order or process in nature and in man. The fact that a sunset is only an
appearance indeed adds to its appeal, for the poetic mind remains
altogether free to create its own splendors. Baudelaire does not pretend to interpret the things of nature as they are. The sunset to him
hardly exists as a real object or even as an objective source of light that
organizes the rest of the visible world. In comparison to English
Romantic images of the sun, Baudelaire's sunset is a splendidly meaningless phantasmagoria.

The most interesting analogies to Baudelaire's image in English
Romantic poetry appear, not surprisingly, in Byron, the one English
Romantic genuinely admired by the French.[8] The rainbow, for example, in the shipwreck of *Don Juan* offers as much motive for metaphor as Baudelaire's sunset:

> . . . a heavenly Chameleon,
>   The airy child of vapour and the sun,
> Brought forth in purple, cradled in vermilion
>   Baptized in molten gold, and swathed in dun,
> Glittering like crescents o'er a Turk's pavilion
>   And blending every color into one.
>   (Canto II. xcii)

In *Don Juan*, Byron indulges his delight in the exotic picturesque.
He obviously enjoys describing the rainbow as a fabulous spectacle,
though the metaphor of birth and baptism is detailed enough to suggest the absurdity of making natural spectacles reflect human patterns
of experience. The spiritual import of natural appearances is even

more loudly deflated by Byron's chatty mockery in the following stanza:

> Our shipwrecked seamen thought it a good omen—
>   It is as well to think so, now and then;
> 'T was an old custom of the Greek and Roman,
>   And may become of great advantage when
> Folks are discouraged; and most surely no men
>   Had greater need to nerve themselves again
> Than these, and so this rainbow look'd like Hope—
>   Quite a celestial Kaleidoscope.
>
> (Canto II. xciii)

Byron's satire accepts the fun of the rainbow as a kaleidoscope for the imagination, while ridiculing the spiritual interpretation of natural appearances: Biblical, pagan, or transcendental. Although "folks" need to comfort themselves by seeing in nature "omens" or symbols of divinity, to Byron the rainbow is only a bastard appearance, "the airy child of vapour and the sun." Byron shows that he can make a freak of physics sound as splendid as a myth, but he mocks the English Romantic blend of traditional religious symbol and imaginative perception. He stays closer to the eighteenth-century moralist—Johnson, Rousseau, or the *Encyclopédie*—his eye still on the human need for imaginary comforts in the shipwrecks of experience.

The appearance of sunset is as absurdly splendid to Baudelaire as the rainbow is to Byron. Yet Baudelaire does not use the impression of absurdity to satirize transcendental readings of nature, in the manner of Byron. The English transcendental imagination is not really at stake for Baudelaire. The important figure of English Romantic poetry, in Baudelaire's view, *is* Byron, not Wordsworth or Coleridge. Baudelaire seems unaware of the difference between Byron's descriptive style and the Wordsworthian sublime, just as he is unaware of the difference between the poetic principles of Poe and of Coleridge. The French know English Romantic poetry and criticism only through its most blasphemous followers; the versions of English Romanticism most easily assimilated into French were those in which the most sacred articles of Romantic faith were least seriously proposed.

Without having to disentangle himself from English Romantic beliefs, Baudelaire is free to turn the exotic picturesque to a different kind of poetic seriousness. He makes the play of light in the sky signify

more than a kaleidoscope. Natural appearances are not "omens," in
the English Romantic sense of mediating between the divine and the
human, but neither are they interesting merely as colorful shows.
Baudelaire makes a new kind of symbol out of natural things. He
creates a symbol that has spiritual meaning, yet without attributing
spirit to nature itself, for the symbol originates altogether in the
human mind and it postulates only the spirit of the human observer.[9]

The poet, according to Baudelaire, discovers in the sunset a symbol
(or rather, an allegory) of his own soul, "la merveilleuse allégorie
d'une âme chargée de vie, qui descend derrière l'horizon avec un
magnifique provision de pensées et de rêves" (the marvelous allegory
of a soul charged with life which descends behind the horizon with a
magnificent store of thoughts and dreams). The symbol is exclusively
self-reflective. It asserts only the poet's vitality, his rich inventiveness
in the midst of empty appearances. It does not pretend to be a symbol
established in the truth of things, in Coleridge's sense. A plant does
truly grow, in the way Coleridge says. Sunlight does permeate a
meadow. But a sunset, of course, has no thoughts or dreams. Only the
poet does. He can make whatever dream or thought he pleases out of
this spectacle of light. What he pleases to make most of all is a symbol
of his own magnificent decadence.

Baudelaire uses a loosened version of English Romantic terminology
(without, for example, Coleridge's important distinction between
symbol and allegory) to define a quite different kind of symbol. He
does not argue against the English view; he creates what becomes the
counter-romantic symbol while seeming simply unaware of what he is
destroying.

The differences, however, between the transcendental symbol and
Baudelaire's self-reflective symbol are both subtle and profound.
Baudelaire's natural symbol does not call forth the awe expressed in
the English Romantic "Lo!" or "Behold!" That awe depends on the
power of the symbol to evoke the presence of some reality beyond the
self. Even if the act of symbolic vision goes on altogether within the
mind, the symbol creates the impression of a drama that is not totally
internal. Whether nature speaks to the imagination directly through
the senses, or whether images of nature live in the mind, a drama goes
on between the self and some representation of reality beyond the self.
The mind grants the symbol authority to act as the agent of reality.

The English Romantic symbol, therefore, does more than project
feelings. It can cause feelings to change; it makes an impression, like a

new presence on the scene. Wordsworth's vision of the sunrise, for example, chastises him when he comes home from the party, and the image of the sunrise in memory acts again, in a different way, to check the poet's lapse into foolish regret. Coleridge is less likely to feel his mind turned round as with the might of waters, but quieter dramas of the spirit are also set in motion for Coleridge by symbols which impress the mind like a new knowledge of reality.

Baudelaire's natural symbol reflects the spirit of the poet without being granted the power to act upon the mind as only a separate reality can do. The poetic spirit appropriates images from nature to entertain and to manifest itself, but the outer world makes no more demands on the self than a mirror does. Mirrors can stimulate or reflect inner conflict, but except in fairy tales they only echo what the observer projects onto them. The purely self-reflective symbol, therefore, offers no foundation for the feelings of revelation, rebuke, or reassurance which in English Romanticism signify the human spirit touched, and in a sense disciplined, by a reality beyond its own invention.

By withholding objective status from the natural symbol, Baudelaire empties the entire act of symbol-making of the disciplinary power so important to Wordsworth and Coleridge. One may say either that Baudelaire releases the natural symbol from the monotonous awe of English Romanticism or that he confines the poet to the different monotony of his own isolated consciousness. Stated either way, the self-reflective symbol tends to make the act of gazing at the self through symbols a more private and more indulgent activity than it was for the English Romantics. The symbol may be as gloomy as an abyss, yet the self encounters in it no pressure from outside: no summons, no news, no correction to personal bias. At its most enjoyable, the making of the self-reflective symbol has the luxurious freedom associated with the autumns and sunsets favored by this kind of imagination. The decadent spirit luxuriates in its own rich coloring, as if it could fill the external void with its own variegated splendor. Baudelaire turns the making of symbols from nature into one of the pleasures of decadent culture rather than a summons away from culture to natural and divine allegiances.

Although Baudelaire defines the self-reflective symbol more or less clearly in his criticism, there is no single example of his conception rich enough to stand next to "Appendix B" of *The Statesman's Manual.* To see the full possibilities for poetry offered by Baudelaire's idea of the natural symbol, one needs to turn back from the criticism to the poetry. The beautiful poem, "Chant d'Automne," shows better than any example in Baudelaire's prose how the decadent imagination uses symbols from nature to embody an internal drama of the human spirit:

I

Bientôt nous plongerons dans les froides ténèbres;
Adieu, vive clarté de nos étés trop courts!
J'entends déjà tomber avec des chocs funèbres
Le bois retentissant sur le pavé des cours.

Tout l'hiver va rentrer dans mon être: colère,
Haine, frissons, horreur, labeur dur et forcé,
Et, comme le soleil dans son enfer polaire,
Mon coeur ne sera plus qu'un bloc rouge et glacé.

J'écoute en frémissant chaque bûche qui tombe;
L'échafaud qu'on bâtit n'a pas d'écho plus sourd.
Mon esprit est pareil à la tour qui succombe
Sous les coups du bélier infatigable et lourd.

Il me semble, bercé par ce choc monotone,
Qu'on cloue en grande hâte un cercueil quelque part.
Pour qui?—C'était hier l'été; voici l'automne!
Ce bruit mystérieux sonne comme un départ.

II

J'aime de vos longs yeux la lumière verdâtre,
Douce beauté, mais tout aujourd'hui m'est amer,
Et rien, ni votre amour, ni le boudoir, ni l'âtre,
Ne me vaut le soleil rayonnant sur la mer.

Et pourtant aimez-moi, tendre coeur! soyez mère,
Même pour un ingrat, même pour un méchant;
Amante ou soeur, soyez la douceur éphémère
D'un glorieux automne ou d'un soleil couchant.

Courte tâche! La tombe attend; elle est avide!
Ah! laissez-moi, mon front posé sur vos genoux,
Goûter, en regrettant l'été blanc et torride,
De l'arrière-saison le rayon jaune et doux!

I

(Soon we shall sink into cold darkness. Farewell, bright light of our too brief summers! I already hear the mournful thud of the wood falling on the courtyard pavement. The whole winter will take hold of my being: anger, hatred, shivers, horror, hard and strained labor; and, like the sun in its polar hell, my heart will be nothing but a red and icy block. Shuddering, I listen to each falling log. The scaffold being built has no duller echo. My mind is like the tower yielding to the heavy, relentless blows of the battering ram. Lulled by this monotonous thud, it seems to me that a coffin is being nailed somewhere in a great hurry. For whom?—Summer was yesterday; now comes autumn! This mysterious sound tolls like a departure.

II

I love the greenish light of your long, slanted eyes, my sweet beauty, but everything tastes bitter to me today; and nothing, neither your love, nor the boudoir, nor the fireside, can equal the sun ablaze upon the sea. And yet do love me, tender heart! be a mother even to a thankless or a wicked soul. Lover or sister, be the fleeting sweetness of a glorious autumn or of a setting sun. Brief task! The grave is waiting; it is greedy! Ah! as I lament the white torrid summer, let me, with my head on your knees, taste the sweet yellow rays of the afterseason!)

The mood of sad splendor in "Notes nouvelles sur Edgar Poe" reappears in "Chant d'Automne" with richer undertones and as part of a complex poetic design. At the end of the poem, the mellow light of autumn recalls the sunset in the essay. "Le rayon jaune et doux" becomes the symbol of the pleasure to be savored between the light and the darkness of the soul.

Although the symbol fully appears only in the last line of the poem, as often in Baudelaire, the symbolism of the seasons appears in the first stanza. The poem's design does not represent the same movement toward the discovery of a symbol as when Coleridge progresses from the happy smiles of the meadow to the symbol of growth in the plant. The relation of winter to summer, darkness to light is altogether clear from the beginning. Baudelaire's design is more geometric than progressive. Although the symbol of autumnal light is withheld until Part II, we know that it will appear; it is the evident missing part of an implied triangle of images.

The forward movement of the poem, within Baudelaire's design, differs from the unfolding of an English Romantic meditation. The remarkable change in music, subject, even form of address between Parts I and II seems contrived to break rather than follow the natural progress of thought. The love song in Part II interrupts the earlier foreboding of darkness and death. The poet had come to the verge of an ominous departure. Then, with a marvelous air of leisure, a new song begins. The lover in Part II complains and broods as if there were no hurry at all, or as if a new song could actually delay the inevitable.

There is time to dwell on feelings of nostalgia, regret, remorse, fear. The poet has time to savor the feelings of autumn, to luxuriate in the contemplation of symbol.

But no amount of symbol-making has power to change the poet's essential perception of his predicament. His insight does not increase as the poem progresses, for the clearest insight appears in the first line: "Bientôt nous plongerons dans les froides ténèbres." Baudelaire calls attention to an irremediable human situation. The traditional imagery has the same immediate symbolic import as Hugo's "J'avais devant les yeux les ténèbres." Whether these shadows signify total death or only death of the spirit, it is clear that the imagery refers to human darkening. There is no encouragement to think about the meaning of darkening as a process or even as a sensory experience of nature. Baudelaire laments the loss of the human summer—"nos étés trop courts"—and what he dreads is the human counterpart of winter. He fully knows the forms of human winter; he names them directly: "colère, / Haine, frissons, horreur, labeur dur et forcé."

Robert Lowell, in his "imitation" of Baudelaire's "Chant d'Automne," rather awkwardly makes the poem more Romantic, in the English sense, by adding to the first stanza perceptions of nature not mentioned by Baudelaire:

> Now colder shadows . . . Who'll turn back the clock?
> Goodbye bright summer's brief too lively sport!
> The squirrel drops its acorn with a shock,
> Cord-wood reverberates in my cobbled court.[10]

No squirrel drops acorns in "Chant d'Automne." Even Lowell's "colder shadows" and "bright summer" give an autonomous presence to nature not granted by Baudelaire's language. While Lowell is attracted to Baudelaire's self-reflective symbol, he also shows the traces of deeply rooted English habits of imagery. Lowell changes Baudelaire so that actual events in nature may seem to set in motion the movement of thought. *Now* autumn comes, and the perception of that chill presence arouses feeling and thought. Hopkins begins "Hurrahing in Harvest" similarly: "Summer ends now; now, barbarous in beauty, the stooks rise." Baudelaire's "Bientôt" expresses human foreboding independent of any actual events in the outer world. The poet's mood does not derive from the sight of squirrels or stooks or even from the perception of changes in the light. He expresses his feelings in terms of natural imagery, but we know that he could see these cold shadows in a windowless room.

The only perception of the outer world in Baudelaire's poem is the thud of the wood being cut, "le bois retentissant sur le pavé des cours." Even that sound, however, has only ambiguous external reality. Its monotony, like that of the clocks and skeins in other poems by Baudelaire, measures time more abstractly than English imagery of the seasons. Perhaps, as in Poe's "The Tell-Tale Heart," the poet hears only the beat of his own life. As the poem proceeds, the sensory origin of the sound comes to matter even less. "Ce bruit mystérieux" is an inward sound, the rhythm of time in the mind, reverberating with the poet's own nightmarish fantasies. He thinks of a scaffold; he feels himself to be the direct object of the pounding. Someone seems to be making a coffin. The meaning of the sound as it relates to the order or law of nature apart from him seems unimportant. The speaker thinks directly about his own plight which the monotonous sound measures out in human terms of punishment, battle, and burial.

By the last stanza of Part I, an expected ending seems almost complete. The poet, lulled finally by "ce choc monotone," becomes strangely detached from his own anxiety. Monotonous sound has not led him to Rousseau's euphoric revery, but his consciousness does seem blunted, as in the moment before sleep or anesthesia or death. The suddenly new rhythm of the love song, then, comes as a marvelous surprise: "J'aime de vos longs yeux la lumière verdâtre, / Douce beauté." After all, there is no ending. The poet's spirit need not yield right away or altogether to the monotonous rhythm of time. Nostalgia, self-reproach, even hopelessness can impose a slower, more varied rhythm which transforms despair into a mellow and luxurious emotion. The green-eyed woman is asked to be correspondingly gentle, undemanding, generous toward the poet's desire to prolong a "volupté" without climax or even clear intensity.

It is this state of feeling that the final symbol of autumn light represents. Although the implacable rhythm of Part I returns in the last stanza, the symbol expresses the spirit's one gesture against the inevitable coming of the end. One may say that autumn, in Baudelaire's poem, "corresponds" to the poet's spirit. Caught in a forward movement, the season resists it with a show of splendid, leisurely richness. But the image of autumn's glory is as limited a metaphor as the sunset's magnificent dreams in "Notes nouvelles sur Edgar Poe." Baudelaire does not attempt to establish through his image any complex truth about autumn as a natural process. His symbol uses light and color to convey the spirit of *human* resourcefulness. The closest representation of objective order in the poem is the "choc monotone" of time. Autumn is a symbol of human resistance to the order of nature rather than an image of new and deeper bonds to it.

In a limited sense, the gesture of the symbol almost succeeds. The poem ends in the motionless beauty of the poetic image, as if the artificial splendor of language (the displacement even of the ordinary forward movement of the sentence) could suspend the very rhythm of time. Ultimately, of course, the symbol cannot stop time. It represents only an illusion of leisure. Baudelaire's very phrasing and syntax acknowledge the transiency of this "douceur éphémère." The poet is helpless against the reality of time, nor does its naturalness make it more acceptable. The symbol affirms no consoling bond between nature and the human spirit. The poet has no philosophy that pretends to offer such a bond. The reflection of the self in a natural symbol does not assimilate human destiny to a larger order, either natural or divine. The poet refuses to comfort himself with any illusions about a larger order. He remains as unambiguous as Rousseau about the isolation of his own consciousness. At the end of the poem, Baudelaire seeks to prolong his taste of autumnal light in the lap of a woman, not in nature itself. Yet he does not really seek union with a woman either, for he seems convinced that the human spirit creates light and darkness alone, in the circumscribed and private world of consciousness.

12
The Language of Nature

In the essay "On Poesy or Art," Coleridge binds the artistic mind to nature by reformulating the venerable idea of art as imitation. Coleridge characteristically steers a narrow course between philosophic positions that are equally unacceptable to him. The artist should not obey external appearances like a slave, for appearances do not equal objective truth. The substance of perception exists only in the mind. Yet to deny that the universe beyond the mind has "internal and actual" life is also untenable, for it leads to "the dreary (and thank heaven! almost impossible) belief that everything around us is but a phantom."[1] Artistic creation must differ from the mere copying of nature, yet it should always aspire to conform to the life *in* nature. The mind is free, but not altogether autonomous. It has both the power and the obligation to obey universal and objective truth. This is the delicate principle which Coleridge's concept of imitation attempts to establish.

Coleridge explains the artist's imitation of nature through the familiar image of nature's language. He wishes to be quite precise about this common metaphor. Only humans have articulate speech, but nature may be understood to have an "unspoken language" which the poet must learn in order to re-create nature in the articulate language of art:

And this is the true exposition of the rule that the artist must first eloign himself from nature in order to return to her with full effect.

221

Why this? Because if he were to begin by mere painful copying, he would produce masks only, not forms breathing life. He must out of his own mind create forms according to the severe laws of the intellect, in order to generate in himself that co-ordination of freedom and law, that involution of obedience in the prescript, and of the prescript in the impulse to obey, which assimilates him to nature, and enables him to understand her. He merely absents himself for a season from her, that his own spirit, which has the same ground with nature, may learn her unspoken language in its main radicals, before he approaches to her endless compositions of them.[2]

The attribution of language to nature makes the artist rather like a translator, especially the translator of an ancient and "unspoken" tongue. Coleridge takes advantage of this analogy in his argument. The Restoration and Augustan debate about literary translation adds another dimension to the classical idea of art as an "imitation" of nature. The dilemma of the translator in relation to an ancient author helps Coleridge to explain the metaphysical problem of the mind's relationship to the universe outside.

The translator confronts the same extreme alternatives as the metaphysician. He can regard himself as the faithful slave of an original text or as totally free. Dryden, in his contribution to the debate, shuns both extremes. The literal translator (Dryden calls him a "Verbal Copyer") produces no work of art. But Dryden also criticizes the irresponsible freedom granted by Denham and Cowley in their loose idea of "imitation." According to Dryden, Denham and Cowley hardly care for the survival of the original authors: " 'Tis no longer to be call'd their work, when neither the thoughts nor words are drawn from the Original: but instead of them there is something new produc'd, which is almost the creation of another hand."[3] Dryden desires a mean between the literal and the autonomous. The translator must reconcile his own freedom and genius with his obligation to a reality known to exist apart from him, though unintelligible without his intervention. Rather than taking the occasion for self-display, the translator commits himself to re-create the life of the original in new form. He works so that "the Spirit of an Authour may be transfus'd, and yet not lost." The translator must take account, therefore, of the differences between languages. He must seek to understand the special character of the original; and then, most important, he must find within himself the means and the will to reproduce that character in his own language.

Coleridge transposes (rather more freely than Dryden would allow) a rather specialized literary debate into the language of metaphysics. The poet's relation to the "unspoken language" of nature replaces Dryden's more practical concern for the relation of one writer's language to another. By using the looser word "imitation," Coleridge affiliates himself with the freer side in the debate about translation. Yet he retains Dryden's sense of responsibility to a reality beyond the translator's own invention.

Both Dryden and Coleridge deepen the meaning of responsibility to another text by directing the artist to reflect upon his own mental operations. Dryden's weighing of the translator's obligation, however, evokes more sense of unresolvable tension than Coleridge's metaphysical principle. All translators must grapple with the interplay, even rivalry, between two individual sensibilities, potentially quite different from each other. Coleridge works around this conflict by postulating "the same ground" between the artistic spirit and nature. Since the mind resembles nature in terms of structure and process, the artist remains faithful to nature even by attending exclusively to the laws of his own mind. Dryden recommends introspection in a different way; we must "look into our selves," Dryden explains, "to conform our Genius to his." Where Dryden admits the possibility of radically different kinds of genius, Coleridge sees the particular forms of genius—in man and in nature—all governed by the same universal laws. The artist therefore need not bend his mind to an alien genius; he is free to obey the highest laws of his own human nature.

Coleridge uses the metaphor of nature's language to convey the same resemblance of mental to natural structure represented by the symbol of the plant in *The Stateman's Manual*. The photosynthesis of light by the plant is exactly what Coleridge means by nature's unspoken language, for Coleridge emphasizes the "radicals" of language, language as living structure guided by laws of growth and organization. The emphasis is somewhat different from Wordsworth's metaphor of Nature's voice. Whereas Wordsworth recalls what Nature's "changing face" said to him at various times, Coleridge directs attention to the grammar of language more than to its coloring. His critical theory seeks the permanent principles of language, thereby diminishing the importance of individual expression. The "main radicals" of language do not vary with either the individuality of the artist or with what may be thought of as the individuality of nature in its "endless compositions." Coleridge's metaphor of language thus allows the artist to turn away from the particular appearances of nature. The artist who follows "the severe laws of the intellect" can close his eyes to the external text of nature without ceasing to be altogether faithful to it.

Baudelaire also uses a metaphor of language to argue against copying nature in art, but instead of Coleridge's "unspoken language," Baudelaire develops the significantly different image of nature as a dictionary: "La nature n'est qu'un dictionnaire" (777). Baudelaire's metaphor appears in the characteristic French syntax for exposing illusion: "ne . . . que." Nature is only a dictionary; it is no more than a dictionary. Natural objects, with all their particular meanings, associations, and connotations exist outside the mind, but only as words do. To copy the appearances of nature is as meaningless as to copy words from a dictionary:

> "La nature n'est qu'un dictionnaire," . . . Pour bien comprendre l'étendue du sens impliqué dans cette phrase, il faut se figurer les usages nombreux et ordinaires du dictionnaire. On y cherche le sens des mots, la génération des mots, l'étymologie des mots; enfin on en extrait tous les éléments qui composent une phrase et un récit; mais personne n'a jamais considéré le dictionnaire comme une composition dans le sens poétique du mot. Les peintres qui obéissent à l'imagination cherchent dans leur dictionnaire les éléments qui s'accordent à leur conception; encore, en les ajustant avec un certain art, leur donnent-ils une physionomie toute nouvelle. Ceux qui n'ont pas d'imagination copient le dictionnaire. ("Le Gouvernement de l'imagination," 777)

> ('Nature is only a dictionary,' . . . Properly to understand the extent of meaning implied in this sentence, you should consider the numerous ordinary usages of a dictionary. In it you look for the meaning of words, their genealogy and their etymology—in brief, you extract from it all the elements that compose a sentence or a narrative: but no one has ever thought of his dictionary as a *composition*, in the poetic sense of the word. Painters who are obedient to the imagination seek in their dictionary for the elements which suit with their conception; in adjusting those elements, however, with more or less art, they confer upon them a totally new physiognomy. But those who have no imagination just copy the dictionary.)

The image of the dictionary, justly recognized as a key to Baudelaire's criticism,[4] illustrates the complexity of his relation to English Romantic theory. Baudelaire himself is battling against contemporary "realism," especially in painting. Encouraged by the example of Delacroix and by his reading of Poe, he argues against landscape copyists by insisting that only the imagination orders the discrete elements of art into significant form. The copyists falsely regard nature itself as a composition: "Ils copient un mot du dictionnaire, croyant copier un poëme" ("Le Paysage," 812) (They copy a word from the dictionary, believing that they are copying a poem). Some interpreters of Baudelaire treat his image of the dictionary as identical to Coleridge's "unspoken language," and it is true that Baudelaire sometimes sounds as though he were directly echoing Coleridge's most important principles. The imagination, Baudelaire explains, both analyzes and synthesizes:

> Elle décompose toute la création, et, avec les matériaux amassés et disposés suivant des règles dont on ne peut trouver l'origine que dans le plus profond de l'âme, elle crée un monde nouveau, elle produit la sensation du neuf. ("La Reine des facultés," 773)
>
> (It decomposes all creation, and with the raw materials accumulated and disposed in accordance with rules whose origins one cannot find save in the furthest depths of the soul, it creates a new world, it produces the sensation of newness.)

Baudelaire's emphasis on the artist's creation of a coherent vital order seems almost identical to Coleridge's famous definition of the "secondary Imagination" in the *Biographia*: "It dissolves, diffuses, dissipates, in order to recreate; or where this process is rendered impossible, yet still at all events it struggles to idealize and to unify. It is essentially *vital*, even as all objects (*as* objects) are essentially fixed and dead."[5] Coleridge's praise of the imagination as the life-giving power in art survives to become the dominant slogan in Baudelaire's argument against mid-century French realism. Putting together principles learned from Delacroix, Poe, and even stranger English sources,[6] Baudelaire introduces the idea of the creative imagination into French critical debate.

Yet those who have studied the new reverence for the creative imagination in Baudelaire's criticism tend to ignore the difference between a dictionary and an "unspoken language." Margaret Gilman, for example, dismisses too quickly the lack of inner meaning in the organization of a dictionary when she paraphrases Baudelaire: "the true artist, the true poet, just as he chooses words from the dictionary with a

careful regard for their meaning and connotation, chooses and ar-
ranges the aspects of nature, of which he has deciphered the inner
meaning."[7] It is not clear what kind of "inner meaning" words in a dictionary may be said to possess, as we have already observed in relation to Johnson's *Dictionary* and the *Encyclopédie*. The French, at
least since the seventeenth century, tend more than the English to treat
words as if they were significant objects intelligible one by one. The
later French Symbolists sometimes behave as if individual words (even
single vowels) were magic objects with secret inner meanings. Baudelaire, to some extent, leads this group, for he too likes to play with
occult correspondences. But critics like Margaret Gilman and Marcel
Raymond exaggerate the importance of the visionary Baudelaire in
quest of the occult.[8] Baudelaire manipulates the image of nature as a
dictionary mainly to show what nature lacks. He proceeds on the
ordinary assumption that meaning in language comes from the ar-
rangement of words in relation to each other. That is why the copyist
produces only a meaningless assemblage of things. The important
point for Baudelaire is to divorce imaginative creation from any form
of imitation; there is no coherent structure of meaning, no Coleridgean "internal and actual" life in nature for the artist to imitate:

> Tout l'univers visible n'est qu'un magasin d'images et de signes aux-
> quelles l'imagination donnera une place et une valeur relative; c'est
> une espèce de pâture que l'imagination doit digérer et transformer.
> ("Le Gouvernement de l'imagination," 779)
>
> (The whole visible universe is but a storehouse of images and signs
> to which the imagination will give a relative place and value; it is a
> sort of pasture which the imagination must digest and transform.)

Coleridge's careful ambiguities and distinctions disappear in Baudelaire's "ne . . . que." The French version is not only clearer, it also discards Coleridge's respect for natural law altogether. Where Coleridge
labors to articulate a concept of re-creation, new and yet faithful to
laws that can be said to govern the original, divine Creation, Baudelaire less ambiguously emphasizes the total and exclusive power of the
artist to create life. The work of art is a living world, a *new* world,
governed by laws that originate altogether within the artist himself.
Baudelaire thus gives no allegiance to Coleridge's intricate relationships between the artistic mind and nature, and between natural
genius and divinity. According to Baudelaire, the creativity of the

artist makes him *like* a god; he can create a world, like God in Genesis. But his imagination does not bring him closer *to* God, for nature and the imagination do not perform the mediating function so important to Coleridge's theory. In Baudelaire's language, the original Creation, Nature as the Creation of God, is only a suggestive metaphor of the artist's autonomy and his responsibility only to the dictates of his own conception:

> Un bon tableau, fidèle et égal au rêve qui l'a enfanté, doit être produit comme un monde. De même que la création, telle que nous la voyons, est le résultat de plusieurs créations dont les précédentes sont toujours complétées par la suivante; ainsi un tableau conduit harmoniquement consiste en une série de tableaux superposés, chaque nouvelle couche donnant au rêve plus de réalité et le faisant monter d'un degré vers la perfection. ("Le Gouvernement de l'imagination," 778-779)

> (A good picture, which is a faithful equivalent of the dream which has begotten it, should be brought into being like a world. Just as the creation, as we see it, is the result of several creations in which the preceding ones are always completed by the following, so a harmoniously conducted picture consists of a series of pictures superimposed on one another, each new layer conferring greater reality upon the dream, and raising it by one degree toward perfection.)

Nature as we know it—"telle que nous la voyons"—is at best one world, "un monde." There is nothing sacred, nothing absolutely real, nothing hidden there that one yearns to reach or assimilate or re-create. Baudelaire's ideal of "la perfection" is abstract, the perfect manifestation of the artist's conception, whatever it is, rather than the perfect assimilation of the human spirit to the one internal and actual order of the universe. Rather than seeking to re-create the life of nature, the artist as directed by Baudelaire *decomposes* the apparent order of nature until it is no more than a dictionary, a reservoir of material (in more than one sense of the word). The artist then uses this store of material to create a living world, a replacement for the dead, natural world and a symbol of his protest against it. All Coleridge's effort to join man to God through nature—all the awkward vocabulary of "union," "mediation," "reconciliation," "coalescence," "co-ordination"—disappears in Baudelaire's characteristically French antitheses.

Although Baudelaire engages in no direct dispute with the English
Romantics, later writers like Yeats and Wallace Stevens know how to
turn the French terms directly against English Romantic values: "It
was only with the modern poets, with Goethe, and Wordsworth and
Browning, that poetry gave up the right to consider all things in the
world as a dictionary of types and symbols and began to call itself a
critic of life and an interpreter of things as they are."[9] Yeats makes the
Romantic faith in imaginative perception seem like a brief interlude of
illusion in the history of art. If nature is only a dictionary, then Romantic theory is both pretentious and restrictive, for it falsely subordinates the poetic mind to what is only an illusion of order. The
French image of nature as a dictionary helps Yeats to see that for all
the celebration of creative freedom in Romantic theory, only quite
limited autonomy is really granted to the artistic mind. The same
recognition may be discerned in Stevens' cryptic pronouncement in
The Necessary Angel: "The imagination is one of the great human
powers," Stevens asserts. "The romantic belittles it. The imagination
is the liberty of the mind. The romantic is a failure to make use of that
liberty."[10] Stevens sounds paradoxical, for we are accustomed to think
that the Romantics inaugurated the imagination as a great human
power. And they did. But to some English as well as French poets after
Baudelaire, Coleridge's idea of the mind's "lawful claims" comes to
look more like an arbitrary infringement of human rights. For the
great power of the imagination to Coleridge (and to Wordsworth also)
is, finally, its power to assimilate the mind to other powers, outside
and beyond the artist's individual human spirit.

In Coleridge's criticism, the artistic mind re-creates human character in fundamentally the same way as it re-creates nature. While
Coleridge is more obscure than Baudelaire at every point, his consistency of principle makes him, in a sense, less elusive. Baudelaire
more often seems to shift his point, or at least to play tricks with it. In
contrast to Coleridge, Baudelaire's view of the imagination seems to
change significantly when human rather than natural appearances are
the subject. The human scene for Baudelaire seems more than a
dictionary of images. The Parisian costume, for example, embodies
contemporary spiritual desolation. The artist creates the symbol, but
its meaning does not derive exclusively from his imagination. The
symbol reveals the inner truth of the contemporary world. Insofar as

the symbol is also self-reflective, it joins the poet to the more general procession of life (or, rather, of death) in modern society.

Baudelaire's interest in modern passion often leads him to grant the human material of art inherent meaning different in kind from what natural objects possess for him. He praises the etchings of Méryon, for example, because they represent the internal and actual life of Paris and the people who live there:

> Nous avons rarement vu, représentée avec plus de poésie, la solennité naturelle d'une grande capitale. Les majestés de la pierre accumulée, les *clochers montrant du doigt le ciel*, les obélisques de l'industrie vomissant contre le firmament leurs coalitions de fumées, les prodigieux échafaudages des monuments en réparation, appliquant sur le corps solide de l'architecture leur architecture à jour d'une beauté arachnéenne et paradoxale, le ciel brumeux, chargé de colère et de rancune, la profondeur des perspectives augmentée par la pensée des drames qui y sont contenus, aucun des éléments complexes dont se compose le douleureux et glorieux décor de la civilisation n'y est oublié. ("Peintres et aqua-fortistes," 848)

> (I have rarely seen the natural solemnity of an immense city more poetically reproduced. Those majestic accumulations of stone; those spires 'whose fingers point to heaven;' those obelisks of industry, spewing forth their conglomerations of smoke against the firmament; those prodigies of scaffolding round buildings under repair, applying their openwork architecture, so paradoxically beautiful, upon architecture's solid body; that tumultuous sky, charged with anger and spite; those limitless perspectives, only increased by the thought of all the drama they contain—he forgot not one of the complex elements which go to make up the painful and glorious décor of civilization.)

Although the cityscape looks as fantastical as a sunset, the city for Baudelaire actually does *contain* passions that correspond to its physical forms. The smokestacks of industry and the intricate scaffolding on old monuments are not merely suggestive appearances. The artistic imagination transforms the objects into symbols (as Baudelaire himself does here in his metaphoric language), but the symbols also reveal the actual inner drama of Parisian life. They represent the perversity of modern worship, how it parodies ancient forms with a grotesque grandeur of its own. Whereas the English Romantic symbol most perfectly becomes lens as well as mirror when it is drawn from nature, only human objects seem to have this double capacity for Baudelaire. The artistic imagination discovers its own grotesque spirit reflected in the cityscape, yet it also apprehends the truth of the object, a separate reality with its own "solennité naturelle."

It is perhaps no accident that Baudelaire's image of the city spires includes one of the few phrases in his writing that can specifically be traced back to the language of Wordsworth and Coleridge.[11] Baudelaire's descriptive style comes closest to English Romantic imagery when his vision is directed toward the city; his reflections upon the artistic value of human and urban appearances bring him closest to Coleridge's idea of the symbol "consubstantial with the reality which it makes intelligible." Baudelaire thus liberates the idea of the symbol to serve all the bizarre manifestations of human passion in contemporary life. Yet Baudelaire's interest in the true symbol of human passion does not so much redirect Coleridge's idea toward different material, as come toward Coleridge from a different and characteristically French direction.

Baudelaire's early essays on portrait-painting, written before his interest in Poe, show the independent French origins of Baudelaire's interest in the symbolic representation of human passion. Baudelaire first considers the idea of symbolic form in his essays on human portraiture, a subject of particular fascination to the French going back through Rousseau to the seventeenth-century moralists and to Montaigne. The portrait of the human figure in painting poses the same questions as literary portraiture, and Baudelaire talks interchangeably about literature and painting. The specific point at stake in the essay "De l'Idéal et du modèle" is Baudelaire's preference for Delacroix over Ingres. As one would expect, Baudelaire opposes the idealization of the human figure as represented by the perfect line in the style of Ingres:

> Mais comme il n'y a pas de circonférence parfaite, l'idéal absolu est une bêtise. Le goût exclusif du simple conduit l'artiste nigaud à l'imitation du même type. Les poëtes, les artistes et toute la race humaine seraient bien malheureux, si l'idéal, cette absurdité, cette impossibilité, était trouvé. Qu'est-ce que chacun ferait désormais de son pauvre *moi*,—de sa ligne brisée? (642-643)

> (But since there is no such thing as a perfect circumference, the absolute ideal is a piece of nonsense. By his exclusive taste for simplicity, the feeble-minded artist is led to a perpetual imitation of the same type. But poets, artists, and the whole human race would be

miserable indeed if the ideal—that absurdity, that impossibility—
were ever discovered. If that happened, what would everyone do
with his poor *ego*—with his crooked line?)

Like the absolute ideal of Beauty in general, the ideal human figure
does not exist—and if it did, it would be boring. Baudelaire starts
from the interesting fact of human individuality, looking for the
devices of art that can best re-create the "pauvre *moi.*" The broken
line of Delacroix is one such device; it is individual, "bizarre," and
that is the mark of beauty in portraiture as in other forms of art.

Portraiture, however, poses a special problem since the "pauvre
moi" of the model is at stake and also the individuality of the artist.
Portraiture involves two human figures, each with his own "bizarrerie." In praising Balzac, Baudelaire simply accepts with admiration
that the ostensible social portraits of the great novelist live only
because they represent, in various forms, Balzac's own individuality.
Baudelaire in his poems more closely follows the example of Rousseau, who simplifies the problem of individuality by portraying only
his own self. In the essays on portrait-painting, however, Baudelaire
does not limit his subject to self-portraiture. The artistic problem in
the essay "De l'Idéal et du modèle" concerns the re-creation in art of
the objective and individual human model.

As always, Baudelaire sets himself against both neoclassicism and
naïve realism. He separates himself from the copyist by affirming
terms like "idéal" and "harmonie," but he redefines the neoclassic con-
cepts to imply the perfect reconstruction of the individual through
artistic means:

> Ainsi l'idéal n'est pas cette chose vague, ce rêve ennuyeux et impal-
> pable qui nage au plafond des académies; un idéal, c'est l'individu,
> redressé par l'individu, reconstruit et rendu par le pinceau ou le
> ciseau à l'éclatante vérité de son harmonie native. (644)

> (Thus the ideal is not that vague thing—that boring and impalpable
> dream—which we see floating on the ceilings of academies; an ideal
> is an individual put right by an individual, reconstructed and
> restored by brush or chisel to the dazzling truth of its native
> harmony.)

To explain what he means by the harmony of the individual model,
Baudelaire draws on Lavater's theory of physiognomy. There are
organizing principles of character manifest in the human form: "Telle

main veut tel pied; chaque épiderme engendre son poil. Chaque
individu a donc son idéal" (643). (Such and such a hand demands such
and such a foot; each epidermis produces its own hair. Thus each
individual has his ideal.) The portraitist must strive to realize the ideal
that is only imperfectly embodied in the actual living form of a person.
The ideal portrait reveals the correspondences between physical form
and the inner life; it perfects the coherence of the model, but without
violating the truth of individual character.

Between the "Salon de 1846" and the "Salon de 1859," Baudelaire
read and translated Poe. Mainly on Poe's authority, the term "imagination" becomes the name of the artistic faculty which re-creates the
inner life of the model in portraiture. But the creation of the coherent
individual figure is still Baudelaire's ideal, now expressed in a more
elaborate critical vocabulary. Holbein's portrait of Erasmus succeeds
because Holbein's imagination creates the perfect visual form to
embody the spirit of Erasmus. Ingres and his followers violate the
individual beauty of their models. By adding an extra fleshiness to the
arm of the Parisian woman, they impose an alien poetry of style to the
painting instead of using the imagination to re-create the true spirit of
contemporary beauty: "la qualité naturellement poétique du sujet qu'il
en faut extraire pour la rendre plus visible" ("Le Portrait," 809) (the
naturally poetic quality of the subject, which must be extracted so that
it may become more visible).

Baudelaire's willingness to grant inner character to human but not
to natural appearances accounts for some of the apparent inconsis-
tencies in his statements about the imagination. Baudelaire tends to
grant more autonomy to the imagination when the object is natural,
but the imagination becomes a power of true insight when the object is
human. There is still a further twist to Baudelaire's view, however,
that comes from his tendency to use the symbol of human passion for
irony and social satire. Baudelaire characteristically undercuts the
inner spirit of the human objects in his world by making a surface of
vitality correspond paradoxically to hidden depths of emptiness. Baudelaire's symbols disclose false promises of passion, like the glittering
clothing of the woman in "Avec ses vêtements ondoyants. . . ." Or,
they embody infernal imitations of spirituality—the spires of industry, for example, vomiting black smoke against the firmament. When
the human object is "le philistin ennemi" (and his temples of material-
ism), the act of imagination becomes the same gesture of the artist
against the deadness of the object that we have already observed in

relation to nature. From Baudelaire's point of view, it is ironically appropriate that the priests of progress worship nature, for the appearances of bourgeois vitality are as empty of inner life as any mere spectacle of landscape.

The essay "Le Portrait" (1859) shows Baudelaire turning the idea of symbolic correspondence to satiric use. He mocks the bourgeois desire for an exact copy of the self in a portrait. Almost in caricature of Rousseau, now every prosperous citizen wants a faithful portrait of his figure for posterity. The gross bourgeois, like Rousseau, exclaims that his own figure offers a subject fully formed. Baudelaire parodies philistine complacency through the imaginary voice of "L'Ame de la bourgeoisie":

> Voilà ce qu'elle me dit aujourd'hui, cette vilaine Ame, qui n'est pas une hallucination: "En vérité, les poëtes sont de singuliers fous de prétendre que l'imagination soit nécessaire dans toutes les fonctions de l'art. Qu'est-il besoin d'imagination, par exemple, pour faire un portrait? Pour peindre mon âme, mon âme si visible, si claire, si notoire? Je pose, et en réalité, c'est moi, le modèle, qui consens à faire le gros de la besogne. Je suis le véritable fournisseur de l'artiste. Je suis, à moi tout seul, toute la matière." (806)

> (Just listen to what she said to me today, that wretched Soul who is no hallucination: 'In truth, our poets are singularly mad to claim that imagination is necessary in all the functions of art. What need is there of imagination in painting a portrait, for example? In painting my soul—my soul which is so visible, so clear, so well-known? I pose, and in reality it is I, the model, who consents to do the bulk of the work. I am the artist's true *supplier*. I myself, all by myself, am the whole thing!')

The bourgeois hates the imagination out of self-love. He regards his own form as sufficient material for the artist. Baudelaire snidely agrees that the plentiful fleshly form of the bourgeois model is material indeed, "toute la matière," only meaningless matter. Here, above all, the imagination is needed to re-create this mass into a form of art:

> Mais je lui réponds: *"Caput mortuum*, tais-toi! Brute hyperboréenne des anciens jours, éternel Esquimau porte-lunettes ou plutôt porte-écailles, que toutes les visions de Damas, tous les tonnerres et les éclairs ne sauraient éclairer! plus la matière est, en apparence, positive et solide, et plus la besogne de l'imagination est subtile et laborieuse. (807)

(To which I reply: "*Caput mortuum,* be silent! Hyperborean brute of ancient days, eternal Esquimau, be-spectacled, or rather be-scaled, whose eyes not all the visions of Damascus, not all the thunders and lightnings of the heavens, would be able to lighten! The more positive and solid the *thing* appears to be, the more subtle and laborious is the work of the imagination.)

Baudelaire plays on the neo-Platonic idea of the symbol that most perfectly overcomes the most obstacles to the full manifestation of spirit. To Baudelaire, the bourgeois model presents the most obstacles to spirit because he has absolutely no spirit himself. The artist displays the superiority of his own spirit by protesting against this solid matter in his satiric symbol: "éternel Esquimau porte-lunettes ou plutôt porte-écailles." The satiric portrait does, of course, also reveal the correspondence of matter to spirit in the object, for the solid bourgeois appearance corresponds precisely to true inward grossness.

The symbol of bourgeois grossness is established in the truth of things. The artist elevates the sordid things of the contemporary world to new intensity while at the same time destroying their false appearances of life. Baudelaire does not exactly allow the things of the outer world to fade away; he is more aggressive than indifferent toward his material. His symbols show how the poetic imagination may expose the true deadness of many superficially living things, human as well as natural. The poetic symbol becomes a weapon for criticism, for revenge, and for a somewhat perverse form of spiritual self-assertion. The new, perhaps the only modern form of spirituality is that demonstrated by the artist in his transformation of things into lively symbols of deadness.

Part Five

Nature and Imagination in *Middlemarch*
and *Madame Bovary*

13

Middlemarch: Beyond the Voyage to Cythera

Both Gustave Flaubert and George Eliot seem to exemplify in the genre of the novel Baudelaire's ideal modern artist, "le peintre de la vie moderne":

> Celui-là sera le *peintre*, le vrai peintre, qui saura arracher à la vie actuelle son côté épique, et nous faire voir et comprendre, avec de la couleur ou du dessin, combien nous sommes grands et poétiques dans nos cravates et nos bottes vernies. ("Sculptures," 596-597)

> (The painter, the true painter for whom we are looking, will be he who can snatch the epic quality from the life of today and can make us see and understand, with brush or with pencil, how great and poetic we are in our cravats and patent-leather boots.)

The great novels of the nineteenth century are closer in spirit to Baudelaire's idea of epic than to Wordsworth's, for Wordsworth never clothes himself (nor his other heroic characters) in ties and shiny boots. *The Prelude* transforms ordinary life into an epic theme, but grandeur in Wordsworth's poetry belongs to *common* rather than to modern life. The poet affirms the continuing possibility of grandeur by uncovering the life of passion common to all men by virtue of their shared and permanent human nature. He does not search for the heroic dimension of modernity, but looks to those parts of common experience that seem least colored by contemporary fashion.

Baudelaire's ideal of the modern artist allows, even requires, a sharper sense of irony than Wordsworth ever shows. The modern tone, according to Baudelaire, must be both ironic and heroic, for contemporary aspirations to grandeur are at the same time admirable and absurd. It is this blend of irony and celebration that Baudelaire applauds in Flaubert's portrait of Emma Bovary. His essay in praise of the novel defends Flaubert against false friends as well as enemies. Baudelaire does not admire the novel for its supposedly impartial realism. This is no mere copy of provincial life, but an imaginative creation, a superb portrait of modern heroic aspiration and defeat:

> et finalement la pauvre épuisée, la bizarre Pasiphaé, reléguée dans l'étroite enceinte d'un village, poursuit l'idéal à travers les bas-tringues et les estaminets de la préfecture:—qu'importe? disons-le, avouons-le, c'est un César à Carpentras, elle poursuit l'Idéal! ("Madame Bovary," 1011)

> (and finally this poor exhausted creature, this bizarre Pasiphaë, reduced to the narrow precincts of a village, pursues the ideal through the dance halls and dingy taverns of the prefecture:—does it matter? Let us say it, let us confess it, she is a Caesar in Carpentras; she is pursuing the Ideal!)

George Eliot, in *Middlemarch*, invites comparable admiration for her very different heroine, Dorothea. The "Prelude" of the novel introduces heroic values by invoking Saint Theresa whose "passionate, ideal nature demanded an epic life" (3).[1] In modern provincial England, there are also passionate, ideal natures, though the pursuit of an epic life has become more awkward than it was in the Spanish Middle Ages—and more incongruous also than Wordsworth had suggested.

Provincial life, in Wordsworth's epic, can be heroic without incongruity, for prosaic circumstances never really entangle the poet-hero. Debts, gossip, the clumsy way a man eats his soup—none of the demeaning social details of contemporary life counts for much in the world of *The Prelude*. There is no necessary discrepancy between heroic aspirations and the character of the world in the poem. Undistracted by the trivial forms and mean shapes of the contemporary, the poet encounters a world equal in grandeur to the demands of his own nature.

The novelist—whether Flaubert or Eliot—differs from Wordsworth, if only by attending to the unelevating details of contemporary social life. Passionate, ideal natures want to ignore or transcend sordid details, but the novelist shows the burden of detail to weigh more heavily against heroic possibility than the aspiring characters imagine. Emma Bovary as Pasiphaë in a dusty town of Normandy, Dorothea Brooke in quest of sainthood in provincial drawing rooms—these are necessarily figures of irony, at least in part. Like Rousseau at l'Hermitage, rudely gulping his dinner so that he may rush off to "le pays des chiméres," they are more bound to social reality than they realize. Whereas Wordsworth at the top of Mount Snowdon discovered even more grandeur than he had expected, the novelists, like Rousseau, report incongruity and disappointment, "perhaps only a life of mistakes, the offspring of a certain spiritual grandeur ill-matched with the meanness of opportunity" ("Prelude," 3).

The ill-match between spiritual grandeur and actual opportunity is a favorite source of irony for the nineteenth-century novelist. Yet the analogy between *Middlemarch* and *Madame Bovary* is uncomfortable, especially for the English reader. A taste formed by George Eliot, or even by Jane Austen, is likely to find any form of grandeur hard to discern in Flaubert's novel. When Henry James complained that Emma Bovary is, finally, "too small an affair" to be a tragic protagonist,[2] he expressed the snobbery, or perhaps only the optimism about human character, taught by the English tradition in fiction as well as poetry. Characters like Dorothea (or Emma Woodhouse or Isabel Archer) may think too grandly of themselves, but they are also rightly and openly valued by the narrators of the novels and by their own most discerning friends within the story, an attractive company whose taste we are flattered to share.

No reader, however, wishes to emulate Charles Bovary's dumb infatuation with his wife, and it is hard to find any more worthy guide to admiration in Flaubert's spare narrative. If Emma gains our serious regard, we give it grudgingly, in spite of our own conceit and our own best sense of taste. Baudelaire thus urges us to *confess* that Emma is a heroine. There is a challenge to the complacent reader in Flaubert's portrait, not unlike the way Rousseau dares his audience to claim superiority over him or Baudelaire taunts the reader: "—Hypocrite lecteur,—mon semblable,—mon frère." (—Hypocritical reader,— my likeness,—my brother.)

Baudelaire accepts the twists of Flaubert's vision more readily than does James,[3] for he recognizes in the novel devices of his own art and also attitudes toward human character deeply rooted in the French tradition, at least since moralists like Pascal and La Rochefoucauld unmasked the mere appearances of distinction among men. Baudelaire acknowledges with a certain satisfaction that Flaubert has made his heroine thoroughly crude in education, intelligence, and taste. Emma's vulgarity in one sense represents the common core of human character generally. Emma can be a heroine to Flaubert and to Baudelaire because they see no great variations in the fundamental moral quality of human character. She will do for a heroine as well as any other.

For the same reason, this crude figure can be made to carry the whole impulse of romantic aspiration. The artist's irreverence for human nature has a radical egalitarian element. All kinds of unsatisfied desire may equally represent aspiration toward "l'Idéal." The nineteenth-century French writer learned from Rousseau that the main distinction among people is the relative thoroughness of their discontent rather than the specific form of their desire. To Baudelaire as well as to Flaubert, complacency signifies the worst grossness; uncompromising dissatisfaction is in itself a kind of heroism and perhaps the only mark of spiritual grandeur in modern life.

Baudelaire accepts as a nasty truth that Emma Bovary's catastrophes cannot be blamed on her inferior intelligence, taste, or social class. Even had she been finer, and her desires taken more beautiful, rare, and discriminating forms, the novel persuades us that the basic pattern of her experience would have been the same. To set the romantic sensibility in such a common figure is essential to Flaubert's irony and to his despair. Emma's vulgarity does not so much cause her failure as expose the common truth of romantic desire. The vulgarity of the subject is, after all, only relative; all art gambles on the artist's power to transform fundamentally vulgar matter into beautiful form.

Baudelaire in his own poetry can level social and intellectual distinctions with the same brutality as Flaubert:

> —C'est Cythère,
> Nous dit-on, un pays fameux dans les chansons,
> Eldorado banal de tous les vieux garçons.
> Regardez, après tout, c'est une pauvre terre.

(It is Cythera, we are told, a country known in song; banal Eldorado of all the old bachelors. Look at it: after all, it is a miserable place.)

To Baudelaire, the Cythera of myth and song is not substantially different from the erotic fantasy of an ordinary Parisian sinner. In the poem "Un Voyage à Cythère," "les vieux garçons" refers equally to the singers of the past and to the sordid crowd of everyday dreamers somewhat past their prime. Baudelaire is one of "les vieux garçons" in both senses; he is the poet carrying forward the traditional dream of love and he also belongs to a more ordinary and rather seedy crowd. These two identities work upon each other. The erotic desire of the modern Parisian comes to seem poetic—a new descant upon the supreme theme of Art and Song. At the same time, the basest and most banal of illusions lurks at the heart of all this noble tradition. This is the truth discovered in the fateful "voyage à Cythère." In the form of a corpse grotesquely hung on a gibbet, all superficial distinctions have long been effaced:

> Les yeux étaient deux trous, et du ventre effondré
> Les intestins pesants lui coulaient sur les cuisses,
> Et ses bourreaux, gorgés de hideuses délices,
> L'avaient à coups de bec absolument châtré.
>
> .   .   .   .   .
>
> Ridicule pendu, tes douleurs sont les miennes!
> Je sentis, à l'aspect de tes membres flottants,
> Comme un vomissement, remonter vers mes dents
> Le long fleuve de fiel des douleurs anciennes.

(The eyes were two holes and his heavy bowels were running down his thighs from his gutted belly. And his executioners, gorged with hideous delight, pecking at him with their beaks, had absolutely castrated him. . . . Ridiculous hanged man, your suffering is also mine! At the sight of your flapping limbs, I felt the long bitter stream of old pain rushing up to my teeth like vomit.)

In the character of Emma Bovary, Flaubert creates another modern voyager to Cythera, with the same double identity as Baudelaire in the poem.[4] Emma's tawdry illusions of passion represent the same yearnings that the most beautiful fantasies of the lyric tradition express. Flaubert belittles romantic lyricism through Emma, but he also ennobles her by the company she keeps in her hapless voyage.

Through most of the novel, Emma absorbs herself in dreams of one or another "Eldorado banal." Her first vague malaise in marriage, for example, takes shape as the image of the exotic honeymoon she missed. Later, she invents a new romantic scenario of flight for her aristocratic lover, Rodolphe. But the closest Emma comes to Cythera is an island in the harbor of Rouen on an evening excursion with her second lover, the clerk Léon. That outing cannot initiate the idyll of myth and song. Emma and Léon can only postpone the inevitable collapse of fantasy. They go on to meet every week in a hotel room that is a gaudy imitation of Cythera, with a boat-shaped bed and ornamental shells. Meanwhile, Flaubert brutally accelerates the movement to disaster, counting the weeks and the debts as they accumulate. The lovers cannot transform their sordid circumstances, nor can they avoid the tedium which eventually destroys their romance from within.

The symbolic corpse on the gibbet in "Un Voyage à Cythère" represents the moral and physical truth of the voyager's own condition. At the moment of her death from poisoning, Emma Bovary sees a similar hideous reflection of herself in the figure of the blind beggar who earlier had followed the carriage to her trysts in Rouen. Hearing the beggar's song of love from her deathbed, Emma loses the peace just promised by the ritual of extreme unction; she dies with "un rire atroce" of bitter recognition. Emma laughs grotesquely to hear the beggar persist in a song so grossly contradicted by his physical condition, but she herself can stop the repetitive melody only by dying. Her insight offers no release. For the true voyager to Cythera, insight has no more power over illusion than it has over a body still alive but already decomposed by poison. That is why the dream of Cythera has survived so long.

Yet insofar as Emma finally recognizes her own image in the blind beggar, Flaubert allows her to become, at the last moment, artistic rather than merely sentimental (as he calls her at the beginning of the story). She becomes like a particular kind of artist—Flaubert himself acknowledging: "Emma Bovary, c'est moi," or Baudelaire at the end of many poems: "Tête-à-tête sombre et limpide / Qu'un coeur devenu son miroir!" (Dark and limpid tête-à-tête of a heart become its own mirror!)

For the disillusioned sentimentalist, the self-reflective symbol is a harsh, even melodramatically ugly confrontation. Fantasy yields not to ordinary, matter-of-fact perception, but to new symbolic mirrors that are as violent and punitive as the earlier fantasies were sweet and soothing. What the mirror reflects outdoes the mere natural decay of earthly things. The corpse on the gibbet, the beggar, Emma's body unnaturally putrefied by arsenic—these hellish images reflect the punishment exacted for illusion and debauchery, and they show persistent illusion to be the most poisonous debauchery of all.

Illusions disintegrate and revive, however more genteely, all through nineteenth-century English literature too. But only George Eliot, among English novelists, comes even close to the French fascination with this pattern. Eliot's preeminence here may signify only the wider range of her mastery in general. She studies more patterns of experience, and each one more thoroughly, than other novelists. Yet beneath the diverse surfaces of experience, one or another form of the deceiving imagination is often what George Eliot's probing vision uncovers. Her special interest in this theme in part reflects the influence of Samuel Johnson. George Eliot gives full novelistic life to Johnson's insight into "the hunger of the imagination." It is less generally recognized that, more than any other English novelist, George Eliot had also studied Rousseau's *Confessions*, the first thorough history of the imagination born of desire. Eliot surprised Emerson in 1848 by announcing that the *Confessions* had first awakened her to deep thought. A few years later she remarked that it was worthwhile learning French if only to read the *Confessions*. She was still reading the book aloud to Lewes in 1876.[5] Since she was an expert in the French as well as the Johnsonian version of the desiring imagination, it is especially interesting to see that even Eliot never grants disappointed illusion the respect it commands from the French. George Eliot's irony shows less brutality and less despair than that of Flaubert and Baudelaire, partly because she refuses to accept the common hunger of the imagination as more than a partial truth about human character.

Idyllic fantasy dominates the experience only of an inferior character in *Middlemarch*, Rosamond Vincy. Romantic illusions, of a sort, do mislead Dorothea, and they contribute to the suffering of Lydgate. But Dorothea is not governed by the dream of Cythera (nor by any other myth of paradise), and Lydgate's failure to find a heaven of love is not the center of his tragedy. He becomes tragic only because disappointment in marriage undermines his scientific vocation, a passion inconceivable to Rosamond, as it would be to Emma Bovary and to the whole tradition of romantic desire which she represents.

Rosamond Vincy, however, is cut from the same pattern as Emma

Bovary, even though the English sentimental imagination includes a sharp eye for real linen and dishes. Rosamond is a better-bred Emma, her fantasies refined at Mrs. Lemon's school. Like Emma, Rosamond reads the *Keepsake*. Her edition offers a socially distinguished rather than an exotic idyll, but the message of idyllic happiness is the same. When Lydgate, as suitor, snobbishly mocks the picture of a bridegroom in the *Keepsake*, Rosamond can only believe that he will transport her to an even more elegant "middleclass heaven."

George Eliot drily exposes the conventional illusions upon which Rosamond and Lydgate vaguely agree to live. The sharp difference from Flaubert is that Eliot, in all the spaciousness of *Middlemarch*, allows little room for sentimental fantasy to expand into either lyricism or tragedy. Lydgate's fantasies during courtship reflect lazy conceit more than the unquenchable thirst of the heart. Rosamond's inability to see beyond illusion provokes more disdain from the narrator than any other failure in the novel. Thus when Rosamond turns from the irritation of marriage to flirt with Ladislaw, Eliot briskly dismisses her shallowness: "the easy conception of an unreal Better had a sentimental charm which diverted her ennui" (VIII. 75. 552).

George Eliot allows Rosamond her share of sympathy (granted in fellow-feeling to all blundering mortals), but other characters in *Middlemarch* deserve deeper compassion and admiration. There are better people than Rosamond in the richly populated world of the novel. Rosamond's tenacious desire does not signify spiritual grandeur, only spoiled stubbornness. George Eliot subjects the different forms of human aspiration to intellectual, moral, and spiritual discriminations. Whereas Flaubert allows his mediocre heroine to embody the essence of the romantic imagination, a Rosamond Vincy for George Eliot is only an example of vulgar selfishness at its most exasperating. Although versions of this selfishness lurk in all the characters, George Eliot does not reduce all forms of imaginative aspiration to this common denominator. Rosamond's imagination represents the power of ordinary egotism, but some of George Eliot's characters at least envision other kinds of power. At the center of the novel are Lydgate, Dorothea, and above all, the narrator, all of whom pursue ideals which make idyllic fantasy seem paltry, cheap, and finally, unimaginative.

To start with Lydgate, he does not think astutely about love partly because his best energies go to his ideal of scientific research. George Eliot also venerates this ideal, drawing upon it for metaphors of her own artistic ambition. Although Lydgate fails where we feel that the novelist succeeds, the terms of her success emerge in part through the character most like her in ambition.

Lydgate is no Charles Bovary, doggedly memorizing test questions and bungling stupid operations. He is a skilled practitioner and, beyond that, a pathologist, a "spirited adventurer" in search of the "primitive tissue" common to all living organisms. Research is to him a "delightful labour of the imagination," "the exercise of disciplined power—combining and constructing with the clearest eye for probabilities and the fullest obedience to knowledge; and then, in yet more energetic alliance with impartial Nature, standing aloof to invent tests by which to try its own work" (II. 16. 122).

Lydgate's imagination is the instrument which gives full value to the microscope and the scalpel. In his unfortunately rare moments of intense work, Lydgate reclines in solitary thought. The intuitive power of his own mind completes and transcends the work of observation. Like the poet in English Romanticism, Lydgate cherishes a sublime idea of the creative imagination, "the imagination that reveals subtle actions inaccessible by any sort of lens, but tracked in that outer darkness through long pathways of necessary sequence by the inward light which is the last refinement of Energy, capable of bathing even the ethereal atoms in its ideally illuminated space" (II. 16. 122).

The weightiness of Eliot's language for Lydgate's ideal oppresses some readers, as Coleridge oppressed Pater. Although Eliot regards Lydgate's failure to work with irony, there is no shade of levity in her descriptions of the ideal itself. Eliot sets forth Lydgate's vision with the same philosophic seriousness that Coleridge has for the poetic mind. Lydgate too aspires to a new knowledge of reality. Instead of imagining a world more in accord with desire, he envisions new insight into the existing reality outside his own mind and beyond the reach of ordinary sight. His own life belongs to this reality but the goal is not primarily an image of or for himself. His vision does not mirror the self but transcends and absorbs it in a larger order. If Lydgate were to succeed, the familiar world would be newly revealed to his imagination. Since the energy of his "inner light" is itself a form of universal vitality, he can legitimately hope that his natural powers will lead him to the truth of nature outside. The scientific imagination, like the mind of the poet as portrayed by Coleridge, seeks to use its own power to discover the innermost harmony and order in the universe.

Eliot's description of Lydgate's ideal makes the scientist resemble the poet in his potential power and also in the genesis of his imagination. Eliot does not bind Lydgate's love of "arduous invention" to the chain of private motives discernible in all the characters, including Lydgate in matters of sexual love. Selfish desire accounts for only one kind of imagination: "that joyous imaginative activity which fashions events according to desire" (III. 23. 172-173). Although that kind of imagination is creative—"for images are the brood of desire" (IV.34.237)— what is created has no alliance with impartial Nature. Desires are always partial, for they are rooted in egotism. They distort truth to gratify the self. Eliot, however, does not reduce Lydgate's scientific aspirations to this common source. He is, of course, personally ambitious, and he tends to mistake his plans for accomplishments, but the origin of his aspiration cannot be contained in these characteristics of temperament. For George Eliot, some forms of imagination transcend the lens and scalpel of psychological analysis, as if there were parts of the mind directed purely by the passion for truth, order, vision.

Lydgate's scientific ardor is both natural and inspired, like Wordsworth's dedication to poetry or the mind's complacency in Beauty, according to Coleridge. George Eliot gives a Wordsworthian history of Lydgate's vocation. Instead of analyzing private motives, as she so thoroughly knows how to do, she traces Lydgate's devotion to a mysterious moment of revelation in childhood. As in Wordsworth's story, the trivial domestic life of the child was interrupted by sudden and sublime vision. The narrator describes how, one wet day, the boy out of boredom looked in an old encyclopedia on a high shelf in the library. A chance "spark" kindled his imagination:

> The page he opened on was under the head of Anatomy, and the first passage that drew his eyes was on the valves of the heart. He was not much acquainted with valves of any sort, but he knew that *valvae* were folding doors, and through this crevice came a sudden light startling him with his first vivid notion of finely-adjusted mechanism in the human frame. A liberal education had of course left him free to read the indecent passages in the school classics, but beyond a general sense of secrecy and obscenity in connection with his internal structure, had left his imagination quite unbiased, so that for anything he knew his brains lay in small bags at his temples, and he had no more thought of representing to himself how his blood circulated than how paper served instead of gold. But the moment of vocation had come, and before he got down from his chair, the world was made new to him by a presentiment of endless processes filling the vast spaces planked out of his sight by that

wordy ignorance which he had supposed to be knowledge. From
that hour Lyndgate felt the growth of an intellectual passion.
(II. 15. 106-107)

Like Wordsworth startled by the sunrise coming home from a
party, Lydgate's moment of vocation came as "a sudden light." He
was not driven to this vision by personal need; on the contrary, Eliot
makes a point of his free idleness. Boredom and indifference were
transformed to "presentiment" all of a sudden, before the boy came
down from his chair. The "spark" came from outside, but his own
intelligence enlarged the light, as he transformed the dry encyclopedia
prose into a "vivid notion of finely-adjusted mechanism in the human
frame."

The leap from folding doors to the presentiment of endless processes
in the universe may seem implausible for a ten-year-old boy, though
Eliot argues that it is no more extraordinary than the more familiar
stories of how people fall in love. The normally sober narrator here
records the mysterious birth of a passion. She intends to make it
sound like a miracle, for intellectual passion is a miracle of nature, a
mysterious marriage of the heart to the living universe:

> Ah! need I say, dear Friend! that to the brim
> My heart was full; I made no vows, but vows
> Were then made for me; bond unknown to me
> Was given, that I should be, else sinning greatly,
> A dedicated Spirit. On I walked
> In thankful blessedness, which yet survives.
> (*The Prelude,* IV. 333-338)

George Eliot reaffirms Wordsworth's belief in natural miracles; yet
as a novelist she is also readier to inspect the obstacles to all marriage
vows: "all the possible thwartings and furtherings of circumstance, all
the niceties of inward balance" (II.15.111). To Wordsworth, the poetic
imagination resembles a stream, moving ever to its destination regardless of impediment. Wordsworth shows the poet protected by vows
made for him beyond his knowledge and will. Even the French Revolution cannot long divert him from his true course. George Eliot's
hero, however, must keep his vows by his own determination. He is
more deeply implicated in the social stream than Wordsworth's heroic
self, and the water is polluted or at least confused by different currents. Lydgate is compared to a swimmer, sometimes floating easily

with the current, strong enough to swim against it, but even without sinning greatly, he is subject to fatigue or, as it turns out, landing himself in an inlet of mud. To disdain the contrary currents, to rely on vows made for him, shows a foolish arrogance in George Eliot's novel rather than a protective faith.

Lydgate's dedication eventually gives way to worldly pressure. Though he becomes a wealthy London practitioner, a success by worldly standards, we measure the significance of his falling away by his own Wordsworthian standards. Eliot, moreover, allows us to separate Lydgate's personal failure from the general value of his ideal. His surrender does not signify the inevitable defeat of heroic aspiration. Lydgate's failure commands sympathy, but George Eliot also holds him individually responsible for it. The very presence of the narrator limits the generality of Lydgate's fate, for she shows by her own example that it is hard, but not impossible, to sustain the exercise of disciplined power. The narrator does join intellectual authority and passionate presentiment; her voice shows that practical attention to everyday truth need not undermine a larger vision of hidden structure in the universe.

Lydgate's failure, therefore, is particular and special, like all human failure, no matter how common failure may be. Coleridge explained this in relation to Taste. True Taste is rare, according to Coleridge, but that fact does not invalidate the possibility of Taste. Corruptions of Taste are still to be explained as individual failures due to the accidents and peculiarities of experience. Although George Eliot gives more sympathetic attention than Coleridge or Wordsworth to the commonness of disappointment, she also continues their austere moral judgment of individual failure. Casaubon's futile work on the Key to All Mythologies does not prove that scholarly ambition is itself delusory, nor does Ladislaw's failure to paint invalidate the idea of creative genius in art. We come to know the blundering figures of Eliot's world as distinct personalities. They are subject to the pressures of circumstance and temperament, but however great those pressures are, they do not negate Eliot's belief in the possible strength of human creative power in various forms.

Failure individualizes George Eliot's characters and, in a special Coleridgean sense, the forms of failure are also representative. The crowded, varied world of *Middlemarch* shows in marvelous detail the "endless compositions" of human nature. The characters represent not only social types but also universal principles of moral and intellectual structure or, rather, failures of effective structure. Casaubon, the aging scholar, for example, hides his vaults of information from the light. He represents the futility of a mind distrustful of natural light, seduced from nature by vanity and false faith in dead fact. Eliot's metaphoric language portrays Ladislaw to be the more attractive but also ineffectual reverse of Casaubon. He is the very embodiment of light, but at the start he lacks the discipline needed for any actual *work* of genius.

George Eliot introduces Lydgate as a good bet because he is more actively committed than any other character to the ideal balance and reconciliation of mental powers needed for any great creative accomplishment. However, Lydgate's story ultimately shows another form of partial development and another way in which disordered powers undermine a great ambition. Lydgate, too, is undone by his failure to cultivate the full natural power of his mind.

Wordsworth had already suggested the particular nature of Lydgate's danger in his comparison of poetry to science in the Preface to *Lyrical Ballads:*

We have no knowledge, that is, no general principles drawn from the contemplation of particular facts, but what has been built up by pleasure, and exists in us by pleasure alone. The Man of science, the Chemist and Mathematician, whatever difficulties and disgusts they may have had to struggle with, know and feel this. However painful may be the objects with which the Anatomist's knowledge is connected, he feels that his knowledge is pleasure; and where he has not pleasure he has no knowledge. What then does the Poet? . . . He considers man and nature as essentially adapted to each other, and the mind of man as naturally the mirror of the fairest and most interesting properties of nature. And thus the Poet, prompted by this feeling of pleasure, which accompanies him through the whole course of his studies, converses with general nature, with affections akin to those, which, through labour and length of time, the Man of science has raised up in himself, by conversing with those particular parts of nature which are the objects of his studies. The knowledge both of the Poet and the Man of science is pleasure; but the knowledge of the one cleaves to us as a necessary part of our existence, our natural and unalienable inheritance; the other is a personal and individual acquisition, slow to come to us, and by no habitual and direct sympathy connecting us with our fellow-beings. The Man of science seeks truth as a remote and unknown benefactor; he cherishes and loves it in his solitude; the Poet, singing a song in which all human beings join with him, rejoices in the presence of truth as our visible friend and hourly companion.[6]

Although Wordsworth introduces the example of science to dignify poetry (as George Eliot dignifies her art by scientific metaphor), he ends by reducing science to a more partial form of knowledge than art. Poetry resembles science, Wordsworth argues, in showing the necessary bond between knowledge and passion: knowledge as a form of love, and love as a power of insight. But compared to the poet, the scientist appears a narrow and isolated figure, cut off from "habitual and direct sympathy" by his pursuit of remote truth.

In the figure of Lydgate, George Eliot both continues and reevaluates Wordsworth's perception. The oddity of Wordsworth's position is that, in his poetry, Wordsworth often seems more like his own view of the scientist. In modern society, the sublime poet as represented by Wordsworth seems in more danger of social isolation than the scientist (especially the scientist-physician). The figure of Lydgate at the start of his career promises to refute Wordsworth's theoretical contrast between science and art. By his actual practice of medicine in the provinces, Lydgate intends to maintain the connection with his fellow-being theoretically reserved by Wordsworth for the poet.

But George Eliot's understanding of "sympathy" is more complex than Lydgate's (as well as being more substantial than Wordsworth's). Lydgate loves his fellow-being professionally and from a distance, rather like Wordsworth in his poetry. Lydgate can be tender and generous, but all his generosity presumes the safe distance of his superiority. His dedication to Anatomy does, in fact, isolate him in arrogance, though it does not protect him from the yoke and tug of ordinary circumstance. Moreover, under stress of debt, Lydgate discovers that his ardor for research is not an "unalienable inheritance," in Wordsworth's phrase. Since Lydgate has no other inheritance to live on, he ultimately relinquishes his ambition altogether. Lydgate does grow to deeper acquaintance with everyday truth, but George Eliot makes that knowledge much sadder than Wordsworth suggested. It comes to Lydgate only through his own struggle and through his discovery of his own need for common human sympathy.

George Eliot's humane vision gives new substance to Wordsworth's criticism of the scientist, while it also suggests dangers for the poetic imagination which Wordsworth was reluctant to acknowledge. The sublime poet, too, may isolate himself from common humanity while mistaking his remote generosity for direct and habitual sympathy. As the narrator of a prosaic novel, George Eliot paradoxically seems to exemplify Wordsworth's ideal poet and Lydgate's ideal scientist more fully than either of them. Through the narrator's vision, we come to understand how Lydgate loses faith in his own energy mainly because he lacks the habit of directing his mental energy to the common details of life. In comparison to the narrator, Lydgate suffers from repeated failures of imagination, above all the failure to exert the natural energy of his imagination on the intricate structure of his own character and its connections to society.

Lydgate's falling away from dedication is balanced in the design of *Middlemarch* against Dorothea's natural growth. Heroic vocation and natural growth, the two main threads of Wordsworth's theme in *The Prelude*, are thus separated and interwoven by George Eliot in the histories of her two principal characters.

At the beginning of the novel, Dorothea displays a different arrogance than Lydgate's by her dramatic disdain for mere nature. Thus she so unnaturally marries Casaubon who seems to offer transcendence with his "archangelic" manner and his vaults of knowledge. To marry Casaubon will be as good as marrying Pascal or Milton (after he became blind), but Dorothea must discover that her life, in reality, is bound to the visible and natural world. As for Wordsworth in *The Prelude*, Dorothea's growth requires her to recognize her bond to nature, and she comes to accept that bond with a Wordsworthian mixture of gratitude and regret.

The balance, however, is not quite Wordsworthian. George Eliot presents Dorothea's spiritual yearnings sympathetically, but not with Wordsworthian reverence. At the start, Dorothea's spirituality mainly takes the form of various "shortsighted plans." She desires the "communion with Divine perfection" described in religious books, yet there is no Wordsworthian suggestion that she has ever directly experienced that communion, even as a child. Her experience seems limited to impulsive gestures toward transcendence in which blindness to common truth outweighs any glimpse of what she calls "the higher inward life."

Nor do Dorothea's vague aspirations command the same serious regard as Lydgate's scientific vision. As Dorothea herself realizes, it is not enough to have obscure feelings of sublimity. Full spiritual grandeur requires at least a vision of some correspondent form of action or knowledge. Still, we are encouraged to admire the purity and generosity of Dorothea's vague idealism. The quality of her desires raises her above a Rosamond Vincy. However confused and partial her judgment, however entangled in false perceptions, what Dorothea longs for is freedom from her own limitations rather than indulgence of them. She has no vocation, yet she does have an intuitive conviction that a vocation *should* reconcile knowledge, feeling, piety, and action. And this intuition speaks for the presence in her character of the same impulse toward unity and truth that we see in Lydgate and the narrator. Instead of disdaining Dorothea's restlessness, therefore, we share her regret that the actual world does not help her to discover what she should do or know.

Dorothea experiences disappointment, yet her story does not become tragic like Lydgate's. It is significant that from the start George Eliot makes Dorothea more beautiful by showing her to be more "natural" than she herself acknowledges. We feel affection for her dramatic renunciations—of ornament, for example, or horseback riding. Her asceticism is so passionate that it paradoxically expresses the power of her natural vitality. Her naïve gestures toward martyrdom are more amusing than either inspiring or depressing because we recognize them mainly as signs of youthful energy and individuality. We admire Dorothea apart from her aspirations as well as for them, so that the worth of her experience to some extent remains distinct from her own evaluation of it.

George Eliot gives the character of Dorothea a vigor which signifies a bond to nature deeper than whether or not she gives up horseback riding or even marries Casaubon. Her "full-blooming youth" illuminates her every appearance in the novel, even when she imagines herself denying nature. Her natural energy turns out to be less limited than Lydgate's, despite his clearer consciousness of his own power. Lydgate's openness to nature is intellectual, deliberate, professional. It is concentrated in a particular activity and can thus be taken from him. When he crosses the "perilous margin" into passivity, we are made to feel that the energy of the scientist is, as Wordsworth said, not altogether intrinsic to his character. Dorothea's energy, at the start, causes her unhappiness because she can discover no shape for it adequate to her ideals. But Dorothea's natural power also proves more enduring than Lydgate's, for it pervades her character. Her openness to nature is habitual, even unconscious: "But there was nothing of an ascetic's expression in her bright full eyes, as she looked before her, not consciously seeing, but absorbing into the intensity of her mood, the solemn glory of the afternoon with its long swathes of light between the far-off rows of limes whose shadows touched each other" (I. 3. 20).

George Eliot's landscape has a "solemn glory" of its own to match and deepen Dorothea's vitality, even when Dorothea is consciously entertaining illusions of her "visionary future" with Casaubon. Through scenes and metaphors which connect Dorothea to the deep and continuing power of nature, George Eliot subtly keeps Dorothea safe from the potential destructiveness of her unnatural marriage. Wordsworth explains how his early experiences in nature preserve him from harm in London and even in the French Revolution. Dorothea, like all the characters in *Middlemarch,* is more vulnerable to chance and circumstance, but George Eliot also grants Dorothea's bond to nature protective power. It is as if vows had been made for her that she should be safe from her own illusions. The novelist does help nature by arranging for Casaubon to die suddenly, but we also feel that Dorothea possesses within herself a living force of nature which can sustain her even when her circumstances are most oppressive.

When she returns from her honeymoon in Rome, for example, Dorothea laments that she has to depend upon inward vision to keep up her spirit in the "shrunken" winter scene. We are perhaps more impressed that Dorothea does have this creative power in abundance. It is implicit in her glowing appearance and in her energetic movement of thought and feeling:

> In the first minutes when Dorothea looked out she felt nothing but the dreary oppression; then came a keen remembrance, and turning away from the window she walked round the room. The ideas and hopes which were living in her mind when she first saw this room nearly three months before were present now only as memories: she judged them as we judge transient and departed things. All existence seemed to beat with a lower pulse than her own. . . . What breadths of experience Dorothea seemed to have passed over since she first looked at this miniature! She felt a new companionship with it, as if it had an ear for her and could see how she was looking at it. Here was a woman who had known some difficulty about marriage. Nay, the colours deepened, the lips and chin seemed to get larger, the hair and eyes seemed to be sending out light, the face was masculine and beamed on her with that full gaze which tells her on whom it falls that she is too interesting for the slightest movement of her eyelid to pass unnoticed and uninterpreted. The vivid presen-

tation came like a pleasant glow to Dorothea: she felt herself
smiling, and turning from the miniature sat down and looked up as
if she were again talking to a figure in front of her. But the smile dis-
appeared as she went on meditating, and at last she said aloud—
    "Oh, it was cruel to speak so! How sad—how dreadful!"
    She rose quickly and went out of the room, hurrying along the
corridor, with the irresistible impulse to see her husband and
inquire if she could do anything for him. (III. 28. 202-203)

Throughout the novel, Dorothea's feelings move, turn, rise, beat with
the pulse of her inner life. The outer world may wither, but Dorothea
continues a spirited inward drama of memory, longing, anger, desire,
guilt, and sympathy. Her inner brightness glows like a gem. It also
melts and flows—animating furniture, pictures, rooms, her own
clothing, finally even the unnatural poise of Rosamond.

Dorothea does not especially value the naturalness so basic to our
perception of her character. She yearns to transcend nature, partly
because she narrowly identifies nature with the constraints of social
convention. She knows that her neighbors think it natural for her to
wear inherited jewelry and marry the "blooming" Sir James. Yet while
she is right to feel confined by conventional judgments of her destiny,
she is wrong to mistake local opinion for natural truth. George Eliot
makes the story of Dorothea's growth an education in Wordsworthian
distinctions. She learns to differentiate the traditional from the conventional, the truly natural from what passes for nature according to
literary and social custom. Dorothea has her own "gem-like brightness" without ornament, and she comes to recognize that she may
choose a natural rather than either a merely conventional or grossly
unnatural husband.

Yet insofar as even the truly natural does not altogether satisfy
Dorothea's spirit, George Eliot follows Wordsworth further to the
perception of more subtle and perhaps unfulfillable human longings.
Dorothea cherishes the idea of herself transformed to a grandeur and
perfection beyond what even the most beautiful forms of nature show,
"that submergence of self in communion with Divine perfection which
seemed to her to be expressed in the best Christian books of widely-
distant ages" (I. 3. 18). Even after she discovers that Casaubon cannot
guide her along the path to this ideal, the ideal itself remains alive
within her. Later, when Dorothea thinks she has been betrayed by
Ladislaw, she suffers, but she also revives the vision of herself initiated

into spiritual perfection: "She yearned towards the perfect Right, that it might make a throne within her, and rule her errant will" (VIII. 80. 577). Although her ideal from the start has a more ethical form than Wordsworth's "bliss ineffable," it represents an analogous vision of the self lost and absorbed in more-than-natural glory.

We are made to regard Dorothea's last vision of transcendence with complex irony. After wrestling all night with her grief over Ladislaw's supposed betrayal, Dorothea greets the dawn as if it signaled her resurrection to saintly power. We see her anguish, and we admire how she transcends private pain through a vision of helping those who have hurt her: "It was not in Dorothea's nature, for longer than the duration of a paroxysm, to sit in the narrow cell of her calamity, in the besotted misery of a consciousness that only sees another's lot as an accident of its own" (VIII. 80. 577). Yet we also know that Ladislaw has not, in fact, betrayed Dorothea. As in *The Prelude*, despair is a delusion rather than the awakening from illusion to reality. Dorothea has less cause for grief than she believes, and her saintly visit to Rosamond is going to initiate Dorothea herself into the natural stream of the world more than she imagines. The morning light, like Dorothea herself, is more natural than spiritual. It favors the free movement of natural feeling and is not really conducive to the martyrdom of lively young women. Though we admire Dorothea's mastery of selfish passion, we also see the natural boundary of her destiny. We see that she is undaunted by a hard night on the floor and we expect that her power will prove to be different—more enjoyable, but also more paltry—than she realizes.

In *The Prelude*, Wordsworth tries to affirm continuity between love of nature and spiritual perfection, though we have observed that Wordsworth's reconciliation of the two is often ambiguous and qualified. In George Eliot's view of Dorothea, the disparity between nature and spirit in a way becomes even more open than in Wordsworth. The poet can at least remember being lost in "the sentiment of Being," even while he sings songs of natural love, but Dorothea cannot be both wife and saint. Moreover, Dorothea would rather be a wife. She accepts the renewed possibility of natural love with joy. She gives up saintliness without hesitation, regardless of whether or not it is an ideal within her power to fulfill.

Yet beyond these ironies, George Eliot still continues Wordsworth's effort to avoid a sharp sense of opposition between nature and spirit in

Dorothea. The same qualities of character inform Dorothea's natural love and her yearning for transcendence. The same generous energy, the same ardor for what promises release from a narrow and stifling social lot quickens both Dorothea's love for Ladislaw and her visions of martyrdom. George Eliot diminishes the impression of a struggle between higher and lower parts of the self. Nature and spirit are not opposed in Dorothea's character, even though they are not altogether reconcilable either. Ladislaw is the right husband for Dorothea because he responds to the very spirit in her character that leads her to yearn for sainthood.

It is not necessary here to debate again Eliot's characterization of Ladislaw. I essentially agree with those who find him too insubstantial to carry the role he must play in the novel's design.[7] He must be the "natural" husband for Dorothea. But he is never quite plausible as a living man. Dorothea's natural power seems fully conveyed in the novel through her youthful womanly appearance and her restless energy of thought, language, and gesture. George Eliot's language for Ladislaw associates him too schematically with "the spirit of morning" without fully rendering how this natural spirit may manifest itself in the form of an attractive man. Ladislaw is too simply and repetitively a "bright creature," associated with the most ephemeral appearances of nature, its "subtler influences," like "the breaking of sunshine on the water."

What is interesting to me is that English Romantic poetry helps to explain this weakness as well as so many of the strengths of *Middlemarch*. Eliot's difficulty with Ladislaw is analogous to problems in Wordsworth's poetry. Here, as so often in Wordsworth, there seems to be an effort to minimize the price of yielding to natural love, and thus a failure to create a substantial natural image for that love. Though Eliot intermittently tries to humanize Ladislaw through ironic or social detail, he lacks human weight, just as Wordsworth's Lucy or even his birds and butterflies have less natural substance than we might expect. In marrying Dorothea to Ladislaw, George Eliot joins her to nature in its most spiritualized, even disembodied, form—as if to suggest that, in her case at least, natural love could hardly be said to violate the purest desires of the spirit. Victorian reticence about sexuality undoubtedly adds to the problem, especially for the social subject of the novelist. The sexuality of Dorothea and Ladislaw is an aspect of nature assumed but never quite presented. At moments in the novel, to love Ladislaw seems no less remote from ordinary nature than the Romantic poet's devotion to birdsong: "Sometimes, when he took off his hat, shaking his head backward, and showing his delicate throat as he sang, he looked like an incarnation of the spring whose spirit filled the air—a bright creature, abundant in uncertain promises" (V. 47. 345).

The English Romantic poet, with richness and ambiguity, makes birdsong fill the space between nature and spirit, at least in the mind of the poet. George Eliot, as novelist, faces an even more difficult problem, for she attempts to portray an actual marriage between a woman and a man who has all the attributes of the Romantic bird.

Although the unsatisfying character of Ladislaw mars the resolution of the novel, Eliot's conception of Dorothea's marriage still seems to me moving and profound. Those who would simply appropriate Dorothea for the feminist cause fail to grasp George Eliot's complex Wordsworthian commitment to nature in the novel.[8] It is true that in part Dorothea suffers limitations from being a mere woman, for even Ladislaw, the "spirit of morning," can grow to a heroic career in politics. But from another point of view, the limitations of Dorothea's marriage represent only the universal limitations of nature, as perceived without sexual distinction by the Romantic poets too. Eliot does, of course, register disappointment that nature and spirit do not merge more perfectly for Dorothea. She had felt purer and nobler impulses of aspiration before her marriage; yet, as for Wordsworth, what nature offers is rich enough to keep regret from dominating the tone of her experience.

There is, after all, less cause for regret in the novel than in Wordsworth's poetry, perhaps because natural human life in *Middlemarch* is made to seem more satisfying, at least more entertaining and varied than it is in *The Prelude*. George Eliot's natural world has less heroic possibility than Wordsworth's, especially for a woman, but Eliot makes this world so engaging to the imagination that the need for heroism, as well as for perfect spirituality, recedes. Moreover, the acceptance of nature in *Middlemarch*, as in Wordsworth's poetry, does not really contradict faith in spiritual values. The force of Dorothea's nature intimates the life of the spirit even though the full union of nature and spirit remains out of her reach.

14

The Poverty of Nature in
Madame Bovary

Madame Bovary offers no form of reconciliation between the human spirit and nature. Flaubert envisions no counterpart to George Eliot's ideal of natural creative power. Nor does he suggest any recompense for lost illusions in the round of natural life. Instead, Flaubert confirms in yet another way the extreme antithesis between nature and spirit so strongly rooted in the French tradition. Human needs are not soothed by what nature can offer. Human ambitions only distract the spirit from the true poverty of nature, as in Pascal's view of "la misère de l'homme sans Dieu." For Pascal, the discrepancy between the needs of the human spirit and the reality of nature forces the choice of Christian faith. Since Flaubert affirms no Christian belief, the despair of the novel is unmitigated. Emma Bovary lives and dies isolated with her own desires in an empty and indifferent universe.

From the English perspective, Flaubert's harsh vision makes his novel more decisively counter-romantic than *Middlemarch*, in the same way that Baudelaire seems more counter-romantic than the Victorian poets. As with Baudelaire, however, Flaubert's relation to Romanticism takes on a different shape within the French tradition. French Romanticism itself never envisions the "energetic alliance" between the spirit and nature so important to the English. The French counter-romantic in a sense only carries the isolation of human consciousness in French Romanticism to its logical and grim conclusion.

258

Emma's imaginary islands of love express the same disparity between desire and reality central to Rousseau. Persistent desire leads to
catastrophe no less inexorably in the *Confessions* than in *Madame
Bovary*. Flaubert, it is true, debases both sides of the antithesis: the
reality of Yonville is even worse than Rousseau's society, and it includes the natural landscape which to Rousseau represented freedom
from oppressive reality. In *Madame Bovary*, the landscape is as depressing as the social scene. On the other side of the antithesis, Emma's inner life may seem no more sordid than what Rousseau confes-
ses, but Flaubert makes unsatisfied desire less attractive than Rousseau
at least intends to do. *Madame Bovary* is more ambiguous than the
Confessions about the superiority of maladjustment. Whereas Rousseau argues that reality offers nothing as fine as his sensibility, what
Emma desires may seem as dreary as what she has.

Yet the debased level of conflict in *Madame Bovary* does not really
dispute the Rousseauist judgment that reality does not satisfy the
needs of the heart or spirit. Nor does Flaubert simply disdain Emma's
sensibility. Though he stops short of Charles Bovary's infatuation
with Emma, he is not as cynical as the aristocrat, Rodolphe, who discards Emma because her insatiable desires finally become boring.

To understand Flaubert's irony, it is necessary, first, to see how it
differs from the cynicism of the aristocratic lover. Rodolphe has the
same callousness that Rousseau saw in his aristocratic contemporaries. A faded version of the eighteenth-century gallant, Rodolphe
understands only the basest sexual meaning of desire. He casually ex-
ploits other people, seeing them all as mere players in a conventional
sexual comedy. When Emma becomes insistent about her fantasies of
romance, Rodolphe recognizes only "l'éternelle monotonie de la passion, qui a toujours les mêmes formes et le même langage" (II. 12.
500)[1] (the eternal monotony of passion, which always has the same
forms and the same language). Although Rodolphe is satisfied to manipulate the clichés of passion for his own shallow pleasure, he has no
ear for the sincerity that can be heard through the banal—the sincerity
of desperation, at least, if not of love.

Flaubert is an even greater connoisseur of the banal than Rodolphe,
yet he understands its significance differently. Like Baudelaire, Flaubert is both revolted and fascinated by the banal: the banality of desire, of despair—and also of cynicism. Banality is a philosophic as
well as a social problem, for at least part of the artist's insight follows
Rousseau in separating the inevitable banality of all forms of expres-

sion from the genuine human need which no actual form can adequately embody:

> puisque personne, jamais, ne peut donner l'exacte mesure de ses
> besoins, ni de ses conceptions, ni de ses douleurs, et que la parole
> humaine est comme un chaudron fêlé où nous battons des mélodies
> à faire danser les ours, quand on voudrait attendrir les étoiles.
>
> (II. 12. 500)
>
> (since no one, ever, has been able to give the exact measure of his
> needs, or of his ideas, or of his suffering, and since human language
> is like a cracked cauldron on which we beat out melodies to make
> bears dance when we want to move the stars to tears.)

Human desires fall into cliché, but behind cliché there is also a truth
of feeling that is real and poignant. The deepest poignancy comes
from the necessary distortion of feeling by the banality of form. Because no forms—either of experience or language—can contain the
desires they are called upon to satisfy or express, every real lover
seems a clumsy and insensitive bear, and all language of emotion
seems only vulgar cliché. Emma's fantasies are her effort to give form
to her desire for something better than what she has: something more
beautiful, clearer, more lasting. Like anyone else, she can only beat
out her melody on a cracked pot.

Emma's banality, then, cannot be simply disdained, for Flaubert
makes it represent the universal tragedy of desire degraded by all
forms of convention and by the conventionality of all forms. Rousseau implies this tragedy, even while he persists in the struggle to devise forms of expression commensurate to his inner life. Flaubert becomes counter-romantic in the special French sense of denying that
hope. Though French lyricism in the nineteenth century was devoted
to acquiring richer resources of self-expression than were available to
Rousseau, Flaubert shows that a half-century of exotic and picturesque imagery leaves the self as impoverished as it was before. In
Emma's fantasies of passion, any impression of real feeling is displaced
by the banal imagery that is supposed to contain and evoke passion.
Her image of romantic escape with Rodolphe exemplifies the inade-
quacy of all her efforts to express desire:

> Et puis ils arrivaient, un soir, dans un village de pêcheurs, où des
> filets bruns séchaient au vent, le long de la falaise et des cabanes.
> C'est là qu'ils s'arrêteraient pour vivre: ils habiteraient une maison

basse à toit plat, ombragée d'un palmier, au fond d'un golfe, au bord de la mer. Ils se promèneraient en gondole, ils se balanceraient en hamac; et leur existence serait facile et large comme leurs vêtements de soie, toute chaude et étoilée comme les nuits douces qu'ils contempleraient. Cependant, sur l'immensité de cet avenir qu'elle se faisait apparaître, rien de particulier ne surgissait: les jours, tous magnifiques, se ressemblaient comme des flots; et cela se balançait à l'horizon infini, harmonieux, bleuâtre et couvert de soleil.

(II. 12. 504-505)

(And then one night they arrived at a fishing village where brown nets dried in the breeze, alongside the cliffs and the cottages. It was there they would stay to live. They would dwell in a low house with a flat roof, shaded by a palm tree, in the heart of a gulf, by the side of the sea. They would promenade in a gondola, swing in a hammock, and their existence would be as easy and loose as their garments of silk, as warm and starry as the gentle nights which they would contemplate. However, in the vastness of this future that she conjured, nothing in particular stood out; the days, all magnificent, resembled each other like waves, and the vision hovered on the endless horizon: harmonious, azure, and bathed in sunshine.)

The main fault in this idyllic fantasy does not derive from Emma's individual crudity of mind. Her "Eldorado banal" is no worse than the dream of Baudelaire's voyager to Cythera. It is true that her image of silken garments is a vulgar cliché, and so is the fishing village and the hammock by the seaside. But better minds than Emma's have also imagined themselves in gorgeous costumes, contemplating the starry night and comparing themselves to it. Emma's language of fantasy even becomes beautiful intermittently, no less lyrical than the dream of "luxe, calme, et volupté" in certain poems by Baudelaire. Yet it is still a cliché to think of days as waves and to imagine the whole of the dream floating on the infinite horizon, "harmonieux, bleuâtre et couvert de soleil."

Flaubert occasionally allows Emma's vulgar inner voice to rise to a finer lyricism, but only to repudiate any easy contempt for her individual limitations of sensibility. The beautiful phrases in Emma's language work to destroy the distinction between vulgar and high lyricism. Whereas George Eliot contrasts Rosamond's thin melody to Dorothea's rich music, Flaubert exposes all songs of desire to be more or less banal. Whether crude or beautiful, none of it corresponds to external reality and none of it measures the vastness of human need and sorrow. Emma, like everyone, seeks satisfaction by shaping desire into language, image, experience. Or rather she passively allows desire to attach itself to the shapes that flow into consciousness. All shapes, however, inevitably vulgarize what we are made to believe is a deeper, original feeling, if only the feeling of need, emptiness, and despair. Sexual fantasy itself may be only the conventional form and imperfect shape taken by more profound, even spiritual desires: "nous battons des mélodies à faire danser les ours, quand on voudrait attendrir les étoiles" (we beat out melodies to make bears dance, when we want to move the stars to tears).

By focusing on sexuality as the main form taken by human desire, Flaubert stays with the dominant subject of French Romanticism since Rousseau. In the *Confessions*, Rousseau's bizarre sexual history is supposed to testify to the superiority of his nature. His sexual reticence, his absorption in fantasy, even his perversions show the distortions forced upon a pure sensibility by a world that has itself fallen from natural grace. Rousseau struggles to make language contain the truth of his feelings because he is convinced that the heart of his desires will seem rich and pure, if only he can manifest it truly. When Poe includes fantasies of perfect sexual love among the signs of the poetic spirit, he remains faithful to the Rousseauist attitude toward desire. Although Poe shifts the origin of sexual fantasy from nature to spirit, the main distinction for Poe between carnal sexuality and sexual desire as a sign of spirit is simply that the spirit remains unsatisfied by any real object. Rousseau used the same distinction to ennoble his sexuality. Unsatisfied desire is the mark of superiority, whether one traces the desire to a Rousseauist ideal of nature or, in Poe's terms, to the "unquenchable thirst for supernal beauty."

Flaubert, like Baudelaire, in part continues the Rousseauist reverence for desire. Emma's sexual fantasies express her protest against base reality, thus testifying to her superiority. As Baudelaire asserts, "Elle poursuit l'Idéal." Yet in *Madame Bovary*, as in Baudelaire's poetry, sexuality also represents the cruel paradoxes of human nature. Sexual desire may express the purest part of the character, but it also shows the inevitable contamination of the spirit seeking bodily form. Sexuality expresses the mixture of the base and the fine in human nature. To go further, it shows the dissolution of whatever is fine in the baseness of nature within the self.

In *Madame Bovary*, Emma's sexuality ultimately testifies to the weakness rather than the richness of her spirit. Though sexual fantasy may seem to preserve the spirit from base nature, Emma's imagery of passion is no less fatal to the life of the spirit than is the rest of her world. There is less contrast than Emma realizes between her fantasies and the reality of the world she loathes. As Jean-Pierre Richard explains, Flaubert shows both the fantasy and the experience of sexuality to involve utter loss of form. The self dissolves in a liquid tide, sinks into a soft doughy ooze, or fades like waves on an empty horizon.[2] This lack of solidity may be the appeal of sexuality to the spirit, for sexual passion may seem to promise form without the limitations of crude matter. But in Flaubert's vision of life, the most repellent quality of matter is precisely that it has no solid form. The farmland is muddy underfoot. The walls of the houses sweat. Even the language of conversation nauseates by a pervasive softness of texture. If the fantasy of passion offers only more formlessness, sexuality is an illusory escape from nature. Fantasies of love may seem to transcend the muck, as stones in the cattlefield keep Emma and Léon from sinking in the mud on one of their amorous walks. But Flaubert, with brutal irony, suggests that their fantasies lack even the shaky solidity of stones in the mud:

> Les bonheur futurs, comme les rivages des tropiques, projettent sur l'immensité qui les précède leurs mollesses natales, une brise parfumée, et l'on s'assoupit dans cet enivrement, sans même s'inquiéter de l'horizon que l'on n'aperçoit pas.
> La terre, à un endroit, se trouvait effondrée par le pas des bestiaux; il fallut marcher sur de grosses pierres vertes, espacées dans la boue. Souvent, elle s'arrêtait une minute à regarder où poser sa bottine,—et, chancelant sur le caillou qui tremblait, les coudes en l'air, la taille penchée, l'oeil indécis, elle riait alors, de peur de tomber dans les flaques d'eau. (II. 3. 412)

> (Future joys, like tropical shores, send their natural softness, a perfumed breeze, out over the vastness which stretches before them. And one is lulled by this intoxication, without concern for the horizon that one does not see.
> The earth in one spot had been trodden down by cattle; they had to walk on the big green stones spread out here and there in the mud. Often, she stopped a moment to see where to place her foot; then, tottering on the shaky stone, elbows in the air, her figure forward, her glance uncertain, she laughed, afraid of falling into the puddles of water.)

Though more fragrant than a cattlefield, the imaginary landscape of love only extends the ooze of nature beyond the horizon. Sexuality, as

Flaubert describes it, further dissolves the little that is distinct in the self, rather than allowing the spirit to attain the firmer balance or clearer realization which it seeks.

While Flaubert describes sexuality more freely than the Victorian novelist, he also uses it as a symbol of paradox in a more rigid abstract proposition than the English in the nineteenth century are in the habit of contemplating. Nature and spirit cannot be joined in any energetic alliance, yet they cannot be separated either. Sexuality represents both the needs of the spirit and the inevitable defeat of the spirit by the forms human nature gives to its need. All voyagers to Cythera are doomed to failure because the very nature of sexual passion opposes the satisfaction of spirit which it is supposed to provide. The spirit needs form, but it only loses itself further in the formless forms offered by nature.

In the twentieth century, Yeats—among other poets and novelists in English—comes to contemplate Flaubert's kind of paradox more closely. It is, for example, the futility of preserving the spirit in natural form that leads Yeats's old man to set sail for Byzantium. But the English writer before Baudelaire and Flaubert characteristically avoids the antitheses which demand such a radical departure from nature. George Eliot tries to suggest the potentially rich bond between the human spirit and nature through the image of Dorothea's marriage to Ladislaw. Baudelaire and Flaubert, by contrast, expose sexuality to be more a bondage than a bond. Emma is mistaken to imagine that marriage (or adultery) could save her from the muddy farmland, just as she is wrong to expect Charles to cure a hoof-shaped foot through a surgical procedure as clumsy as he is himself.

Flaubert's art radically differs from George Eliot's in that Flaubert exercises his inventiveness within an extraordinarily narrow and rigid conception of human possibility. He insists on the degrading bondage of the human to the natural mainly through Emma's story, but also through all the minor symbolic figures and events in the novel. Charles Bovary's disastrous operation on the foot of the groom, Hippolyte, is another grotesque image of human bondage to nature, as is the blind beggar, and also the peasant woman who has become as mute and placid as a beast. Instead of the range and diversity of George Eliot's scene, different facets of a single degrading truth are all that Flaubert presents. Emma's experience comes to seem a universal predicament because partial reflections of her bondage to nature fill the book. She meets her own image at every turn, even while she mistakes her disgust for freedom.

The novel follows Emma's desire for escape and her illusions of choice while Flaubert systematically condemns her to reenact the same ironies and the same paradoxes from adolescence to death. The scene where Charles visits Emma on her father's farm ironically sets the inflexible limits of experience even before Emma has made her first mistake:

> Il arriva un jour vers trois heures; tout le monde était aux champs; il entra dans la cuisine, mais n'aperçut point d'abord Emma; les auvents étaient fermés. Par les fentes du bois, le soleil allongeait sur les pavés de grandes rais minces, qui se brisaient à l'angle des meubles et tremblaient au plafond. Des mouches, sur la table, montaient le long des verres qui avaient servi, et bourdonnaient en se noyant au fond, dans le cidre resté. . . . L'air, passant par le dessous de la porte, poussait un peu de poussière sur les dalles; il la regardait se traîner, et il entendait seulement le battement intérieur de sa tête, avec le cri d'une poule, au loin, qui pondait dans les cours. Emma, de temps à autre, se rafraîchissait les joues en y appliquant la paume de ses mains, qu'elle refroidissait après cela sur la pomme de fer des grands chenets. (I. 3. 344-345)

(One day he got there about three o'clock; everyone was in the fields. He went into the kitchen, but at first did not notice Emma; the shutters were closed. Through the wooden slats, the sun sent long fine rays across the floor; they broke at the corners of the furniture and trembled on the ceiling. On the table some flies that were crawling up the dirty glasses drowned themselves, buzzing, in the dregs of cider. . . . The air coming in under the door pushed a bit of dust over the stone floor. He watched it drift along and heard nothing but the pulse beating inside his head, along with the faraway clucking of a hen that had laid an egg in the yard. Emma cooled her cheeks from time to time with her palms, which she then cooled off again on the knobs of the huge firedogs.)

Flaubert's simple registering of heat, dust, food, and sweat connects Emma to the atmosphere of her father's farm. Her presence has a sensuous weight somehow related to the dregs of cider and the hen laying eggs in the yard. Emma exaggerates her dissociation from the farm. She is more at home there than either she or Charles realizes. Although Charles is dazzled by her finesse, we see that her white nails, fine teeth, the delicate skill of her tongue seeking a drop of liqueur only enhance the sensuous nature of her appeal without really altering it. Later, Emma's more elaborate ornaments of manner attract Léon, but Emma's appeal to Léon, as to Rodolphe also, is rooted in the hot farmyard where Charles finds her. The pounding in Charles's head does not come from Emma's affectations of elegance, but from the enticing and inextricable mixture in her of delicacy and kitchen-sweat.

Emma, therefore, is not the Rousseauist hero whose pure nature suffers in the base actual world as in a prison. In disdaining the farm, Emma ignores part of her own basic nature. She can never fundamentally escape from the farmyard because it is the origin of what is most powerful in her own nature. Yet Emma is right to hate the farm, as Charles is right to admire her affectations. The confused yearning to rise above nature may ultimately be all that distinguishes human life from the hen in the yard. For Emma to follow her yearning into any form of experience, however, is only to resemble the flies in the farmhouse after all. They climb from the crumbs on the kitchen table only to drown in the dregs of cider.

Flaubert reiterates the same depressing irony in single descriptive images and in the most elaborate scenes, like the episode of the Agricultural Fair. The longer scenes offer the illusion of more varied choices and contrasts, but beneath the surface of detail, Flaubert relentlessly pursues his single theme. At the Fair, Rodolphe seduces Emma with the promise of eternal passion while animals bleat in the background and a dignitary drones congratulations to the peasants. The scene of the Fair and Rodolphe's performance cut in and out of each other, separate but mirror images of simple truths disguised in absurdly pompous clichés. Emma seems to believe that Rodolphe will rescue her from the gross and tedious world represented by the Fair. The Fair is so boring, the audience so stupefied—we cannot help but sympathize with her desire for escape. But there is no real contrast between Rodolphe's high-toned lovemaking and the empty rhetoric of the Fair. The bleating of the beasts unifies the social and personal ironies of the scene more than it underlines incongruity.[3] We know already that Rodolphe's empty phrasing covers a crude sexual intention, just as the Counsellor at the Fair tries to seduce the peasants by calling their chickens "l'ornement de nos basse-cours." Emma fails to reflect upon what she is being awarded, just as the stupid peasants dumbly accept their meager prizes. Moreover, Emma is not simply deceived by lies. Like the audience at the Fair, open-mouthed in hunger and wonder, Emma welcomes the ornaments of rhetoric because she needs to find form and significance for her diffuse longings. Meanwhile the animals bray and Emma's head swirls from the sweet smell of Rodolphe's beard next to her face.

The ornaments of rhetoric both cover and reveal the profound emptiness of all human and natural forms in *Madame Bovary*. The most palpable reality is the crude and anonymous bleating of beasts. In a world so devoid of any higher signs of life, Emma's brief experiences of religious fervor assume special importance. When Emma becomes religious on her sickbed after Rodolphe abandons her, we are persuaded that she needs supernatural love. In contrast to Dorothea, Emma Bovary *has* been betrayed, not just by Rodolphe, but by the age-old promise of passion—even more generally, she has been misled to believe in the promise of happiness through experience. Emma's despair is no illusion. Flaubert's pervasive irony persuades us that only divine love can answer to her need. When Emma echoes the traditional language of religious consolation, she seems to glimpse with accuracy the only form of experience commensurate to the needs of the spirit: "Il existait à la place du bonheur des félicités plus grandes, un autre amour au-dessus de tous les autres amours, sans intermittence ni fin, et qui s'accroîtrait éternellement!" (II. 14. 520-521). (There existed a bliss greater than happiness, another love beyond all loves, without pause and without end, a bliss that would grow forever!)

Flaubert allows Emma to hover at the border of religious conversion. She is in the situation described by Pascal, where need for the supernatural actually generates the experience of faith. T. S. Eliot, reconsidering the religious feeling in Baudelaire's poetry, interprets Baudelaire's suffering similarly: "Indeed, in his way of suffering is already a kind of presence of the supernatural and of the superhuman. He rejects always the purely natural and the purely human; in other words, he is neither 'naturalist' nor 'humanist.' "[4] Yet, T. S. Eliot goes on to insist, the need for the supernatural is finally not the same as faith. Baudelaire's poetry dramatizes "the unsuccessful struggle towards the spiritual life." Eliot's phrase describes Emma's religious drama with equal accuracy, though there is less struggle in *Madame Bovary*, and the supernatural is even less of a real presence in the novel than in Baudelaire's poetry. The vision of heaven attained by Emma on her sickbed is no less banal and no less unreal than her imaginary islands of love. Her harps and saints and flaming angels destroy rather than sustain the feeling of supernatural presence. As in the desscriptions of erotic fantasy, Flaubert evokes a deep feeling of need through Emma's religious imagery, only to bury all feeling in a caricature of lyric vision. In contrast, therefore, to Hugo who envisioned the spirit building a bridge from the abyss to God out of traditional religious images, Flaubert exposes the repertory of religious imagery to contain only more soiled stage props. Emma's vision of beatitude resembles a gaudy provincial mural. It is no more able to embody the divine than is the local priest in his dirty habit.

Emma, moreover, cannot sustain her religious vision once she begins to recover physically. The irony of her return to natural life has some analogy to Dorothea's recovery from anguish in *Middlemarch* but with an altogether different cast to the irony. When Dorothea gets up none the worse for a night of anguish, we see that she is not a saint, but her obvious natural vigor and the promise of happiness in her true situation suggest that she will live past the illusion of saintliness without terrible cost. In *Madame Bovary*, Emma's physical recovery signifies only another paradoxical victory of gross nature. She tries to hold on to her religious feeling by using amulets and a reliquary. But these props, like all other human devices, cannot stop the evaporation of feeling which seems one of the fundamental laws of nature in the novel. The priest has a library send Emma arrogant or boring books which she cannot read. Finally, she tries to stimulate fervor by transferring the language of sensual love to her prayers. What began as a release from earthly passion ends, with terrible irony, in a parody of adultery. In a final irony, God is even less responsive to her appeal than was Rodolphe.

Emma Bovary represents the desiring imagination of the French tradition at the point of ultimate desperation. Less self-sufficient than Rousseau claimed to be, inextricably bound to desires that nature cannot satisfy, Emma finally desires only to die. Suicide seems the inevitable conclusion to her experience. She can fill her emptiness only by gulping poison. She cannot escape her own nature except by disintegrating into nonexistence.

Emma's suicide is the most grotesque, but not the only form of self-annihilation in *Madame Bovary*. One or another form of suicide is the logical end of all experience in the vision of the novel. The old peasant at the Fair embodies another, less self-conscious version. She has yielded herself to nature so thoroughly that she apparently retains no desires, not even for a prize. Although Rousseau might say that she has "le sentiment de l'existence" of natural man, Flaubert is less ready to make an ideal out of such a reduction of spirit. The peasant has been brutalized through poverty and suffering, and she is only as self-sufficient as a beast. Though her tranquillity may be enviable, and though she has more dignity than the dignitaries, she is still an image of self-obliteration rather than of freedom. Nor does she represent transcendence of human limitations, like a Wordsworthian peasant. Closer to Baudelaire's image of "un sommeil stupide," the insensibility of Flaubert's peasant signifies the death of the spirit rather than its release.

The noblest alternative to Emma's suicide, however, is yet another form of self-annihilation, the ambiguous form represented indirectly by the artist himself in the writing of the novel. The artist presumably destroys the sentimental self without either sinking to bestiality or utterly ceasing to exist. He differs from both the peasant and Emma. Instead of losing his spirit in nature, the artist appears to recover his spirit by destroying natural desire in himself, or, at least, by disciplining his nature to desire only the selfless forms of art.

The impersonality of Flaubert's art is famous, indeed it is a critical commonplace, supported by Flaubert's own well-known statements of artistic purpose. He aspires to be the selfless artist, the artist as martyr, sacrificing his life for the pursuit of form. I have already suggested in relation to Baudelaire, however, that the ideal of artistic martyrdom becomes most interesting when it is a less settled commitment than the credo of Art for Art's Sake pretends. The manifestoes simplify and idealize the posture of martyrdom. In the best works of art written out of this creed, it is the effort rather than the achievement of self-obliteration that we see. The desire to destroy the natural self becomes, however indirectly, part of the artist's own inward drama projected into the seemingly impersonal form of the work.

The artist's drama of self-destruction in *Madame Bovary* is necessarily indirect, since Flaubert does succeed in obliterating his direct authorial presence in the narrative. He refuses to establish himself as a feeling, thinking, judging personality, in the manner of George Eliot's narrator. He *begins* to be a presence in Chapter 1, looking back on his schoolboy acquaintance with Charles Bovary. But then he withdraws. One effect of the beginning is to assert this withdrawal as an action in itself, a choice rather than merely a neutral or spontaneous position. Even after Chapter 1, Flaubert as artist does not simply disappear

into his subject as the old peasant gives in to nature. Throughout the
narrative we feel his absence as an active and deliberate gesture. His
eye fixed on a world so disappointing that it drives the heroine to suicide, the artist actively refuses to show any more desire or regret than
a peasant. He appears to attain, by deliberate discipline, the same stoi-
cism that the peasant has instinctively, like a beast. He shows, for
example, no repugnance for the flat and dull landscape. He discloses
its horror fully, yet he presents himself as neither attracted nor re-
pelled by what he describes.

The sentimental imagination, that is, the imagination that originates in the natural self, always seeks forms to embody and satisfy
desire, and thus it always ends in disappointment. The artist, by contrast, appears to free himself from this sequence by reducing his desires to the desire for form alone. If one withdraws all other desires
from nature, Flaubert's style argues, even a blank horizon can become
beautiful. Flaubert attends carefully to the lifeless surface of the landscape, forming elegant designs from the shadings of color and the
subtleties of outline never noticed by Emma. Not that Emma overlooks
any comfort or reassurance in the landscape. There is no connection
between the formal beauty which Flaubert's language gives to the
scene and what the heart needs and wants:

> Il arrivait parfois des rafales de vent, brises de la mer qui, roulant
> d'un bond sur tout le plateau du pays de Caux, apportaient, jusqu'au
> loin dans les champs, une fraîcheur salée. Les joncs sifflaient à ras de
> terre et les feuilles des hêtres bruissaient en un frisson rapide, tandis
> que les cimes, se balançant toujours, continuaient leur grand mur-
> mure. Emma serrait son châle contre ses épaules et se levait.
> Dans l'avenue, un jour vert rabattu par le feuillage éclairait la
> mousse rase qui craquait doucement sous ses pieds. Le soleil se
> couchait; le ciel était rouge entre les branches, et les troncs pareils
> des arbres plantés en lignes droite semblaient une colonnade brune
> se détachant sur un fond d'or; une peur la prenait, elle appelait
> Djali, s'en retournait vite à Tostes par la grande route, s'affaissait
> dans un fauteuil, et de toute la soirée ne parlait pas. (I. 7. 366)

> (Sometimes there were gusts of wind, breezes from the sea rolling
> in a sweep across the whole plateau of the Caux, which brought a
> salty coolness deep into the fields. The rushes, close to the ground,
> whistled; and the leaves of the beeches trembled in a quick rustling,
> while the swaying treetops kept up their deep murmur. Emma
> pulled her shawl around her shoulders and got up.
> In the avenue, a green light dimmed by the leaves lit up the short

moss that crackled softly under her feet. The sun was setting. The sky was red between the branches, and the uniform trunks of the trees planted in a straight line seemed like a brown colonnade against a backdrop of gold. Fear took hold of her; she called Djali, returned quickly to Tostes by the main road and, throwing herself into an armchair, did not speak for the rest of the evening.)

Flaubert's descriptive language attributes no living force to the natural scene. There is no Wordsworthian blessing in this salt breeze, nor does the pictorial beauty of the sunset radiate any glory. It is not Emma's fault that she feels afraid. Flaubert's descriptive style confirms her sense of isolation. The artistic imagination neither enlivens nature nor discovers life in it. The artist differs from Emma only by gazing steadfastly at the spiritless scene. Instead of fleeing in horror, he dispassionately transforms the deadness into the formal artistic design of straight lines against a backdrop of gold.

Flaubert uses the same descriptive style for Emma's ennui:

Tout lui parut enveloppé par une atmosphère noire qui flottait confusément sur l'extérieur des choses, et le chagrin s'engouffrait dans son âme avec des hurlements doux, comme fait le vent d'hiver dans les châteaux abandonnés. (II. 7. 437)

(Everything seemed wrapped in a dark vapor which floated vaguely over the outward surface of things, and misery permeated her soul like the soft moans of the winter wind blowing through ruined castles.)

Flaubert makes artistic objects out of emptiness, whether it be the blank sky or Emma's depression. He positively flaunts his capacity to confront deadness without flinching, without swerving from his pursuit of form. The style is an exhibition which asserts the artist's discipline of his own imagination, for he will not allow his spirit to lose itself in the false imagery of desire. Either he destroys that imagery through irony or he weaves designs of emptiness. He avoids Emma's illusions by using his language to disclose the essential nothingness of the world he represents in words.

Flaubert's artistic language, therefore, creates none of the false promises made by the language of fantasy. Yet the artist's use of imagination to discipline desire also suggests the barrenness of the artistic act, for Flaubert's language leaves the human and natural void as spiritless as it was before.[5] Indeed, the extreme deadness of things in *Mad-*

ame Bovary may even seem caused by gestures of language that are positively aggressive beneath their dispassionate surface. Flaubert's elaborate figurative style often seems intent upon destroying even Emma as a living presence, in the same way as Baudelaire shows how to destroy the bourgeois model in the essay on portraiture. The artist asserts his own spirit mainly by destroying all sense of spirit in the world outside his own mind. Even Emma's ennui becomes more a blankness, an absence of life given positive presence only by virtue of the artist's verbal inventiveness. All that remains is the artist's gesture of style in the void, perhaps a perverse form of self-display after all.

Since Flaubert withholds the kind of guidance to judgment so generously offered by George Eliot's narrator, it is difficult, within the novel, to measure Flaubert's own view of his performance. Yet there is one figure who, if not a surrogate for the artist, at least resembles his posture sufficiently to invite special regard. In his eulogy for the famous and austere doctor, Larivière, Flaubert briefly abandons his ironic reserve. The doctor stands out from the design of the novel, for he appears only once (at Emma's deathbed) and is quite superfluous to the action.[6] In a novel without another superfluous figure, the visiting doctor seems a device to represent Flaubert's most heroic view of his own art:

> Il appartenait à la grande école chirurgicale sortie du tablier de Bichat, à cette génération, maintenant disparue, de praticiens philosophes qui, chérissant leur art d'un amour fanatique, l'exerçaient avec exaltation et sagacité! Tout tremblait dans son hôpital quand il se mettait en colère et ses élèves le vénéraient si bien, qu'ils s'efforçaient, à peine établis, de l'imiter le plus possible; de sorte que l'on retrouvait sur eux, par les villes d'alentour, sa longue douillette de mérinos et son large habit noir, dont les parements déboutonnés couvraient un peu ses mains charnues, de fort belles mains, et qui n'avaient jamais de gants, comme pour être plus prompts à plonger dans les misères. Dédaigneux des croix, des titres et des académies, hospitalier, libéral, paternel avec les pauvres et pratiquant la vertu sans y croire, il eût presque passé pour un saint si la finesse de son esprit ne l'eût fait craindre comme un démon. Son regard, plus tranchant que ses bistouris, vous descendait droit dans l'âme et désarticulait tout mensonge à travers les allégations et les pudeurs. Et il allait ainsi, plein de cette majesté débonnaire que donnent la conscience d'un grand talent, de la fortune, et quarante ans d'une existence laborieuse et irréprochable. (III. 8. 618)
>
> (He belonged to that great surgical school established by Bichat, to that generation of philosopher practicians, now gone, who cher-

ished their art with fanatical devotion, and exercised it with enthusiasm and wisdom! Everyone at his hospital venerated him so much that they tried, as soon as they were on their own, to imitate him as much as possible. Thus could they be seen, in all the neighboring towns, wearing the same merino overcoat and wide black frock, whose buttoned cuffs slightly covered his fleshy hands—beautiful hands, always without gloves, as if to be readier to plunge into suffering. Disdainful of medals, titles, and academies, cordial, generous, fatherly with the poor, and practicing virtue without believing in it, he would almost have passed for a saint if the keenness of his intelligence had not made him feared like a demon. His look, sharper than a scalpel, penetrated right into the soul and detected every lie through all disavowals and timidities. So he went through life, full of that benign dignity which goes with consciousness of a great talent, and with wealth, and with forty years of a hardworking and irreproachable existence.)

The physician as hero (and the novelist as physician) at first seems incongruous in *Madame Bovary*, especially in comparison to *Middlemarch*, where the medical ideal of joining knowledge and practical sympathy offers a rich analogy to the novelist's values. Though Flaubert shares George Eliot's desire to give the art of the novel a dignity distinct from the holy priesthood of poets, the analogy to medicine may seem less natural in his case. Flaubert's posture of stoic uselessness has little in common with the virtues usually associated with the medical profession. Larivière, however, is a more unusual doctor than Lydgate even aspires to be. Lydgate and Larivière are both "praticiens philosophes"; they both follow the great Bichat. But their philosophy differs as sharply as George Eliot's from Flaubert's.

Larivière has none of Lydgate's passion for the secret of living structures. As a philosopher, Larivière is ironic rather than visionary, stoical rather than inspired. He has a sharp, penetrating glance rather than Lydgate's "inward light" of creative imagination. His most remarkable skill is to expose hypocrisy and illusion, as if diseases were mainly failures of moral lucidity. Indeed, Larivière is more a moralist than a physician in the usual sense. He continues the long and noble tradition of the moralist in French culture. It is not clear whether he ever cures a patient. Emma, for example, cannot be cured. Larivière is neither a pathologist nor a healer but a diagnostician, a fierce moral intelligence, heroic by virtue of his courage to probe hidden, disgusting, and unchangeable truth.

Larivière appears to fulfill his ideal successfully. He shows none of

Lydgate's "spots of commonness," partly because he seems to have no common life of his own. Although a worldly figure, he seems devoid of worldly desires—his love, anger, energy all concentrated on the selfless exercise of his art. He does not live in the world he serves; he participates in no common action (not even the action of the novel). After all, he resembles a saint (or demon) more than an ordinary mortal. He is a debonair saint, without illusions or desires, yet by that very achievement, he exercises extraordinary personal power. For a model of selflessness, his fame seems paradoxically attached to the power of his personal style, a style that is austere and yet dangerous, mysterious, heroic.

Insofar as Larivière represents Flaubert's heroic ideal of the artist, he shows how discipline becomes a substitute for personality and the equivalent of virtue. Rousseau, we have observed, aspired to similar austerity in his period of personal reform, but Rousseau was forced to acknowledge that, in his case at least, the natural self survived, ultimately to undermine the artificial selflessness of the moralist and social critic. Flaubert's brief idealized portrait of Larivière does not hint at any comparable weakness. Moreover, Flaubert seems unaware that he has made his noble doctor a theatrically glamorous figure. In this instance, Flaubert seems insufficiently ironic, for he does not remark how the effect, if not the intention, of Larivière's selflessness is still to render the self an object of fear and admiration. Although we need not take the rather wooden set piece about Larivière too seriously in the novel, it reflects similar, more interesting paradoxes in Flaubert's own performance.

The limits of self-effacement are even more vivid for the artist than for the doctor. Whereas Larivière merely waits to plunge into misery when called, Flaubert actively summons the wretched objects of his scrutiny himself, out of his own imagination. While this may always be true of every artist, it is especially true of Flaubert. For all the apparent impersonality of the novel, Flaubert never creates the impression of a living objective world imposing its various forms of suffering on his mind. We do not grant the kind of autonomy possessed by George Eliot's most minor characters to Flaubert's blind beggar or the groom Hippolyte with his hoofed foot—or even to Emma. Flaubert's sordid and grotesque figures seem too clear in their significance, the correspondence between their physical and figurative aspect is too complete, their appearances in the action too neatly calculated—in other words, they are too artificial to represent compositions of nature, in the English sense. Despite the natural and social detail in Flaubert's novel, we tend to think of his characters as symbols rather than as objects of perception. They are symbols in Baudelaire's sense, that is, they are composed from the dictionary of nature, but they are significant, expressive, alive, only in relation to the artist's own single-minded design.

The tightness of Flaubert's design in *Madame Bovary*, along with the consistent sordidness of image and event, in the end leaves the impression of a private, even obsessive vision. The novel seems to express the dark underside of an individual sensibility rather than the hidden structure of reality outside the individual mind. Moreover, Flaubert's vision of emptiness in effect denies George Eliot's kind of objective order to the universe. Flaubert's verbal negations acknowledge no living structure outside the mind for the imagination to imitate or obey.

Flaubert's self-effacement, then, may be more apparent than real. He refuses to display his sensibility directly, but what he creates shows him still poised before the mirror of his own consciousness. For the French counter-romantic, disillusionment does not reduce what George Eliot calls "the layers of reflecting glass" between the self and the outside world. Like Baudelaire, Flaubert shows illusion yielding only to new forms of self-projection, forms that have all the harshness of moral recognition, but without the impartiality that George Eliot makes the goal of moral vision in *Middlemarch*.

Left to his own devices in an empty world, the self of the disillusioned sentimentalist does not simply disappear. Flaubert and Baudelaire show how the artistic imagination fills the void left by desire with new, ironic forms to express the feelings of disgust which are the antithesis of desire. In the absence of any transcendent spirit in the universe, the artist, like Larivière, takes on the role of saint and demon. He is like a deity, but he is a punitive rather than a redeeming spirit. The self-punishing imagination becomes one heroic alternative to sentimental desire as the mind exposes the futility and the inevitable contamination of its own nature.

George Eliot maintained the English Romantic faith that experience, in the mind and in nature, could open the individual self to the larger spirit of life outside. The French, from Rousseau through Baudelaire and Flaubert, tend to deny the presence of any spirit beyond the self. Even when the French artist in the nineteenth century comes to scorn Rousseau's idolatry of his own desires, he still follows Rousseau in

taking the limited evidence of his own feelings as truth. The artist ob-
jectifies the inner drama of consciousness in symbols that seem as
solid, even more solid than nature, but the symbols are essentially
new forms of confession, inner dialogue, and dream. The rhythm of
experience is still only the movement between desire and disappointment, even though the private source of that rhythm is partially concealed by the objective appearance of the artistic form. The power of
this art continues to derive from the same intensity of private conviction that constitutes Rousseau's power, rather than from the effort to
open up the prison of self characteristic of the English writer in the
nineteenth century. Baudelaire and Flaubert even glory in the exclusively inward sources of their vision, just as did Rousseau, for the isolated human consciousness remains for them the only source of truth,
order—and glamour. Like Rousseau in the *Confessions*, Baudelaire
and Flaubert assert the courage of the isolated self to confront its own
condition to be the supreme heroic virtue, even if the mirror of the self
now clearly discloses only irremediable perversity, guilt, and despair:

> Tête-à-tête sombre et limpide
> Qu'un coeur devenu son miroir!
> Puis de Vérité, clair et noir,
> Où tremble une étoile livide,
>
> Un phare ironique, infernal,
> Flambeau des grâces sataniques,
> Soulagement et gloire uniques,
> —La conscience dans le Mal!
>
> (L'Irrémédiable)

(Dark and limpid tête-à-tête of a heart become its own mirror! Well
of Truth, clear and black, where a livid star trembles. An ironic,
infernal beacon, torch of satanic graces; unique comfort and glory,
—consciousness in Evil!)

Notes

Index

Notes

CHAPTER 1. *THE STORY OF A LIFE*

1. William Hazlitt, "On the Character of Rousseau," *Complete Works*, ed. P. P. Howe (London, J. M. Dent, 1930), IV, 92.

2. See, for example, Irving Babbitt, "The Primitivism of Wordsworth," *The Bookman*, 74 (1931), 1-10. For Babbitt's general argument, see *Rousseau and Romanticism* (New York, 1919). Many other studies in both French and English pursue analogies between Rousseau and Wordsworth, without Babbitt's moral distaste for the Romantic characteristics they are said to share. See, for example: Emile Legouis, *The Early Life of William Wordsworth: 1770-1798* (London, 1897), pp. 55-59; Jacques Voisine, *Jean-Jacques Rousseau en Angleterre à l'époque romantique* (Paris, 1956), pp. 121, 138, 162, 203, 211, and passim; Herbert Lindenberger, *On Wordsworth's "Prelude"* (Princeton, 1963), pp. 139-142, 178; Lionel Trilling, *Sincerity and Authenticity* (Cambridge, Mass., Harvard University Press, 1972), pp. 92-122. Recent critics tend to restrict their studies to analogies rather than influence, for modern scholarship has uncovered only meager evidence of Wordsworth's direct knowledge of Rousseau's writing. Voisine cites only two references to Rousseau by Wordsworth: a brief allusion to an episode in *Emile* in the Preface to *The Borderers* (1797) and a passing criticism of Rousseau's "paradoxical reveries" in the *Convention of Cintra* (Pamphlet, 1809). Although Wordsworth's library is known to have included an edition of the *Confessions* (a French edition of 1782, containing Part One of the *Confessions* and the *Rêveries du promeneur solitaire*), the extent of his familiarity with Rousseau's autobiographical writings is unknown. See Voisine, pp. 2-3, 202n.

3. Hazlitt, "On the Living Poets," *Complete Works*, V, 163. The political implications of Rousseau's "egotism" were first, and more harshly, stated by Burke in his "Letter to a Member of the National Assembly" (1791). For Burke, Rousseau's social and political writings were less nefarious than the autobiography, "those mad confessions of his mad faults." The very impulse to autobiography in Rousseau, the "philosopher of vanity," expressed for Burke the same egotism unleashed in society at large in the French Revolution: "It was this abuse and perversion, which vanity makes even of hypocrisy, which has driven Rousseau to record a life not so much as checkered, or spotted here and there with virtues, or even distinguished by a single good action." *The Works of Edmund Burke* (London, 1866), IV, 27. English response to the *Confessions* in the eighteenth century is studied by Henri Roddier, *Jean-Jacques Rousseau en Angleterre au dix-huitième siècle* (Paris, 1950), and by Voisine, pp. 100-123. See also Edmond Gosse, "Rousseau in England in the Nineteenth Century," *Aspects and Impressions* (New York, 1922), pp. 169-191.

4. All quotations from Rousseau's autobiographical writings are from *Oeuvres complètes*, vol. I: *Les Confessions, autres textes autobiographiques*, ed. Bernard Gagnebin and Marcel Raymond, Bibliothèque de la Pléiade (Paris, 1962). This volume also includes *Rousseau juge de Jean Jaques, Dialogues, Les Rêveries du promeneur solitaire, Lettres à Malesherbes*, and "Ebauches des Confessions." Quotations from this edition are referred to in the text by page number; the original spelling of this text has been retained.

5. Montaigne, "Du Repentir," *Essais, Oeuvres complètes*, ed. Albert Thibaudet and Maurice Rat, Bibliothèque de la Pléiade (Paris, 1965), pp. 782-783.

6. La Bruyère, *Les Caractères ou les moeurs de ce siècle, Oeuvres complètes*, ed. Julien Benda, Bibliothèque de la Pléiade (Paris, 1934), p. 81.

7. Pascal, Preface, "L'Homme sans Dieu," *Pensées, Oeuvres complètes*, ed. Jacques Chevalier, Bibliothèque de la Pléiade (Paris, 1960), p. 1104.

8. The line of descent from Montaigne to the moralists of the seventeenth century interested in the study of the self is discussed by A. J. Krailsheimer, *Studies in Self-Interest: From Descartes to La Bruyère* (Oxford, 1962).

9. The complexity of Rousseau's antiaestheticism is brilliantly analyzed by Jacques Derrida, *De la Grammatologie* (Paris, Editions de Minuit, 1967), pp. 262-264, and passim.

10. La Bruyère, *Les Caractères*, p. 85.

11. Montaigne, "De la Vanité," *Essais, OC*, p. 973.

12. William Wordsworth, *The Prelude*, ed. E. de Selincourt and H. Darbishire (London, Oxford University Press, 1959). Quotations from *The Prelude* are from the 1850 text in this edition, unless otherwise specified, and are referred to by book and line numbers.

13. Meyer H. Abrams, *The Mirror and the Lamp* (New York, Oxford University Press, 1953), p. 22.

14. Ibid., p. 98.

15. Ibid.

CHAPTER 2. *ROUSSEAU AND THE VOCABULARY OF FEELING*

1. Rousseau's view of language as a source of evil as well as perfectibility is interpreted by Derrida, *De la Grammatologie*, passim, and by Paul de Man, "Theory of Metaphor in Rousseau's *Second Discourse*," *Romanticism: Vistas, Instances, Continuities*, ed. David Thorburn and Geoffrey Hartman (Ithaca, 1973), pp. 83-114.

2. Derrida, *De la Grammatologie*, p. 202: "Both Rousseau and Lévi-Strauss combine contempt for writing with praise for the power of the spoken word. Nevertheless, in the texts which we are about to read, Rousseau also distrusts the illusion of the fully present spoken word, the illusion of presence in language thought to be fully transparent and innocent." The point is explained further and is, indeed, the main subject of Derrida's fascinating book.

3. In addition to Derrida and De Man, see also the first clear conceptualization of Rousseau's paradoxical attitude toward language in the ground-breaking book by Jean Starobinski, *Jean-Jacques Rousseau: La transparence et l'obstacle* (Paris, Gallimard, 1957), pp. 175, 177: "What made Jean-Jacques write was . . . his need to overcome his timidity, the need to prove his worth in a different way. He writes in order to assert that he is worth more than he seems; but he also writes to proclaim that he is worth more than what he writes. He pleads not to be taken literally, not to be imprisoned in his words. . . . In everything that Rousseau writes on the subject of language, one finds a very clear understanding of the conditions which make recourse to conventional signs inevitable, along with an acute regret for the absence of more direct modes of communication."

4. See Martin Turnell, *The Classical Moment* (London, 1947), pp. 11-14.

5. Rousseau's theory is most fully stated in the famous second *Discours: Discours sur l'origine et les fondemens de l'inégalité parmi les hommes, Oeuvres complètes*, ed. Bernard Gagnebin and Marcel Raymond, Bibliothèque de la Pléiade (Paris, 1966), III, 131-194.

6. La Rochefoucauld's interest in "la paresse" is mentioned by Krail-sheimer, *Studies in Self-Interest*, p. 86.

7. La Rochefoucauld, *Oeuvres complètes*, ed. L. Martin-Chauffier, Biblio-thèque de la Pléiade (Paris, 1935), p. 288. See also pp. 347-348.

8. Babbitt implies this judgment, though his criticism of Rousseau's "Ro-mantic love" is, of course, more complex and not at all dismissive, since Bab-bitt sees Rousseauism as the dominant tendency in Western literature of the past two hundred years; see *Rousseau and Romanticism*, pp. 220-239.

9. *Encyclopédie, ou Dictionnaire raisonné des sciences, des arts, et des métiers*, ed. Diderot and d'Alembert (Geneva, 1757), II, 410.

10. La Rochefoucauld, *OC*, p. 254: 'Il n'y a que d'une sorte d'amour, mais il y en a mille différentes copies"; "Il est du véritable amour comme de l'appar-ition des esprits: tout le monde en parle; mais peu de gens en ont vu."

11. La Bruyère, *Les Caractères*, *OC*, pp. 152-154.

12. La Rochefoucauld, *OC*, p. 253. The more common sentence of the *Maximes* begins, "Il y a . . .," for La Rochefoucauld characteristically anal-yzes what he believes to exist rather than speculating upon hypotheses. See, for examples, pp. 244, 260, 269.

CHAPTER 3. *"LOVE" IN* THE PRELUDE

1. Josephine Miles observes that the word "love" appears in Wordsworth's poetry more than any other word except "man," "life," and the common verbs: *Wordsworth and the Vocabulary of Emotion* (Berkeley, University of California Press, 1942), p. 18.

2. Wordsworth, "Essay, Supplementary to Preface (1815)," *The Poetical Works of William Wordsworth*, ed. E. de Selincourt (London, Oxford Univer-sity Press, 1944), II, 428.

3. Johnson, "Preface to the English Dictionary," *The Works of Samuel Johnson* (London, 1806), II, 50.

4. Ibid., pp. 47-48.

5. *A Dictionary of the English Language* (London, 1755).

6. Yves Bonnefoy offers a similar contrast between French and English poetic language in "Shakespeare et le poète français," *Preuves*, No. 100 (1959), pp. 42-48.

7. Johnson explains in the Preface that he includes few if any contempo-rary examples: "My purpose was to admit no testimony of living authors, that I might not be misled by partiality, and that none of my contemporaries might have reason to complain." *Works*, II, 46.

8. Coleridge criticizes "mental bombast" in Wordsworth in Chap. XXII of *Biographia Literaria, edited with his Aesthetical Essays*, ed. J. Shawcross (Oxford, Clarendon Press, 1907), I, 109. See also Hazlitt, "Observations on Mr. Wordsworth's poem, *The Excursion*," *The Round Table, Works*, IV, 121. Josephine Miles, in *Wordsworth and the Vocabulary of Emotion* (pp. 66-69), mentions the objections of contemporary critics to Wordsworth's "particular instances" of general human passion, citing reviews which complain of his "drivelling to the redbreast."

9. Josephine Miles mainly emphasizes the universalizing force of Words-worth's formal naming of emotion. She places him directly in the tradition of the eighteenth century by his effort "to use in poetry those words which meant the same to the greatest number of persons over the greatest length of time"

(p. 55). F. R. Leavis also emphasizes the "essential sanity and normality" of Wordsworth's language. See his *Revaluation* (New York, Chatto and Windus, 1936), p. 174.

10. Further paradoxes in Wordsworth's "love of man" are discussed by David Ferry, *The Limits of Mortality* (Wesleyan, Wesleyan University Press, 1960), pp. 51-111.

CHAPTER 4.   *THE SOURCES OF IMAGINATION*

1. "bewilder": 1. lit. "To lose in pathless places, to confound for want of a plain road," *Oxford English Dictionary*.

2. Geoffrey Hartman, *Wordsworth's Poetry: 1787-1814* (New Haven, Yale University Press, 1964), pp. 6-7.

3. See Richard Onorato, *The Character of the Poet: Wordsworth in "The Prelude"* (Princeton, 1971) for a psychoanalytic study of *The Prelude* more subtly attentive to the poetry than most psychoanalytic interpretations of literature.

4. Abrams, *The Mirror and the Lamp*, p. 63; among the many studies of this subject, another especially useful essay is "Wordsworth and the Empirical Philosophers," by Hugh Sykes Davies in *The English Mind: Studies in the English Moralists*, ed. H. S. Davies and G. Watson (Cambridge, Eng., 1964), pp. 153-174.

5. Addison, *The Spectator*, No. 413, *The Works of Joseph Addison*, ed. Henry G. Bohn (London, 1893), III, 402-403.

6. Johnson, *Rasselas*, *Works*, III, 406.

7. Addison, *The Spectator*, No. 413, *Works*, III, 403.

8. Modern psychology has, of course, attended to the possible "motives" of religious vision. The classic text is by Sigmund Freud, *The Future of an Illusion* (1937) in *The Complete Psychological Works of Sigmund Freud*, ed. James Strachey (London, 1961), XXI, 5-56. William James in *The Varieties of Religious Experience* (New York, 1923) tries to mediate between psychological explanations of religious experience and the traditional theological view of response to an external, objective power.

9. Onorato, for example, begins his psychoanalytic study with attention to what he regards as unpersuasively affirmative language in "Tintern Abbey" (pp. 32-50, 82-87).

10. Epicurus, "Extant Works," trans. C. Bailey, *The Stoic and Epicurean Philosophers*, ed. Whitney J. Oates (New York, Random House, 1940), pp. 36, 51.

11. Johnson, *Rasselas*, *Works*, III, 405-406.

12. Rousseau, *Emile*, *Oeuvres complètes*, ed. Bernard Gagnebin and Marcel Raymond, Bibliothèque de la Pléiade (Paris, 1969), IV, 305.

13. Derrida, *De la Grammatologie* (p. 288, and passim), recognizes this idea of development to be at the center of Rousseau's concept of history: social and political as well as personal.

14. Starobinski, *Jean-Jacques Rousseau*, p. 9: "The discovery of appearances, here, is by no means the result of a reflection on the illusory nature of perceived reality. Jean-Jacques is not a philosophical 'subject' who analyzes the spectacle of the external world and then calls it into question as a mere appearance distorted by the delusive mediation of the senses."

15. Marc Eigeldinger, *Rousseau et la réalité de l'imaginaire* (Neuchâtel, La Baconnière, 1962), p. 183.

16. Wordsworth's veneration for the self is contrasted to Rousseau's tenderness by Roy Pascal, *Design and Truth in Autobiography* (London, 1960), p. 44.

CHAPTER 5.   *THE CHARM OF MEMORY*

1. Johnson, *The Rambler*, No. 41, *Works*, IV, 239.
2. Coleridge, *Biographia Literaria*, ed. Shawcross, II, 109-110.
3. Johnson, *The Idler*, No. 72, *Works*, VII, 236-237.
4. Georges Poulet cites Rousseau when defining Romantic memory in these terms in "Timelessness and Romanticism," *Journal of the History of Ideas*, 15 (1954), 3-22. See also his *Studies in Human Time*, trans. E. Coleman (Baltimore, 1956), pp. 175-177.
5. See C. -A. Sainte-Beuve, "Les Confessions de J. -J. Rousseau" (1850), *Causeries du Lundi*, ed. C. Pierrot (Paris, Garnier, 1943), III, 91: "In everything, Rousseau, as a painter, has the sense of *reality* . . . in that he wants each scene which he remembers or invents, each character he introduces, to be framed and to move in a clearly defined space, the least details of which may be engraved and retained in memory."
6. Note to *Confessions, OC*, I, 1344: "Bergson, in *Matter and Memory* echoes both Rousseau and Proust: 'Our past is that which no longer acts, but could act; it is that which will act when inserted into a present sensation whose life it will borrow.' " See also Justin O'Brien, "La Mémoire affective avant Marcel Proust," *Revue de la littérature comparée*, 19 (1939), 19-36.
7. The psychological "denial" in the rowboat episode is interpreted by Onorato, *The Character of the Poet*, pp. 268-274. The partly unconscious feelings of guilt and fear in Wordsworth's memories are also emphasized by Jonathan Bishop, "Wordsworth and the 'Spots of time,' " *English Literary History*, 26 (1959), 45-65.
8. Johnson, *The Idler*, No. 72, *Works*, VII, 236.
9. John Locke, *An Essay concerning Human Understanding*, ed. A. S. Pringle-Pattison (Oxford, Clarendon Press, 1924), p. 81.
10. Johnson, *The Rambler*, No. 41, *Works*, IV, 240.
11. The distinction between true and false happiness was a favorite point of Johnson's when criticizing Rousseau. Boswell reports a conversation on the same subject with Rousseau about Johnson. See *Boswell on the Grand Tour*, ed. F. Brady and F. A. Pottle (New York, McGraw-Hill, 1955), II, 252: "I gave him very fully the character of Mr. Johnson. He said with force, 'I should like that man. I should respect him. I would not disturb his principles if I could. I should like to see him, but from a distance, for fear he might maul me.' . . . I told him Mr. Johnson's *bon mot* upon the innovators: that truth is a cow which will yield them no more milk, and so they are gone to milk the bull. He said, 'He would detest me. He would say, Here is a corrupter: a man who comes here to milk the bull.' "
12. *Encyclopédie*, VIII, 370.
13. Mme de Staël, "Lettres sur le caractère et les écrits de J. -J. Rousseau," *Oeuvres complètes* (Paris, 1820), I, 81-82.

CHAPTER 6.   *THE SENTIMENT OF BEING*

1. The key significance of the phrase is emphasized by: Renato Poggioli, "The Pastoral of Self," *Daedalus*, No. 88 (Fall 1959), pp. 686-699; Herbert

Lindenberger, *On Wordsworth's "Prelude,"* p. 178; Lionel Trilling, *Sincerity and Authenticity,* pp. 62-72, 92-122.

2. Lindenberger (p. 178n) suggests that Wordsworth may have been echoing Rousseau.

3. Second *Discours, OC,* III, 164.

4. Ibid., p. 193.

5. David Hume, *A Treatise of Human Nature,* ed. L. A. Selby-Bigge (London, 1955), p. 252.

6. Second *Discours, OC,* III, 135.

7. *Emile, OC,* IV, 253.

8. Ibid., p. 249.

9. Ibid., pp. 771-772.

10. See Note to *Confessions, OC,* I, 1308.

11. See Robert Osmont, "Contribution à l'étude psychologique des *Rêveries,"* *Annales,* 23 (1934), 7-135. See esp. pp. 77-96.

12. Rousseau is quoting from a story by La Fontaine, "Diable de Papefiguière"; see Note to *Confessions, OC,* I, 1601.

13. *Emile, OC,* IV, 251.

14. Pascal, *OC,* p. 1138.

15. Jean Wahl, *Tableau de la philosophie française* (Paris, 1946), pp. 94-95. Cited in Note to *Confessions, OC,* I, 1800.

16. Osmont, p. 120. Like many French commentators on Rousseau, Osmont tends not to distinguish "la réalisation mystique du moi" (the mystical realization of the self) from a "vision mystique de la nature" (mystical vision of nature).

17. The *Concordance* lists seven appearances of the word "sentiment," four of which are from *The Prelude.* See *A Concordance to the Poems of William Wordsworth,* ed. Lane Cooper (London, 1911).

18. See the brilliant discussion by William Empson, "Sense in *The Prelude,"* *The Structure of Complex Words* (New York, 1951), pp. 289-305.

19. David Ferry emphasizes the tension in Wordsworth's poetry between what he calls the "sacramental" and the "mystical" in *The Limits of Mortality* (see esp. pp. 122-123, 159-160, 171); I am interested in the characteristics of Wordsworth's language which keep him from casting that sense of tension into the antitheses common to Rousseau.

20. Trilling, *Sincerity and Authenticity,* p. 122.

CHAPTER 7.
VICTOR HUGO AND WORDSWORTHIAN PERCEPTION

1. The poem appears in *Les Feuilles d'automne* (1831). Hugo's earlier published volumes of poetry were: *Odes et poésies diverses* (1822), *Odes et ballades* (1826), *Les Orientales* (1829). All quotations from Victor Hugo's poetry are from *Oeuvres poétiques,* ed. Pierre Albouy, Bibliothèque de la Pléiade, 2 vols. (Paris, 1964). Volume and page numbers refer to this edition.

2. Baudelaire, "Victor Hugo," *L'Art romantique, Oeuvres complètes,* ed. Y. -G. Le Dantec, Bibliothèque de la Pléiade (Paris, 1954), pp. 1084-1091. All quotations from Baudelaire's poetry and prose are from this edition and are referred to in the text by page number.

Baudelaire's tone toward Hugo goes from the inflated public homage of the essay, "Victor Hugo," to the private jeering in the critical fragments of "Fusées": "Cet homme est si peu élégiaque, si peu éthéré, qu'il ferait horreur même à un notaire. Hugo-Sacerdoce a toujours le front penché, —trop penché pour rien voir, excepté son nombril" (1202). (This man is so unelegiac, so unethereal; he would horrify even a notary. Hugo the High Priest always has his head bowed, too bowed to see anything except his navel.) The questionable sincerity of Baudelaire's homage to Hugo in the essay, "Victor Hugo," is remarked by Margaret Gilman, *Baudelaire the Critic* (New York, Columbia University Press, 1943), pp. 186-189.

3. W. B. Yeats, "The Autumn of the Body" (1898) in *Essays and Introductions* (New York, Macmillan, 1961), pp. 192-193. See also his "The Symbolism of Poetry" (1900), pp. 153-164.

4. George Eliot, review of *Les Contemplations* in "Belles Lettres, 1856," *Westminster Review*, 66 (1856), 264. Victorian criticism of Hugo's poetry is described by Kenneth Ward Hooker, *The Fortunes of Victor Hugo in England* (New York, 1938).

5. G. H. Lewes, "Victor Hugo's Latest Poems," *Fortnightly Review*, 3 (1865), 181-190.

6. See Lindenberger, *On Wordsworth's "Prelude,"* pp. 51, 56.

7. I disagree, obviously, with the view common in French criticism that Victor Hugo's poetry is remarkable for its imaginative perception of nature. Marc Eigeldinger states this view in *Le Dynamisme de l'image dans la poésie française* (Neuchâtel, La Baconnière, 1943), pp. 82-87. The terms in which Eigeldinger praises Hugo seem related to his serious (but characteristically French) misunderstanding of English Romantic poetry, particularly the poetry of Wordsworth whom Eigeldinger identifies as a poet of the humble picturesque: Wordsworth's poetry "attends only to the humble and modest aspects of nature; it strives to register unnoticed details. . . . It was in imitation of the English Lake poets that Sainte-Beuve conceived of an intimate and familiar poetry, close to daily reality, unafraid of either banality or even vulgarity" (p. 49).

8. Geoffrey Hartman writes interestingly about Victor Hugo's encyclopedic gathering of spiritual imagery in "Reflections on Romanticism in France," *Studies in Romanticism*, 9 (1970), 244-247. George Henry Lewes explains Hugo's inexhaustible imagery in terms of his general weaknesses: "His imagery is all the more inexhaustible because for the most part it is not drawn from actual experience of nature or human nature, but compounded out of verbal suggestions; often therefore incongruous, very often incapable of being realized in thought. It is not representative, but kaleidoscopic," "Victor Hugo's Latest Poems," p. 183.

9. Ferry, *The Limits of Mortality*, pp. 170-171.

CHAPTER 8.   *VICTOR HUGO: FROM SPECTACLE TO VISION*

1. See Abrams, *The Mirror and the Lamp*, pp. 291-292.

2. Wordsworth, "Preface to the Edition of 1815," *Poetical Works*, ed. De Selincourt, II, 436.

3. Hugo's practice of putting the metaphor in apposition to the substantive has been observed, though interpreted differently, by J. -B. Barrère, *La Fantaisie de Victor Hugo* (Paris, 1949), pp. 197-198; see also H. Temple Pat-

terson, "The Origin of Hugo's Condensed Metaphor," *French Studies*, 5 (1951), 343-348; Eigeldinger, *Le Dynamisme de l'image dans la poésie française*, p. 109.

4. I am indebted to David Ferry's excellent reading of this poem in *The Limits of Mortality*, pp. 17-19.

5. The manuscript of "Relligio" is dated 1854, making it a late poem, but Albouy observes that it closely echoes a prose text by Hugo dated 1840, in Notes to *Oeuvres poétiques*, II, 1647.

6. The allusion to *Paradise Lost* is noted by Albouy, Notes to *Oeuvres poétiques*, II, 1603. Albouy further describes the use of Miltonic imagery by Hugo (and other French Romantic writers) in *La Création mythologique chez Victor Hugo* (Paris, 1968), pp. 24-27, 128-129, 372, and passim. Hugo probably knew *Paradise Lost* only through the well-known translation by Delille (1805) and the translation in prose by Chateaubriand (1836). Hugo's meager knowledge of the English language is remarked by Geraud Venzac, *Les Premiers Maîtres de Victor Hugo* (Paris, 1955), p. 402, n. 5 and, in more detail, by Edmond Estève, *Byron et le romantisme français* (Paris, n.d.), pp. 299-300. Originally published as thesis in 1907.

7. Anne D. Ferry, *Milton's Epic Voice* (Cambridge, Mass., 1963), pp. 129-132.

8. Although Baudelaire seems to have written "De Profundis clamavi" a few years before Hugo's "Le Pont," Baudelaire's poem need not be taken as a direct reply to this poem by Hugo for my comparison of the poets. Forms of "des visions de l'ombre intérieure" appear in poems by Hugo written through the 1840s.

CHAPTER 9.
THE LOVELY BEHAVIOR OF THINGS: HOPKINS AND BAUDELAIRE

1. "Hurrahing in Harvest," *Poems of Gerard Manley Hopkins*, 4th ed., ed. W. H. Gardner and N. H. MacKenzie (New York, Oxford University Press, 1967).

2. Yeats, "The Autumn of the Body," *Essays and Introductions*, pp. 192-193.

CHAPTER 10.   *BEAUTY AND TASTE*

1. W. B. Yeats, "The Symbolism of Poetry," *Essays and Introductions*, pp. 191, 193.

2. T. S. Eliot, "Baudelaire" (1930), in *Selected Essays: 1917-1932* (New York, Harcourt, Brace, 1932), p. 341.

3. For a detailed discussion of Poe's influence on Baudelaire, see Patrick F. Quinn, *The French Face of Edgar Poe* (Carbondale, Ill., 1957). Quinn is mainly interested in the French response to Poe's stories, as translated by Baudelaire.

4. There is no mention of Coleridge in Baudelaire's criticism. There is only one mention of Wordsworth (in Baudelaire's version of De Quincey's *Confessions of an English Opium-Eater* [ed. Pléiade, p. 513]).

5. "Principles of Genial Criticism," in Shawcross, II, 233.

6. Ibid., p. 232.

7. James V. Baker provides a useful summary of twentieth-century con-

troversy about Coleridge's critical writing in the chapter, "Coleridge, Critics, and the Future," in *The Sacred River: Coleridge's Theory of the Imagination* (Louisiana, 1957), pp. 254-288.

8. See Francis Jeffrey, review of "Essays on the Nature and Principles of Taste," *Edinburgh Review* (May 1811). Reprinted in *Selections from the Essays of Francis Jeffrey,* ed. Lewis E. Gates, Athenaeum Press Series (Boston, 1894), p. 151. Jeffrey is reviewing the 2d edition of Alison (1811).

9. "The terms Beauty and Sublimity are applied by all men to Sounds, and even sometimes to smells. In our own experience, we very often find, that the same Emotion is produced by Sounds, which is produced by Forms or Colours; and the nature of language sufficiently shows, that this is conformable also to general experience. There seems no reason therefore for limiting the objects of Sublimity or Beauty to the sole class of visible objects." Alison, 3d ed. (Edinburgh, 1812), I, 289-290.

10. Jeffrey on Alison, in Gates ed., pp. 156-157.

11. The German influence on Coleridge's critical writing has been discussed by most commentators. Particularly useful is Abrams, *The Mirror and the Lamp,* pp. 88-94, 201-213; J. A. Appleyard, *Coleridge's Philosophy of Literature* (Cambridge, Mass., 1965); the issue of Coleridge's plagiarism from Schelling and Schlegel is discussed by Norman Fruman, *Coleridge, the Damaged Archangel* (New York, 1971) and, more sympathetically, by Walter Jackson Bate, *Coleridge,* Masters of World Literature Series, ed. Louis Kronenberger (New York, 1968), pp. 131-138.

12. "There is beauty in that wheel, and you yourself would not only admit, but would feel it, had you never seen a wheel before. See how the rays proceed from the centre to the circumferences, and how many different images are distinctly comprehended at one glance, as forming one whole, and each part in some harmonious relation to each and to all." "Principles of Genial Criticism," in Shawcross, II, 233.

13. Ibid., p. 243.

14. Ibid., p. 225.

15. Edgar Allen Poe, "The Poetic Principle," *Works,* ed. E. C. Stedman and G. E. Woodberry (Chicago, 1895), VI, 10.

16. Poe's repudiation of Coleridge's most important principles is described well by Richard Fogle, "Organic Form in American Criticism: 1840-1870" in *The Development of American Literary Criticism,* ed. Floyd Stovall (Chapel Hill, 1955), p. 98. I agree with Fogle more than with Floyd Stovall who emphasizes Poe's resemblance to Coleridge, despite changes in critical vocabulary. See Stovall, "Poe's Debt to Coleridge," *Edgar Poe the Poet* (Virginia, 1969), pp. 126-174.

17. Poe, "The Poetic Principle," *Works,* VI, 29.

18. I. A. Richards, *Coleridge on Imagination* (New York, Harcourt, Brace and Co., 1935), pp. 10-11: "The critical theories can be obtained from the psychology without initial complication with the philosophical matter. . . . The psychology and the metaphysics (and theology) are independent. For Coleridge's own thought, they were not; they probably could not be; to a later reader they may, and as a rule, will be."

19. Rousseau's first *Discours* was directed to the question set by the Academy of Dijon for the prize of 1750: "Si le retablissement des sciences et des arts a contribué à épurer les moeurs." Rousseau won the prize with his argument for the negative position. In 1751, Rousseau's life as a polemicist

began in earnest with the refutations and counterrefutations of his argument about the relation between culture and virtue. The debate took place in the press and in correspondence with figures like Voltaire, Grimm, and the King of Poland. Geoffrey Hartman remarks the greater social bias of French compared to English Romanticism in "Reflections on Romanticism in France" in vol. 9, *Studies in Romanticism*, p. 240.

20. Quinn dates Baudelaire's first reading of Poe to January, 1847. His translations of Poe's stories began in July, 1848. See Quinn, *The French Face of Edgar Poe*, pp. 70-72, 86-89.

21. The influence on Baudelaire of Stendhal's idea of "le beau moderne" is discussed by Gilman, *Baudelaire the Critic*, pp. 47-49.

22. The relationship of Baudelaire's term, "bizarre," to Poe's idea of "novelty" is suggested by Gilman, p. 87. Poe, however, does not emphasize a historical or cultural approach to "novelty."

23. Eliot, "Baudelaire," p. 340.

24. From Lecture X (1818), *Coleridge's Miscellaneous Criticism*, ed. Thomas Raysor (Cambridge, Mass., Harvard University Press, 1936), pp. 159-160.

25. "Principles of Genial Criticism," in Shawcross, II, 239.

CHAPTER 11.   *SYMBOLIC LIGHT*

1.Walter Pater, "Coleridge" (1865) in *Appreciations, Works of Walter Pater* (London, 1901), V, 69.

2. "Appendix B," *The Statesman's Manual, Complete Works of Coleridge*, ed. W. G. T. Shedd (New York, 1853), I, 461-463.

3. I discuss the importance of "conscience" to Coleridge's criticism of Wordsworth in Chapter 5 above, pp. 78-79.

4. Abrams cites an important analogue to Coleridge's description of the plant in a passage by Herder, quoted in Abrams, *The Mirror and the Lamp*, p. 204. To me, the most satisfying explanation of Coleridge's idea of "organic growth" is by Richard Fogle, *The Idea of Coleridge's Criticism* (Berkeley, 1962), pp. 24-27, 68, 108, and passim.

5. Note (1827) to "Appendix B," *Works*, ed. Shedd, I, 460.

6. *Biographia Literaria*, ed. Shawcross, I, 100.

7. "Notes nouvelles sur Edgar Poe" (1857), *Oeuvres de Edgar A. Poe*, trans. Charles Baudelaire, ed. Y. -G. Le Dantec, Bibliothèque de la Pléiade (Paris, 1940), p. 700.

8. See Edmond Estève, *Byron et le romantisme français*. The extent of Baudelaire's actual knowledge of Byron's poetry is not discussed by Estève and is difficult to establish. In his critical essays, Baudelaire characteristically names Byron in his roster of great foreign writers, cited in invidious comparison to the French. Baudelaire says little about the names on the list; they appear more as part of a formula of taste than as subjects of critical commentary. In addition to Byron, the list includes (in varying order): Shakespeare, Ariosto, Dante, Scott, Goethe, sometimes supplemented by Heine, Poe, Tennyson, and, on one occasion, Crabbe. See pp. 695, 708, 784, 858, 1086, 1175.

9. See Stephen Spender, *The Destructive Element* (London, Jonathan Cape, 1935), p. 134: "The true descendent of Baudelaire is discovering not an outward reality, but, in external objects, his own spiritual individuality." I agree more with Spender than with critics like Margaret Gilman and Marcel Raymond who make Baudelaire sound like a transcendentalist. See Marcel

Raymond, *De Baudelaire au surréalisme* (Paris, 1952), p. 22; Gilman, *Baudelaire the Critic*, p. 51.

10. Lowell, "Autumn," *Imitations* (New York, Farrar, Straus and Giroux, 1958), p. 51.

CHAPTER 12. *THE LANGUAGE OF NATURE*

1. Coleridge, "On Poesy or Art," *Works*, ed. Shedd, IV, 333.

2. Ibid., pp. 332-333.

3. Dryden, "The Preface to Ovid's Epistles," *The Poems of John Dryden*, ed. James Kinsley (Oxford, Clarendon Press, 1958), I, 184.

4. Baudelaire adapted the image of the dictionary from Delacroix. See Gilman, *Baudelaire the Critic*, p. 38.

5. *Biographia Literaria*, ed. Shawcross, I, 202.

6. The peculiar route of Baudelaire's knowledge of Coleridgean theory is suggested in an essay of the "Salon de 1859" where he quotes (in English) a version of Coleridge's distinction between Fancy and Imagination, taken from a spiritualist compendium by Catherine Crowe, *The Night Side of Nature* (London, 1848). Crowe uses the distinction to promote receptivity to belief in ghosts and wraiths. See Baudelaire, *OC*, p. 776. The allusion to Crowe and its bearing on Baudelaire's knowledge of Coleridge is discussed by Gilman, pp. 128-131.

7. Gilman, p. 165.

8. Raymond, *De Baudelaire au surréalisme*, pp. 22-26.

9. Yeats, "The Autumn of the Body," *Essays and Introductions*, p. 192.

10. Wallace Stevens, "Imagination as Value" (1948) in *The Necessary Angel* (New York, Knopf, 1951, rpt. Vintage), p. 138.

11. In a note to his translation of Baudelaire's critical writing, Jonathan Mayne suggests that Baudelaire probably had the quoted phrase *"clochers montrant du doigt le ciel"* from Gautier (*Fantaisies*, III), who quoted it as the only line of Wordsworth that he knew. *The Mirror of Art*, ed. Mayne, p. 287n. The phrase, also in quotation marks, appears in *The Excursion*: "And O, ye swelling hills, and spacious plains! / Besprent from shore to shore with steeple-towers, / And spires whose 'silent finger points to heaven' " (VI. 17-19). The oddly indirect route from Coleridge to Baudelaire is further suggested by Wordsworth's Note to the first edition of *The Excursion*, attributing the phrase in question to Coleridge. Wordsworth's Note is printed by De Selincourt, *Wordsworth's Poetical Works*, V, 456: " 'An instinctive taste teaches men to build their churches in flat countries with spire-steeples, which as they cannot be referred to any other object, point as with silent finger to the sky and stars, and sometimes, when they reflect the brazen light of a rich though rainy sunset, appear like a pyramid of flame burning heavenward.' See 'The Friend,' by S. T. Coleridge, No. 14, p. 223. —W." Baudelaire shows no awareness of these English sources, nor of how he has wrenched the borrowed phrasing away from its original significance.

CHAPTER 13.
MIDDLEMARCH: *BEYOND THE VOYAGE TO CYTHERA*

1. Book, chapter, and page numbers in my text refer to *Middlemarch*, ed. Gordon S. Haight, Riverside ed. (Boston, Houghton Mifflin, 1956).

2. Henry James, "Gustave Flaubert," *Notes on Novelists* (New York, 1914),

pp. 81-84. Despite his criticism, James admired Flaubert; he was considerably less enthusiastic about Baudelaire's poetry. See his "Charles Baudelaire," *French Poets and Novelists* (London, 1878), pp. 72-83.

3. Flaubert expressed his appreciation of Baudelaire's response to *Madame Bovary* in a letter (October 21, 1857): "I thank you very much, my dear friend. Your article gave me the *greatest* pleasure. You have entered the arcana of the work as if my brain were yours. You have understood and felt it in *depth*": Flaubert, *Correspondance* (Paris, L. Conard, 1927), IV, 229.

4. In another letter to Baudelaire, Flaubert names "Un Voyage à Cythère" (and also the sonnet, "Avec ses vêtements ondoyants . . . ") among his favorite poems in *Les Fleurs du Mal*. Flaubert, *Correspondance*, IV, 205.

5. Gordon S. Haight, *George Eliot: A Biography* (New York, 1968), pp. 60, 65, 485.

6. Wordsworth, "Preface to *Lyrical Ballads*," *Poetical Works*, ed. De Selincourt, II, 395-396.

7. See especially F. R. Leavis, *The Great Tradition* (London, 1948), pp. 75-76.

8. See, for example, Kate Millett, *Sexual Politics* (New York, 1970), p. 139.

CHAPTER 14.   *THE POVERTY OF NATURE IN* MADAME BOVARY

1. *Madame Bovary*, *Oeuvres de Flaubert*, vol. I, ed. A. Thibaudet and R. Dumesmil, Bibliothèque de la Pléiade (Paris, 1946). Quotations from this edition are referred to by part, chapter, and page number in the text.

2. Jean-Pierre Richard, "The Creation of Form in Flaubert," trans. Raymond Giraud in *Flaubert: A Collection of Critical Essays*, ed. Raymond Giraud, Twentieth-Century Views (N. J., Prentice-Hall, 1964), pp. 36-56. From *Littérature et sensation* (Paris, 1954), pp. 125-147.

3. See Leo Bersani, *From Balzac to Beckett: Center and Circumference in French Fiction* (New York, 1970), p. 169.

4. T. S. Eliot, "Baudelaire," in *Selected Essays*, p. 339.

5. Leo Bersani criticizes the tedium of this style, pp. 181-191.

6. The portrait of Larivière is commonly recognized to be based on the figure of Flaubert's father. See Benjamin F. Bart, *Flaubert* (Syracuse, 1967), p. 307; Francis Steegmuller, *Flaubert and Madame Bovary: A Double Portrait* (New York, 1939), p. 360.

Index

291